The Wit

of Seventeenth-Century Poetry

Edited by Claude J. Summers

& Ted-Larry Pebworth

University of Missouri Press

Columbia and London

Copyright © 1995 by
The Curators of the University of Missouri
University of Missouri Press, Columbia, Missouri 65201
Printed and bound in the United States of America
All rights reserved
5 4 3 2 1   99 98 97 96 95

Library of Congress Cataloging-in-Publication Data

The wit of seventeenth-century poetry / edited by Claude J. Summers and Ted-Larry
    Pebworth.
        p. cm.
    Essays deriving from a conference held at the University of Michigan.
    Includes bibliographical references and index.
    ISBN 0-8262-0985-8 (alk. paper)
        1. English poetry—Early modern, 1500–1700—History and criticism—
Congresses. 2. Humorous poetry, English—History and criticism—Congresses.
3. English wit and humor—History and criticism—Congresses. I. Summers, Claude J.
II. Pebworth, Ted-Larry.
PR545.H87W58 1995
821'.409—dc20   94-31210
                                                                                                        CIP

♾™ This paper meets the requirements of the
American National Standard for Permanence of Paper
for Printed Library Materials, Z39.48, 1984.

Designer: Stephanie Foley
Typesetter: Connell-Zeko Type & Graphics
Printer and binder: Thomson-Shore, Inc.
Typefaces: Medici Script and Goudy

The Wit of Seventeenth-Century Poetry

For *Mary and Michael Schoenfeldt*

Contents

Acknowledgments

This book and the scholarly meeting from which it originated have profited from the great effort, wide learning, and scholarly generosity of the conference steering committee. Diana Treviño Benet, Achsah Guibbory, Judith Scherer Herz, Robert B. Hinman, John R. Roberts, and Michael C. Schoenfeldt helped referee the submissions to the conference and offered valuable suggestions for revision. Their contributions have been extensive, and we join the authors of the essays in expressing gratitude for their insights and devotion. It is also our pleasant duty to acknowledge the support of the Horace H. Rackham Graduate School of the University of Michigan, John D'Arms, Dean; and of the following administrators at the University of Michigan–Dearborn: Emily L. Spinelli, Chair, Department of Humanities; John W. Presley, Dean, College of Arts, Sciences, and Letters; and Robert L. Simpson, Provost and Vice-Chancellor for Academic Affairs.

The Wit of Seventeenth-Century Poetry

Claude J. Summers and Ted-Larry Pebworth

Introduction

"*Wit*," says Davenant in the Preface to *Gondibert*, "is not onely the luck and labour, but also the dexterity of the thought" reflected in a work of literature.[1] Davenant's observation stands at the midpoint of a century obsessed with wit: defining it, analyzing it, amplifying it, using it, rejecting it, and using it to reject it. The very obsessiveness with which the topic is broached in the seventeenth century is an index both of its central significance for the period's poetry and of its resistance to easy definition and categorization. Wit variously and alternately and sometime simultaneously signifies in the seventeenth century ingenuity, fancy, pseudological argument, inventiveness, flagrant sophistry, adroit craftsmanship, facile wordplay, complexity of thought and statement, baroque excess, arcane imagery, strained conceits, mere cleverness, high and low humor, the agile manipulation of standard tropes, the startling discovery of unsuspected resemblances between unlike phenomena, the perception of the order and connectedness of the Creation, and truth, sometimes apprehended as through a veil darkly. In the period, wit may be either a term of commendation or an epithet of abuse, a sign of subtle intelligence or a mark of facetiousness. As practiced in seventeenth-century poetry, it may be obvious or subtle, local or universal. Wit is at once a series of lucky (or unfortunate) strokes and a habit of thought, both a poetic technique and a means of comprehending the world.

For T. S. Eliot, seventeenth-century wit exemplified a rare fusion of thought

1. *Discourse upon Gondibert*, in *Literary Criticism of Seventeenth Century England*, ed. Edward W. Tayler (New York: Knopf, 1967), 271.

1

and feeling, of intelligence and sensual experience concentrated in verse. Expanding upon Eliot's insights, A. J. Smith regards the distinctive metaphysical wit of the seventeenth century as akin to an epistemological exercise: "Wit focuses an interest in the rendering of our ambiguous state when sensation and idea interfuse in the language itself, opening an absolute consequence in the momentary encounter and registering the shock of metaphysical predicaments posed in the play of the senses."[2] From this perspective, wit is not merely mental gymnastics, verbal tours de force, or virtuoso play—though it may embody all of these—but a sensibility rooted in the religious and literary culture of late Renaissance Europe. As expressed by seventeenth-century English poets such as Donne and Herbert, this sensibility yields an intellectual verse that is fully inflected with passion and that is capable of apprehending and dramatizing all the dualities of early modern consciousness.

The centrality of wit to seventeenth-century poetry can hardly be disputed. What makes wit so vexed and slippery a topic for study, however, are the variety of conceptions of it, the range of attitudes toward it, and the multiplicity of its manifestations in the period. Moreover, wit is itself an important marker of historical change; it is always historically and culturally (as well as individually) specific: the wit of Donne is not exactly that of Jonson but still less is it that of the cavalier poets or of Marvell or of Dryden. Yet these very obstacles to glib generalizations actually facilitate—even demand—approaches from various vantage points and also testify to wit's function as a fundamental key to the theory and practice of seventeenth-century poetry, one that both transcends and subsumes the overly familiar categories of religious and secular, metaphysical and classical, plain style and baroque. Thus, to study the wit of seventeenth-century poetry is necessarily to address concerns at the very heart of the period's shifting literary culture.

Indeed, as the essays collected in this volume demonstrate, to explore seventeenth-century wit in the final years of the twentieth century is to engage issues of politics and religion, of secular and sacred love, of literary theory and poetic technique, of gender relations and historical consciousness, of literary history and social change, as well as both larger concerns of literary

---

2. See especially Eliot's "The Metaphysical Poets," originally published in *TLS* in 1921 and reprinted in *Selected Essays* (London: Faber and Faber, 1932). A. J. Smith, *Metaphysical Wit* (Cambridge: Cambridge University Press, 1991), xi.

production and smaller ones of local effects. The wit of seventeenth-century poetry is a topic that raises persistent questions of thematics and authorial intent even as it also interrogates a wide spectrum of cultural issues.

The original, abbreviated versions of the essays included here were presented at the tenth biennial Renaissance conference at the University of Michigan–Dearborn, October 16–17, 1992.[3] The final versions printed here have benefited from the stimulating exchanges and responses afforded by the conference, and they intersect, reinforce, and challenge each other in significant and interesting ways. But the essays were written independently and without consultation among the authors. No topics or approaches were suggested or assigned, and none were proscribed. All the essays are historically grounded and critically based, but they vary widely in their historical perspectives and critical techniques and in their scope and focus. The only criterion for selection has been that each essay contribute to the understanding and informed appreciation of the wit of seventeenth-century English poetry.

In the wide-ranging essay that opens the collection, Helen Wilcox takes up the highly problematic issue of wit in devotional poetry. Although the presence of wit in devotional works might argue an unconscionable hubris on the part of an author and its intrusion could be criticized as too low and

3. Selected papers from the first nine Dearborn conferences have been published: those from the 1974 conference as *"Trust to Good Verses": Herrick Tercentenary Essays*, ed. Roger B. Rollin and J. Max Patrick (Pittsburgh: University of Pittsburgh Press, 1978); those from the 1976 conference on seventeenth-century prose as a special issue of *Studies in the Literary Imagination* 10:2 (1977), ed. William A. Sessions and James S. Tillman; those from the 1978 conference as *"Too Rich to Clothe the Sunne": Essays on George Herbert*, ed. Claude J. Summers and Ted-Larry Pebworth (Pittsburgh: University of Pittsburgh Press, 1980); those from the 1980 conference as *Classic and Cavalier: Essays on Jonson and the Sons of Ben*, ed. Claude J. Summers and Ted-Larry Pebworth (Pittsburgh: University of Pittsburgh Press, 1982); those from the 1982 conference as *The Eagle and the Dove: Reassessing John Donne*, ed. Claude J. Summers and Ted-Larry Pebworth (Columbia: University of Missouri Press, 1986); those from the 1984 conference as *"Bright Shootes of Everlastingnesse": The Seventeenth-Century Religious Lyric*, ed. Claude J. Summers and Ted-Larry Pebworth (Columbia: University of Missouri Press, 1987); those from the 1986 conference as *"The Muses Common-Weale": Poetry and Politics in the Seventeenth Century*, ed. Claude J. Summers and Ted-Larry Pebworth (Columbia: University of Missouri Press, 1988); those from the 1988 conference as *On the Celebrated and Neglected Poems of Andrew Marvell*, ed. Claude J. Summers and Ted-Larry Pebworth (Columbia: University of Missouri Press, 1992); and those from the 1990 conference as *Renaissance Discourses of Desire*, ed. Claude J. Summers and Ted-Larry Pebworth (Columbia: University of Missouri Press, 1993).

distracting for the heights of religious verse, wit was a natural part of most seventeenth-century poets' patterns of creativity and habits of thought. Despite the recurrent tension between wit and devotion in the period, the qualities of the two, Wilcox observes, "may actually be perceived as remarkably similar" in that both "wit and devotion function primarily by taking the ordinary and transforming it, making it surprising, special, holy." Considering devotional poetry by such diverse figures as Donne, Jonson, Beaumont, Crashaw, Herbert, Traherne, Margaret Cavendish, Henry Colman, and An Collins, Wilcox finds that its most effective wit is dependent on "the given material of faith and tradition . . . the inhabiting of a shared set of ideas," and that, unlike the case in secular verse, wit in devotional verse finds its fulfillment "not in keeping control but in abandoning it, surrendering to the faith which it seeks to express and serve."

P. G. Stanwood and Lee Johnson also consider wit in religious poetry, that of Herbert and Milton, but their subject is metaphysical wit's discovery of "infinity in time" and its profound desire "to engage and order experience." In an essay that might have as accurately been entitled "The Wit of Structure" as "The Structure of Wit," they examine the differing structures—visual, numerological, and typological—of Herbert's "Coloss. 3.3," "Trinitie Sunday," "Aaron," and "Man." Then they turn to the insufficiently appreciated wit of Milton's poetic structures: the "falling" passages in *Paradise Lost* 3 and 4, the staggering of Satan in book 6, the acrostic on his name in book 9; the harmonic structure of "At a Solemn Music"; the sonnet forms embedded in Uriel's speech in *Paradise Lost* 3; and the symmetrically witty structure of the "unmeditated" hymn of Adam and Eve in book 5. They conclude that "Herbert frequently designs whole poems that use to large advantage discrete details of language and even the mapping of words on the page" and that Milton's effects are similar, but typically larger and more ambitious. Following the winding metaphysical stair, both poets leave witty structures everywhere.

In another wide-ranging essay, Erna Kelly investigates the kinds and uses of wit particular to women writers in the period. Concentrating on works by Bradstreet, Cavendish, and Behn, she examines three kinds of poetry that lend themselves to gender awareness: poems about the writing of poetry, poems using metaphors traditionally associated with women (such as cooking and attention to dress), and amatory verse. In examples of all three of these kinds of poetry, she finds that women's wit is often employed in reexamining "male descriptions of and prescriptions for women's experience." That wit is frequently subversive, especially when used to gain entrance into the male world of letters or to question male perceptions of sexuality, but it is also constructive in its refiguration and elevation of female experience.

To the modern reader, one of the more unusual subjects of seventeenth-century religious verse is the circumcision of Christ. Beginning with poems on that subject by Herrick, Crashaw, Milton, and Quarles, and passages on it in sermons by Donne and Andrewes, Jim Ellis discusses the theological and hermeneutic significance of the act and its relationship to wit. Noting that this first shedding of Christ's blood "prefigures and guarantees the last," the act of salvation itself, he points out a further significance. Just as a literal circumcision served the Jews to mark out a community and demonstrate a submission to the law, so the Christian's "circumcision" of his wit, the cutting away of "those urgings or desires that come from the body and the senses," marks out his own community and his submission to grace. This circumcision of wit leads to a reading of the body and the world that is metaphysical rather than literal. After exploring the changes in attitudes toward the body and toward the making of contracts taking place in the late Renaissance, Ellis concludes by examining the religiopolitical implications of the circumcision of wit. By associating Puritans with the Jews of the Old Testament and by connecting them with a naive or literal reading style, writers such as Donne and Herrick mark out themselves and their fellow Anglicans as the true New Covenant community of believers.

In the first of a series of essays that focus on the meaning of wit for individual authors, Catherine Gimelli Martin offers a subtle and revisionist reexamination of the wit of Donne's *Songs and Sonnets*. Reacting against recent criticism of Donne and applying to his amorous verse Freud's theory of play, she finds that his poetics are not "imperial," but rather "bourgeois." His conversion of private lovemaking into a public display intended for courtly or coterie audiences clothes a celebration of the body in the language of power. "By self-consciously enlarging the scope of gendered human interchange in the private sphere," Martin concludes, "Donne's lyrics enlarge the private sphere itself" and "participate in an implicitly subversive critique of the hierarchical limits imposed by the divine right ideology of the Stuart court."

Robert Evans considers the nature of and reactions to wit in a poet much less usually associated with wit than Donne, Ben Jonson. Noting Jonson's debt to Quintilian, Evans concludes that wit, "in the ideal Jonsonian sense, involved both prodigious invention and apt expression" and that "any undue emphasis on wit as mere verbal play or linguistic self-indulgence . . . earned Jonson's scorn." Exploring both the private and the public wit in *Epigrammes,* he finds that Jonson's thinking about wit, his association of it with learning and judgment, had a social dimension that led him "to champion a particular ideal of wit in the face of the differing expectations."

M. C. Allen argues that the purpose of wit in Herbert's *The Temple* is pastoral, discerning in the work an ingenuity more characteristic of a priest than of a scholar or courtier. Reading the wit of the poetry through the lens of *The Country Parson,* Allen finds that Herbert's ingenious devices and techniques are consistently utilized in the service of pastoral care and that his wit is relational rather than doctrinal. Moreover, Herbert's pastoral wit typically adopts the mode of such priestly offices as preaching, catechizing, admonishing, and praying. Allen's approach to Herbert via pastoral wit leads him to question the current emphasis on the poet's spiritual struggles and to reconsider his place in literary history, finding him in some ways more similar to Jonson than to Donne.

Roger Rollin explores the various kinds of wit in Herrick's *Hesperides.* He finds wit as apt expression in abundance and even "conceited wit" in such poems as "His Winding-sheet." But arching over all, Rollin finds, is a "witty design" to both *Hesperides* and *Noble Numbers* as collections. Both works open and close with sequences, both contain strings of related poems, and both progress by juxtapositions of complement and discrepancy. This is a pattern, Rollin concludes, "whose contradictions, ironies, self-referentiality, and dialectic . . . constitute a very special kind of seventeenth-century wit."

In a probing essay focused on Richard Lovelace, Sharon Seelig suggests that wit is deeply implicated in complex questions of gender, audience, power, and dominance. Contending that cavalier wit is not only a matter of quick turns of phrase, reinterpretations of familiar situations, or intellectual domination, but of sexual mastery as well, she demonstrates that in many of Lovelace's poems a dominant male controls—visually, verbally, or rhetorically—an objectified female subject. The poet's wit, as expressed in sensuous and complex images, is fundamentally a wit of control. Seelig concludes that "Lovelace is not only more disturbing than we may have supposed . . . but also more versatile: in the sensuous, even shocking images of Lovelace's poetry there are intriguing similarities, not only with the metaphysicals, whom he sometimes inadequately imitates, but also with that which is usually termed baroque and associated with Crashaw." Lovelace's wit is both an expression of his fascination with power and confinement and a reflection of a particular way of knowing and seeing the world.

Lorraine Roberts points out that Richard Crashaw, too often cited only for the extravagance of his conceits, in fact thought of wit as meaning "something much more substantive than ingenuity or fancy" and as functioning "on the level of wisdom as well as that of cleverness." Drawing upon the parallel of Bernini, the master of baroque sculpture, Roberts argues that Crashaw's real wit resides in the overall idea, the *concetto,* that underlies and informs each poem. She analyzes "The Flaming Heart," "Hymn in the Holy Nativity," and "The Weeper" from that perspective. "In all Crashaw's poetry," she asserts, "wit is meant to manifest the 'Truewit' of God—Christ and his love of mankind"; and she concludes, "The wit of the poet in rendering this truth can also be seen as a conspiracy between ingenuity and wisdom, fancy and judgment, surface devices and structural concept."

In a dense and subtle essay, William A. Sessions argues that Marvell's ironic, ambiguous, dialectical wit is ultimately a wit of survival, an expression of and reaction to the seventeenth-century's social and political disillusionment. The counterbalances so characteristic of Marvell's elusive transtextuality, Sessions argues, "operate as a formal cathartic means of self-historicizing for reader and audience, a kind of mask put on to prepare the reader for entry (or reentry) into time and history." Marvell's mower, in particular, enacts dialectics of *eros* and *thanatos* and of choice and time that he must somehow endure. Marvell's wit inscribes a new kind of hero for an age in which conventional heroism was no longer possible, a modern georgic figure who survives in an utterly changed world haunted by failure and the prospect of annihilation.

Katherine Quinsey's essay on Dryden's problematic *Religio Laici* fittingly concludes this exploration of the nature of wit in seventeenth-century poetry. As Quinsey remarks, "The heart of the poem's subject—the nature of religious authority—harbors the same questions of language and truth that lie at the heart of the seventeenth-century debate on wit." The poem concerns the criteria for judging and discovering truth, and the means of transmission and expression of truth, as well as the nature of interpretation. Dryden's poem ultimately presents both human and poetic wit as weak and fallacious, deluded and deluding, in the face of "Sacred Truth." It suggests that "reliable interpretation is the province of a community of minds over time," that that community is made up of "Men of wit," and that the criteria for that interpretation are unity of thought and expression and a sense of the creative spirit lying behind the work. In effect, then, this poem that seems to deny individual wit at the same time relies on a community of wits through time for interpretation.

In their varied approaches and diverse conclusions, these essays illustrate the richness of seventeenth-century wit and its susceptibility to a number of critical techniques and vantage points. They illuminate important authors and significant texts and broach many of the crucial questions that animate the study of seventeenth-century poetry in the dwindling years of the twentieth century. Thus, the essays collected here demonstrate the continuing vitality of seventeenth-century wit, both as a topic in its own right and, especially, as a means of understanding the complexity and range of seventeenth-century poetry.

Helen Wilcox

"No More Wit Than a Christian?"

The Case of Devotional Poetry

The lament of the unfortunate Sir Andrew Aguecheek in Shakespeare's *Twelfth Night*, that he has "no more wit than a Christian" (a weakness that he subsequently puts down to his being "a great eater of beef" [1.3.82–83]) aptly introduces the dilemma of the seventeenth-century writer of religious verse. Christianity and wit were not obvious bedfellows. The word *wit* does not appear at all in the great English exemplum of seventeenth-century Christian language, the Authorized Version; and although the overall pattern of biblical narrative may be seen in Dante's terms as a divine comedy, this tale of redemption was generally not felt to be the kind of comedy that demanded or deserved wit. "Honest wit and merriment" were fine in their place—even according to Luigi Cornaro's "Treatise of Temperance and Sobrietie"—but that proper place was "a most pleasant comedie,"[1] not the interaction of human beings with God. In George Herbert's "The Church-porch," a poem attempting a mediation between the values of the world and the Christian faith, wit comes in for some harsh dealing: it is said to be an "unruly engine" and is bluntly dismissed as "newes only to ignorance." While "usefulnesse" is seen as the outcome of "labour," Herbert describes "wit" as merely the product of "ease" (ll. 241, 230, 291). Henry Vaughan summed up the sense of wit as a transient and potentially dangerous distraction to the religious poet when he characterized the world, in his poem of that name, as a place tasting of

---

1. "A Treatise of Temperance and Sobrietie," trans. George Herbert, in *The Works of George Herbert*, ed. F. E. Hutchinson (Oxford: Clarendon Press, 1941), 302. All further references to Herbert are to this edition.

"Wit's sour delights."[2] Perhaps, then, Sir Andrew's jibe at the typically un-witty Christian was well founded; the values of wit—leisure, ingenuity, one-upmanship, trickery—were not those of faith and devotion.

I

The work of early- and mid-seventeenth-century religious poets in English may seem at first to confirm this view of an unbridgeable gulf between true wit and true devotion. John Donne was intensely aware of the danger of being "mov'd to seeme religious / Only to vent wit,"[3] and this comment implies an association of wit with superficiality, as a kind of mental agility unconnected with genuine spiritual activity. Much of the most characteristically witty reli-gious poetry of this period does indeed display intellectual and verbal skills that appear to be at odds with the avowed purpose of the writing.[4] The ingenuity of acrostics and other demonstrative poetic forms, for instance, perhaps distracts a reader with multiple linguistic and visual effects. Consider one of the devo-tional acrostics of Elisabeth Major in which her own name (and being) are constructed vertically, even as the name of Jesus and the self-denying instinct of her prayer to him are expressed horizontally. The poem concludes:

> M ercy, O Saviour, teach me to ask aright,
> A nd then for comfort, 'tis thy chief delight:
> I beg and faint, I fear and hope again,
> O Lord, I see all self, and earth is vain,
> R enouncing all, on thee Lord, I remain.[5]

The devotional intention here is to "renounce" the self and, by means of Christ's mercy, be absorbed into the loving presence of God; but the effect of the wit, reasserting Major's name by simultaneously making use of all the dimensions of the verse, seems to run counter to this objective. Such a

2. "The World," l. 11, in *The Complete Poems of Henry Vaughan*, ed. Alan Rudrum (Harmondsworth: Penguin Books, 1976), 227.

3. "The Litanie" ll. 188–89, in *Complete English Poems of John Donne*, ed. C. A. Patrides (London: Dent, 1985), 464.

4. Judith Dundas discusses the traditional moral opposition between wit and wisdom in her "Levity and Grace: The Poetry of Sacred Wit," *Yearbook of English Studies* 2 (1972): 93–102.

5. *Honey on the Rod* (London: Thomas Maxey, 1656), 212.

criticism could also be made of the dazzlingly complex double acrostic of Henry Colman, "On the inscription over the head of Christ on the Crosse," in which both the beginning and end of the lines (running across two pages) spell out "Jesus of Nazareth the King of the Jews."[6] This impressive achievement serves a spiritual purpose: it highlights the duality of the title, and therefore of Christ's incarnate divinity. The poem even invites the reader on a word search to find the hidden biblical quotation "I am nigh to all that love me" embedded in the central portion of the text, and thus to realize its meaning. But is all this wit, in fact, counterproductive? Is the devotion itself not lost between the invention of the poet and the sanctioned play of the reader?

The extended imaginative exercise of a Baroque conceit, as in poems by Richard Crashaw or Joseph Beaumont, may also tell us more in the end about the poet than about the religious object of the poem. Beaumont's spiritual epic *Psyche* leads its reader along such labyrinths of adoration and excess that we are perhaps blinded rather than enlightened when we confront the glittering heavenly castle made of "living Chrystal" and rich with the "sparkling Diamond" of divine love.[7] In a very different mode, the intensity of a poetic meditation such as Donne's Holy Sonnet "Spit in my face" may also push wit to the limit of its devotional usefulness. The poet's initial demand challenges, and maybe transgresses, the boundary between self-humiliation and self-focus:

> Spit in my face you Jewes, and pierce my side,
> Buffet, and scoffe, scourge, and crucifie mee,
> For I have sinn'd, and sinn'd, . . . [8]

Whether to chastise or to glorify, the poet puts himself center stage; in this poem, that means receiving the tortures of Calvary. The potential for blasphemy here—the poet temporarily edging Christ off the cross and taking his place as redeemer of humankind—is inherent in the activity of wit in wider terms. Successful poets, as Herbert pointed out in "Jordan (II)," almost inevitably "weave" themselves "into the sense" of the text and thus vie with their maker. This presumption applies to the writer not only as poetic subject but

6. *Divine Meditations (1640)*, ed. Karen E. Steanson (New Haven: Yale University Press, 1979), 146–47.

7. *Psyche: or Loves Mysterie* (London, 1648), 3.34, 40. See also *The Minor Poems of Joseph Beaumont, D.D.*, ed. Eloise Robinson (Boston: Houghton Mifflin, 1914).

8. Holy Sonnet XI, in *Complete English Poems*, ed. Patrides, 441.

also as artistic creator; by striving for the witty excellence of "trim invention," the poet threatens rivalry with the divine wit of creation itself. Indeed, it is in the nature of most secular wit to thrive on a combative challenge; but such a spirit is surely inappropriate to the "sweetness" of devotional writing "readie penn'd" in love (pp. 102–3).

One apparently simple solution to this dilemma of the unwarranted wit of a Christian is to disclaim all such poetic pretensions. This is precisely what An Collins did in her *Divine Songs and Meditations* of 1653; in "The Discourse" she states unhesitatingly that any "error" in her text should be put down to "want of art," not to a failure of "true intent of mind." Anxious to explain her vocation further, she continues:

> Some may desirous be to understand
> What moved me, who unskilful am herein,
> To meddle with, and thus to take in hand,
> That which I cannot well end or begin;
> But such may first resolve themselves herein,
> If they consider, 'tis not want of skill
> That's more blameworthy than want of good will.[9]

By means of a defiantly plain style, but also through the ironic use of rhyme, she draws attention to spiritually unmatched pairs such as "skill" and "good will," confirming her aesthetic commitment to truth and faith rather than wit and art. In a similar vein, Herbert's vision of a "true Hymne" was a musical verse whose "fineness" was most clearly sensed not in artful wit but when "the soul unto the lines accords" (ll. 9–10). In "The Pearl," Herbert describes the Christian's struggle through the ways of worldly wisdom and pleasure, asserting ultimately that the escape route is to be found not through the "quick returns" of the poet's "groveling wit" but by means of the "silk twist" of divine grace "let down from heav'n" (ll. 12, 37–38). There is, however, a danger in this aesthetic of grace-in-plainness, the antiwit stance so favored by Calvinism and vividly depicted in Herbert's "British Church" as the desire to wear "nothing"—which can itself become a pride in nakedness. The stress upon plainness may license not only a zealous purity of style but also the plodding

9. In *Her Own Life: Autobiographical Writings by Seventeenth-century Englishwomen*, ed. Elspeth Graham et al. (London: Routledge, 1989), 57.

didacticism of a Christopher Harvey, thereby upholding witlessly feeble art as the keeping of faith. As Eldred Revett wrote, commenting that unfallen humanity knew no pride, "Pride first began, when first began defect": there can indeed be a perverse poet's pride in imperfection.[10]

At this stage, the argument comes an uncomfortable full circle. Wit in devotion is rejected from both sides, as part of an inappropriate human striving for perfection—an unconscionable hubris—and as something too low and distracting for the heights of religious verse. This circle of rejection does not, however, solve the problem, though it perhaps explains why the poets' dilemma was so intense and painful. Devotional poets continued to wrestle with wit, on account of one of the strongest residual arguments in its favor: if profane poetry is witty, sacred poetry has an obligation to be all the more so. If poetry expresses, as Marlowe claimed, the "highest reaches of a human wit,"[11] then the highest reaches of human spirituality in verse must find their appropriate match in the constructions of such a wit. The qualities of poetic wit and of devotion, when viewed from a more positive perspective, may actually be perceived as remarkably similar, particularly in the case of the seventeenth-century English lyric. Both wit and devotion function primarily by taking the ordinary and transforming it, making it surprising, special, holy. This happens, for example, most famously to the down-to-earth elements, the bread and the wine, in the communion service. It is also true of the drop of dew in Marvell's poem of that name; the "little globe" of "orient dew" puts the poet in mind of the soul that, like the dew,

> Remembering still its former height,
> Shuns the sweet leaves and blossoms green;
>
> And, recollecting its own light,
> Does, in its pure and circling thoughts, express
> The greater heaven in an heaven less.[12]

10. See Harvey's *The Synagogue* (1640), a laborious blow-by-blow imitation of Herbert's *The Temple*; Revett, *Selected Poems, Humane and Divine* (1657), ed. Donald Friedman (Liverpool: Liverpool University Press, 1966), 63.

11. *Tamburlaine the Great* (part 1), in *Christopher Marlowe: The Complete Plays*, ed. J. B. Steane (Harmondsworth: Penguin Books, 1969), 5.2.105.

12. *Andrew Marvell: Selected Poetry and Prose*, ed. Robert Wilcher (London: Methuen, 1986), 18–19.

Marvell and his contemporaries accepted that the "less" could be expressive of the "greater," a fundamental principle of both Christianity and wit. A religious approach to the familiar will enable "things of ordinary use," according to Herbert in his advice to a Country Parson, to serve as "lights even of Heavenly Truths" (*Works*, 257). Equally, wit facilitates the release of hidden spiritual significance in a lowly object such as the "bee" in a poem by the midcentury lyricist Cardell Goodman, as the symbolic "Treasure" concealed in the insect's "Amber Cabinetts" is gradually revealed by the poet's devotional imagination. The bee comes during the course of the poem to signify Christ, "our Love" who "with healing wings / Came humbly downe,"

> The Bee which did his honey poure
> Upon each growing herb and flowre.
> Butt yet, att last, this Innocence
> By men (Alas)
> Surprized was
> Without resistance or defence;
> And as a Sacrifice he dide
> Out dropd the Honey, from his side.[13]

The wit of this conclusion, like the "honey" or redeeming blood and water of Christ, is an unexpected gift to the reader, sudden but satisfying in both aesthetic and spiritual effect.

Certain aspects of seventeenth-century wit, then, begin to seem suitable for devotional writing: not the wit of sleek thinking and competitive brilliance, but a sharing of surprises, the discovery of holiness hidden in the everyday world, the wit of revelation as of Traherne's "News from a forrein Country." The effect of this wit is typified in Vaughan's effortless shifting of our perspective in a line such as "I saw Eternity the other night," or in the ending of Herbert's "Redemption" when a neat worldview is turned upside down by a confrontation with the "ragged noise and mirth" at the foot of the cross (l. 12).[14] The language and subjectivity of the lyrics are transformed by

13. *Beawty in Raggs Or Divine Phancies put into Broken Verse*, ed. R. J. Roberts (Reading: University of Reading, 1958), 11.

14. Traherne, "On News," in *Centuries, Poems, and Thanksgivings*, ed. H. M. Margoliouth (Oxford: Clarendon Press, 1965), 1:125; Vaughan, "The World," in *The Complete Poems*, ed. Rudrum, 227.

their absorption into a typological or biblical-historical identification; the wit of Vaughan and Herbert, as in the extracts from Marvell and Goodman, comprises an originality of perspective and expression, but also a common source in the Bible and mystical tradition. The appropriateness of this wit lies in its merging of startling individuality with larger patterns of language, liturgy, and history, a creative reconciling of what Herbert called the "Mine" and "Thine" ("Clasping of hands," l. 20).

The wit of discovery, personal and communal, is one means of reconciling invention and faithfulness. There is a certain aptness, too, in the exuberant verbal creativity of Donne's poetic arguments as a means of, albeit indirectly, celebrating the wonder of the creation; wit not only shows forth but also celebrates, polishing and enjoying creativity. As Donne wrote in his *Devotions*, God is "figurative" and "metaphoricall" as well as "literall," and so should his creations be also. There is, in addition, a fitting sense of divine glory inherent in (to borrow Crashaw's phrase for Mary Magdalene's tears) the "Still spending, never spent" expansiveness of Crashaw's textual richness.[15] A further parallel lies in the dependence of both devotion and sacred wit on the effect they achieve. While devotion is clearly concerned with the state of an individual's soul, its main focus lies outside the worshiper, on the object of worship. Wit, too, though often apparently arising from the poet's obsessive desire to be ingenious, requires a reader for its full effect. Devotional wit may even be defined by its influence on the audience, bearing in mind that this could be both human and divine.[16] As Herbert wrote in "The Forerunners," "if I please him [God], I write fine and wittie" (l. 12).

In the same poem, however, Herbert says farewell to his "lovely" and "embellished" language (ll. 13, 33), a reminder that religious wit is always only an interim skill. Thus wit in a devotional context is not only a slippery concept in its unpredictable link with readers' responses but is also unstable in always requiring the poet's willingness to dismantle that which has been built, to sacrifice the transient even in its most beautiful and expressive

15. Donne, "Expostulation," 19, in *Devotions upon Emergent Occasions,* ed. Anthony Raspa (Montreal: McGill-Queen's University Press, 1975), 99; Crashaw, "Saint Mary Magdalene or the Weeper," l. 5, in *The Poems: English, Latin, and Greek of Richard Crashaw,* ed. L. C. Martin (Oxford: Clarendon Press, 1927), 79.

16. See A. D. Nuttall, *Overheard By God: Fiction and Prayer in Herbert, Milton, Dante and St. John* (London and New York: Methuen, 1980).

forms.[17] The power of this religious wit lies, ironically, in the frequent realization that the project to unite wit and devotion, however right and necessary, must inevitably fail. Even that supreme craftsman, Ben Jonson, admitted that his best "gift" to God was not a witty verse but a "confused" heart.[18] Paradoxically, knowledge of the hopelessness of the task to find words for the Logos highlights just how far words can go.

II

Among the many tests of the wit of seventeenth-century devotional poets was the challenge to describe in words the wordless communication of God and the human soul in prayer. In some ways, poets who attempted to find verbal emblems for prayer were at the same time struggling to give expression to the essence of religious wit itself, since prayer shares in some of the qualities already identified with wit: creativity, self-expression, newness of perspective, identification, transformation, revelation, and abandonment. Let us, then, take a close look at two short poems on prayer, to clarify in detail some of the qualities of seventeenth-century Christian wit. The first text, Herbert's "Prayer (I)," published in *The Temple* in 1633, will no doubt be familiar; the second, "Prayer" by Eldred Revett, from his 1657 volume *Selected Poems, Humane and Divine,* probably less so.

> Prayer the Churches banquet, Angels age,
>   Gods breath in man returning to his birth,
>   The soul in paraphrase, heart in pilgrimage,
> The Christian plummet sounding heav'n and earth;
> Engine against th'Almightie, sinners towre,
>   Reversed thunder, Christ-side-piercing spear,
>   The six-daies world transposing in an houre,
> A kind of tune, which all things heare and fear;

17. See Dundas, "Levity and Grace," 102. A parallel argument is advanced with respect to the self-dismantling nature of the poems themselves in my "'Curious Frame': The Seventeenth-Century Religious Lyric as Genre," in *New Perspectives on the Seventeenth-Century English Religious Lyric,* ed. John R. Roberts (Columbia: University of Missouri Press, 1994).

18. "The Sinner's Sacrifice To the Holy Trinity," in *Ben Jonson: Poems,* ed. Ian Donaldson (Oxford: Oxford University Press, 1975), 125.

Softnesse, and peace, and joy, and love, and blisse,
    Exalted Manna, gladnesse of the best,   10
        Heaven in ordinarie, man well drest,
The milkie way, the bird of Paradise,
    Church-bels beyond the starres heard, the souls bloud,
    The land of spices; something understood.

Prayer
(1)
A *Fleece* of *Angell-downe* that flyes
    In a golden cloud of Breath;
Still upward to the kindred skyes
    And above them hovereth
        A *Soule*,
In *Parcell* ushering the whole.

(2)
A most illustrious *break* of *Day*,
    From the *Night* of Death and *sin*,
A Bright and *Emissary* Ray
    Of a cheerful *light within*;   10
        A *Spice!*
Smoaks from the Heart *in sacrifice*:

(3)
A *Spirit* hath got leave to *play*
    From its *Chains* of *Flesh* and *Blood*.
A soul *escap'd* to *learn* the way
    To its longed for abroad;
        A thought,
Then up *in the third Heavens caught*.

(4)
A *talking* with the *Holy One*,
    A Familiar conference: 20
A *wrestling* for a sparkling throne
    Got by *holy violence*
        A *Plate*.
And *Clapper* to Saint *Peters* Gate.[19]

19. Revett, *Selected Poems*, ed. Friedman, 62.

What are the elements of devotional wit to be found in these two poems? To begin with, it is important to consider structural features as an aspect of poetic wit. In both poems (Revett was, of course, substantially influenced by the earlier poet), the syntactical patterning is unusual, with the absence of a central verb (prayer *is*) emphasizing the nonnarrative nature of prayer as these poets perceived it. The oddity of prayer—lacking a logical sequence, taking multiple forms, and giving many varied sensations—is thus stressed in the witty handling of poetic structures. In terms of poetic form, Revett uses each stanza to develop one cluster of metaphors, giving the poem a characteristically spacious quality in contrast to the intensity of the tumbling epithets in Herbert's sonnet. The fact that his poem is a sonnet, however, enables Herbert to change the mood after the octet, leaving behind imagery of weapons and music for the simplicity of "Softnesse, and peace, and joy." This whole line in its plainness is the first sign of the poem's will to abandon metaphoric descriptions, more fully realized in the second half of its last line.

This fundamental structural wit, dependent on the poet's having an eye and an ear for poetic configuration, is built upon by localized outbursts of what we might call explicit wit. This takes the form of wordplay, for example, in Herbert's fourth line, where the plummet "sounding heav'n and earth" carries the primary meaning of measuring but also has a secondary implication that prayer both expresses heaven and earth and is resounding throughout them. Revett plays with the word *abroad* in line 16, punning on an implied reference to the escaped soul's longed-for "abode" as well as its freedom to be "abroad." There is more than a hint of paradox, too, in Revett's phrase "holy violence," the apparently contradictory entangling of spiritual conversation and aggression (also present in Herbert's "Engine against th'Almightie"). Herbert's wit expresses itself in ironies of reversal rather than in paradoxes on this occasion; the "Exalted Manna" of prayer is an image delighting in the simultaneous downward movement of the manna falling from heaven and the upward action of this nourishment being offered back in thanksgiving (recalling the uplifting of Christ on the cross and of the consecrated host in the Eucharist).

This latest instance of wit within the two poems draws attention to the fact that devotional wit is dependent upon the given material of faith and tradition. Unlike much secular wit, the poetic ingenuity of the religious lyricists does not function simply as originality but as the inhabiting of a shared set of ideas, many of which underpin the puns, paradoxes, and metaphors of indi-

vidual texts. Revett's poem also contains a direct echo of a biblical passage—
"up *in the third Heavens caught*" (see 2 Cor. 12:2)—and invokes Old Testament
sacrifices and a New Testament heaven with Saint Peter at the gate. Herbert
not only assumes a biblical background for "Angels age," the "sinners towre,"
and the "Christ-side-piercing spear" but also invokes a liturgical context with
references to the "Churches banquet" (both the communion and the ulti-
mate heavenly feast) and the "houre" of a church service that can "transpose"
the ordinary world.[20] This is wit that, however individual and perceptive,
nevertheless acknowledges and celebrates its communal sources.

Both poems, not surprisingly in view of their subject, reach out to find a
means of expressing mystery. Through exotic metaphors—a *"Fleece of Angell-
downe"* in Revett's opening line, "The milkie way, the bird of Paradise"
toward the end of Herbert's sonnet, and the land of "spices" found in both—
they strain to lift their work, as well as prayer itself, above the "kindred skyes."
But this sense of wit stretched to its limits in figurative language should not
blind us to the working of wit in another direction, through the poem's
conceptual framework. The center of Herbert's wit in "Prayer (I)" lies in his
perception of the reciprocity of the actions in prayer, repeatedly suggested
through phrases such as "Reversed thunder" and whole lines such as "Heaven
in ordinarie, man well drest" (also vivid on account of the mingling of an
everyday item such as clothing with the extraordinary notion that is heaven).
The dominant idea in Revett's "Prayer" is that of the part representing the
whole, suggested in the *"Emissary* Ray" or thought escaping upward, "In
Parcell ushering the whole." Although the two poems therefore go their sep-
arate ways, perhaps more than we would at first have sensed, they still have in
common this element of wit as conception, not necessarily as full-blown
"conceit" but as the kernel of an intellectual structure.

Each poem in its own way builds toward a conclusion. In Revett's more ex-
pansive style, there is a gradual familiarizing with the otherworldliness of
prayer; at the beginning it was "golden" and definitely upwardly mobile, but
by the end, although the throne is still "sparkling," the action of prayer has

---

20. "Angels age" is set in opposition to the average span of a human life (Ps. 90:10); the
"towre" refers to the idea of prayer as protective (as in 2 Sam. 22:51) as well as troublingly
reminding us of the Tower of Babel (Gen. 11:4); and prayer, like the spear that pierced the
crucified Christ, releases the "blood and water" of salvation (John 19:34).

become, simply, "A *talking* with the *Holy One*." The closing line with its final definition of prayer as the "*Clapper* to Saint *Peters* Gate" is startlingly direct, and in reality not a closing but an opening, an optimistic anticipation of the biblical promise "knock, and it shall be opened unto you" (Matt. 7:7). By contrast, Herbert's equivalent of the homely door-knocker, in his case the welcoming sound of "Church-bels" heard "beyond the starres," is not the poem's conclusion but part of a crescendo of definitions that is halted dramatically just five syllables before the end of the sonnet. The profundity of Herbert's vision allows him to glimpse the folly of thinking that words, however witty, could ever adequately define prayer. So the poem ends in the powerful plainness and humility of the transparent phrase "something understood"; prayer is finally to be entered into, not described.

Is Herbert's "Prayer (I)" a reminder of the dangers of wit in devotional poetry? Does ingenuity get in the way of spirituality here? Perhaps part of the brilliance of this sonnet is that it allows descriptive wit to run almost its full course and then, with a different but related wit, supplies a twist, a reassessment, that vital new perspective, in the last half line. What is "understood" in the closing phrase is not just God, and the Christian, and prayer, but wit itself. Looking back over the poem in the light of its conclusion—always a fruitful and necessary action in reading Herbert—we can see that religious wit, like prayer in Herbert's terms, is a "transposing" mechanism, rewriting the world in another key. It is, like the "Churches banquet," at once a private and a communal activity, inspired by individuality but also with its roots in shared traditions and texts. Unlike secular wit, it finds its fulfillment not in keeping control but in abandoning it, surrendering to the faith that it seeks to express and serve.

III

It is possible, then, to see both the nature of seventeenth-century religious wit and its complex relationship with devotion in a reading of these two poems. The poets and their contemporaries were deeply sensitive to the pitfalls of wit in spiritual language, aware that, as Donne wrote, the "infirmitie / Of him which speaks, diminishes the Word."[21] But they were able to demonstrate that a devotion to words in all their variety and potential need not represent

---

21. "The Litanie," ll. 190–91, in *Complete English Poems*, ed. Patrides, 465.

rivalry to devotion to the Word, nor indeed to something beyond words. Wit in the religious context was not the "Bravery" and "glistering Shews" that Margaret Cavendish, Revett's exact contemporary, identified as that which worldly poetic art craved;[22] devotional wit revealed itself rather in a variety of modes from structural and conceptual patterns to localized sharpness of observation or wordplay. Most crucially, Christian wit found that its "beauty" lay in "the *discovery*," as Herbert wrote in the early sonnet "Sure, Lord, there is enough in thee," preserved in Walton's *Life*. By means of an aesthetic of revelation and interaction, wit and beauty and truth were found to be compatible in seventeenth-century English devotional lyrics. As Herbert wrote in "The Church-porch," "nothing that's plain, / But may be wittie, if thou hast the vein" (ll. 239–40). The implication is that there is a seam of wit even in the plainest of words or concepts, provided that the approach taken is sympathetic and alert to the possibility of "discovery," the unearthing, showing forth, and ultimately the releasing, of an idea. This does not represent a deep-seated incompatibility between wit and Christianity, as was assumed in the remark by Sir Andrew Aguecheek with which we began, but a close interrelation of the two, rather along the lines of Polixenes' vision of art and nature in *The Winter's Tale*:

> Yet nature is made better by no mean
> But nature makes that mean; so over that art
> Which you say adds to nature, is an art
> That nature makes. . . .
>   . . . This is an art
> Which does mend nature—change it rather; but
> The art itself, is nature.
>   (4.4.89–92, 95–97)[23]

Despite the dangers inherent in wit for the Christian poet, the workings of wit and devotion, the artful and the natural, are profoundly connected in their essential activities and assumptions. As Polixenes might have said, it is a case of the devotion being "made better" by such wit; but the wit itself, is devotion.

22. "I *Language* want," from *Poems, and Fancies* (1653), in *Kissing the Rod: An Anthology of Seventeenth Century Women's Verse*, ed. Germaine Greer et al. (London: Virago Press, 1988), 173.

23. As Sir Thomas Browne confirmed, this "nature" is itself "the art of God." See *Religio Medici*, The First Part, paragraph 16, in *Sir Thomas Browne: The Major Works*, ed. C. A. Patrides (Harmondsworth: Penguin, 1977), 78–81.

P. G. Stanwood and Lee M. Johnson

The Structure of Wit

"Is all good structure in a winding stair?"

To define "wit" is no easier than to tell the meaning of "nature"; for these terms, used freely by both writers and critics from the Renaissance through the Romantic period, can describe so many different features of style and even culture. Wit has persistently chased after most of us, and yet remained elusive. Many of us began teaching with George Williamson's *The Proper Wit of Poetry*, and thirty years on, we are still traveling the witty route with A. J. Smith's *Metaphysical Wit*. The first book is an indispensable though essentially descriptive work; the second is a critical study within a historical framework that tries to discriminate between "metaphorical" wit, on the one hand, and "metaphysical" wit, on the other. In his early chapters, Williamson also describes metaphorical wit in the frequent sense of rhetorical forms that surprise us for their unexpected ingenuity, through fanciful exaggeration, resemblance, dissimilitude, incongruity, contradiction, or covert imitation. Smith traces "the line of wit" through such continental rhetoricians and theoreticians as Serafino and Tebaldeo to the conceited virtuosity of Maurice Scève, Jean de Sponde, and Agrippa D'Aubigné; he likewise moves across the landscape of English ingenuity from Wyatt onward. Once we reach Donne and the poets of the earlier seventeenth century, we discover metaphysical wit; now the counters and comparisons of courtly art that trivialized or ignored the inner life at last serve "to follow out the intricate interrelation of divine being with human nature, timeless events with history."[1] In other words,

---

1. See Smith, *Metaphysical Wit* (Cambridge: Cambridge University Press, 1991), 135; cf. Williamson, *The Proper Wit of Poetry* (Chicago: University of Chicago Press, 1961), 15.

metaphysical wit discovers infinity in time, provides a transcendent vision of life and a means to truth, and *effigiates*, that is, portrays the secular in the sacred, the sacred in the secular. This kind of wit seeks to go beyond ornament, ingenuity, and clever invention. Our wish is to clarify this broad species of wit by showing how it may be reinforced and corroborated by the form and structure of poetry itself, for metaphysical wit may in part be induced through structural mediation. It is this sort of "structural wit" that interests us here.

Let us illustrate wit that is merely metaphorical, of the sort that we mean mostly to exclude from our discussion, with an example. Sidney is a master of elegant wit, finding out expressive comparisons, with his "sunburnt brain" and "truant pen" (*Astrophel and Stella*, sonnet 1). "With how sad steps, Oh Moon, thou climb'st the skies!" leads to the hopeless question, "Oh Moon, tell me, / Is constant love deemed there but want of wit?" (sonnet 31). Such conceits are metaphorically but not metaphysically witty, and often they become egregious through repetition, extreme novelty, or absurdity—Sidney himself satirizes complaining poet lovers for their "living death, dear wounds, fair storms, and freezing fires" (sonnet 6).[2]

Metaphorical wit may derive from yoking conventionally contrary ideas together, and also unexpectedly remote ones; but metaphysical wit desires more deeply to engage and order experience. Therefore, Donne's description of twisted eye-beams that "did thred / Our eyes, upon one double string" is a good example of metaphysical wit. Not only does it point to an unusual resemblance but it also unfolds the greater experience of the whole poem. But we can see a less happy use of wit in Cleveland; he merely opens up a grotesque metaphor by declaring near the ending of "*The Rebell* Scot,"

> Sure *England* hath the Hemerods, and these
> On the North Posterne of the patient seize,
> Like Leeches: thus they physically thirst
> After our blood, but in the cure shall burst.
>   (ll. 83–86)

Similarly, Dryden offers, with a gratuitous comparison, an account of the smallpox that carried off the Lord Hastings:

---

2. Sidney is quoted from *The Poems of Sir Philip Sidney*, ed. William A. Ringler Jr. (Oxford: Clarendon Press, 1962).

> Like rose-buds, stuck i' th' Lily-skin about.
> Each little pimple had a tear in it,
> To wail the fault its rising did commit.[3]

Our aim is to elucidate not the metaphorical wit represented by these examples from Cleveland and Dryden, but the metaphysical wit typical of Donne; we wish to identify the kinds of poetic structures that metaphysical wit launches and brings to life, for such wit may depend upon interpretive patterns and figures as well as cogent comparison. To trace this process, we will draw particularly from the poetry of Herbert and Milton, who seem best to uphold our theme and display its development.

The familiar pattern poems of George Herbert, "The Altar" and "Easter-Wings," display metaphysical wit, adopting almost equally familiar antique models; but those earlier poems are built from very limited exercises of invention. The well-known shaped poems of the Greek Anthology are notable for their clever depictions of wings, pillars, and axes. The acrostic verses of Publilius Optatianus Porfyrius, a contemporary of Constantine, who made him prefect of the city of Rome for two terms in 329 and 333, have no equal for ingenuity, but they are premetaphorical, in A. J. Smith's taxonomy; they could not be further from the kind of metaphysical wit that tries seriously to unfold truths or portray transcendent visions. Optatian certainly constructed his poems with intense elaboration, but the finished buildings, pushed together with such devotion, have the significance of a *Times* crossword. In a recent (and rare) discussion of his verse, one critic writes:

> With the possible exception of Sisyphus, antiquity has no more compelling paradigm of expended effort than the poet Optatian moving his own stones to and fro in these unprecedented mosaics. . . . As impressive as the poems are as finished products, they are irresistibly more impressive as activities. How much time, how much intellectual labor, how many discarded versions, how much paper, how much ink has been so conspicu-

---

3. Cleveland is quoted from *The Poems of John Cleveland*, ed. Brian Morris and Eleanor Withington (Oxford: Clarendon Press, 1967), 31. John Dryden's first printed work, "Upon the Death of the Lord Hastings," appeared in the second edition of *Lachrymae Musarum* (1650). See *The Best of Dryden*, ed. Louis I. Bredvold (New York: Ronald Press, 1933), 1–4. We have quoted lines 58–60.

ously consumed for this gigantic enterprise? And finally, to what purpose and under what strange compulsion?[4]

In the accompanying illustration from Optatian (figure 1), internal letters form a symbol (a *chi* and *rho*); when removed from the poem, these letters provide additional verses disposed into a metrical scheme, so that the Christian monogram usefully honors the "pious and eternal emperor Constantine, / restorer of the world." We can appreciate Optatian's tinkering with words, an art indicative of joinery, quite unconcerned with universal principles. His accomplishments are marvelous, but profoundly trivial.

Although no one could surpass Optatian for acrostic verse, others carried on the fertile tradition of making pictures out of verse, or in some way combining the two. We may see evidence of this activity in another illustration (figure 2), this one attributed to Hrabanus Maurus (circa 784–856) from his *De laudibus sanctae crucis* (In praise of the holy cross). Hrabanus makes an acrostic not only of Christ's crown but also of his navel. When the letters enclosed in the crown are read, the result is "Rex regum et Dominus dominorum" (King of kings and Lord of lords); and the letters surrounding the head (in the hair itself) spell "Iste est rex iustitiae" (He is the king of justice). Only the three Greek letters about the head stand apart, not belonging to a separate line; A, M, and Ω are meant to signify the beginning, the middle, and the end, or Christ's comprehending of all things. The whole poem is a meditation on the Passion; the central line, which runs through the umbilical "O," is "Nazareus cum offensio sit, ac scandalum iniquis" (When the Nazarene is hated and there is the scandal of wickedness).[5]

To travel from Optatian and Hrabanus to the seventeenth century reveals both "times trans-shifting" and wit's. In Herbert, for example, verbal dexterity leads from invention to vision, where the literal connotes "something

4. See W. Levitan, "Dancing at the End of the Rope: Optatian Porfyry and the Field of Roman Verse," *Transactions of the American Philological Association* 115 (1985): 266. See also Elizabeth Cook, *Seeing through Words: The Scope of Late Renaissance Poetry* (New Haven: Yale University Press, 1986), esp. chap. 2, "Figured Poetry," and chap. 3, "George Herbert." Optatian was edited by E. Kluge (Leipzig: Teubner, 1926).

5. Hrabanus Maurus appears in *Patrologia Latina*, ed. J.-P. Migne et al. (Paris, 1833–1903), vols. 107–12; *De laudibus sanctae crucis* (circa 810) is in vol. 107 (see esp. pp. 149–52). The illustration reproduces one figure from an early-tenth-century English manuscript of Hrabanus at Trinity College, Cambridge (MS B.16.3).

XIV.

```
        5        10        15        20        25        30        35
   SANCTE·DECVS·MVNDI·ACRERVM·SVMMA·SALVTIS
   LVX·PIA·TERRARVM·TE·SOLO·PRINCIPE·SAECLIS
   IN·MENSVM·GAVDERE·BONIS·DATVRA·VREA·VENIT
   SVMMO·MISSA·DEO·FVSI·SPATER·ALME·TYRANNIS
 5 IVSTITIA·IN·TERRAS·ET·GLORIA·CANDIDA·VERI
   TEQVE·DVCE·MAGE·GRATA·FIDES·ET·IVRA·RENATA
   TOTAQVE·PERCVLSIS·INGENTI·MOLE·TYRANNIS
   ASPERA·VIS·POSITA·EST·BELLI·RES·ITALA·IVRE
   SCEPTRA·DABIT·POPVLIS·VOTO·PIVS·ORBIS·EOI
10 AVGVSTE·INVICTAS·MVNDI·TRANSIBIS·IN·ORAS
   TEQVE·SVPLEX·TOTIS·DVCIBVS·STIPATA·SYENE
   ORATIVRA·CVPIT·LVCISSI·BIGA·VDIANOSTRAE
   OPTATA·MAT·FALLAXEN·PERFIDA·TELA·FVGARVM
   PARTHVS·DEPOSVIT·RVITORIS·VNDIQVE·RVBRI
15 LITORIS·AETHERIO·ENVTV·CERTAMINE·AMORIS
   MEDVS·ARABS·MOX·OMNISO·VAT·LAVDARE·SERENI
   ORIS·LVSTRATVI·DAT·VERIS·SANCTE·TROPAEIS
   HAEC·MAGE·FELICES·T·ITVLOS·VT·VINCAS·AMORE
   AVREA·PERPETVO·RESTAVRANS·SAECVLA·MVNDO
20 NDVS·ET·AVRORAEM·ILESQVOS·FLVMINE·NILVS
   TANGIT·FECVNDIS·VENTVRVS·FRVGIFER·VNDIS
   ORANTES·PIA·IVRA·PETENT·GENS·NOBILIS·ORTV
   AETHIOPES·CVNCTI·PARENT·OPTATAQVE·MVNDI
   TEMPORA·LAETA·DEDIT·NOBIS·FELICITAS·AEVI
25 ENSVPLICES·PERSAE·IVRA·SIBI·REGIA·NOLVNT
   TE·DOMINVM·MALVNT·FVSITVA·SEMPER·ADORANT
   ORAS·VIS·CVPIVNT·TOTI·STIBI·CEDERE·REGNIS
   TV·PIVS·ET·IVSTI·VERE·MEMOR·INCLYTE·LAETIS
   DARES·PONSA·BONO·SEMPER·MITISSIMVS·ORBIS
30 IMPERTIRE·ET·VVM·CLEMENTERE·ET·ADDITON·VMEN
   SINT·MAGE·FELICES·PARITER·QVOS·ALME·TVERE
   ET·REPARATA·IVGANS·MAESTI·DIVORTIA·MVNDI
   ORBES·IVNGE·PARES·DE·TLEGES·ROMA·VOLENTIS
   PRINCIPE·TE·IN·POPVLOS·MITI·FELICIVS·AEVO
35 OMNIA·LAETENTVR·FLORENTIBVS·AVREA·REBVS
```

Versus intexti Summi dei auxilio nutuque perpetuo tutus
orbem totum pacavit trucidatis tyrannis
Constantinus pius et aeternus imperator,
reparator orbis.

Figure 1. This poem by Optatian appears in *Optatian*, ed. E. Kluge (Leipzig: Teubner, 1926).

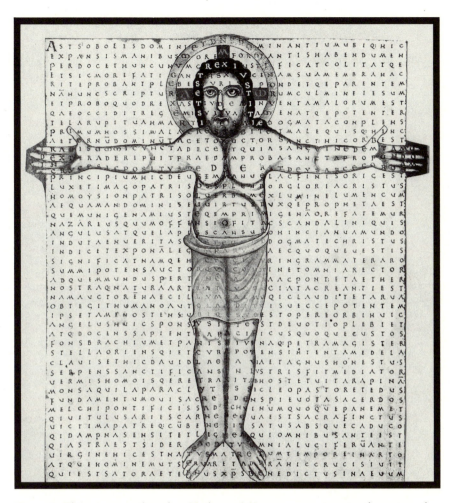

Figure 2. This poem attributed to Hrabanus Maurus appears in a tenth-century il-
luminated manuscript in the possession of Trinity College, Cambridge (MS B.16.3),
and is reproduced by kind permission of the Master and Fellows.

understood," and the whole poetic structure becomes a witty performance. We might compare with these earlier examples of wit Herbert's poem on Col. 3:3, "Our life is hid with Christ in God":

> My words & thoughts do both expresse this notion,
> That *Life* hath with the sun a double motion.
> The first *Is* straight, and our diurnall friend,
> The   other *Hid* and doeth obliquely bend.
> One life is wrapt *In* flesh, and tends to earth:
> The other winds towards *Him*, whose happie birth
> Taught me to live here so, *That* still one eye
> Should aim and shoot at that which *Is* on high:
> Quitting   with   daily   labour   all   *My* pleasure,
> To   gain   at   harvest   an   eternall   *Treasure*.[6]

The ten lines of the poem imitate God's perfection. The poet's "life" is hidden in the poem obliquely—slantingly, from the top left to the bottom right—his discovery helping to interpret the scriptural text on which the poem is founded. Thus the title-verse of the poem is described by the internal text that explains both the poem of which it is a part and the verse on which the poem is constructed: *Our life* becomes *My life*, but both are mutually accessible by being hidden. In such ways does Herbert furnish his metaphysical structure, preferring his own "simple" rooms to the ingeniously decorated lodgings of his predecessors.

The importance of structural wit is regularly manifested in Herbert's verse, sometimes in subtle ways, always in significant ones. The precepts of "The Church-Porch" are like the droplets of water sprinkled with the perirran-terium (or aspergillum), preparing us for the holy mysteries that will be celebrated within the church, not at "The Altar" whose false shape—that of a Hebrew or Old Testament altar, *not* a Christian one—we see; for it is "broken," in need of "new" construction and blessing. The dust of our old life passes through the twenty-four lines of the hourglass in "Church-Monuments" to remind us of our earthly consummation in a fleeting day. The decay of life in Herbert steadily meets the immutable joy of heavenly reward, his structural wit repeatedly supporting this theme by defining it with visual references.

Herbert's "Trinitie Sunday" is written for the feast day that celebrates a

6. *The Works of George Herbert*, ed. F. E. Hutchinson (1941; corrected rpt. Oxford: Clarendon Press, 1959), 84–85. All quotations of Herbert are from this edition.

theological doctrine. He reminds us of the Trinity in several ways, especially through the poetic structure itself:

> Lord, who hast form'd me out of mud,
>   And hast redeem'd me through thy bloud,
>   And sanctifi'd me to do good;
>
> Purge all my sinnes done heretofore:
>   For I confesse my heavie score,
>   And I will strive to sinne no more.
>
> Enrich my heart, mouth, hands in me,
>   With faith, with hope, with charitie;
>   That I may runne, rise, rest with thee.

The poem is thick with threes: three stanzas of three lines each, with sets of rhymes emphasizing the direction of Father, Son, and Spirit—with the associations of creator, redeemer, sanctifier ("mud," "bloud," "good"; "heretofore," "score," "no more"; "me," "charitie," "thee"), though any set of three rhymes can be transposed, with the terms in any order. And key words in each stanza stress the one-in-three constitution of the Trinity: stanza 1 belongs to the Father, who "form'd," "redeem'd," "sanctifi'd"; stanza 2 is that of the Son, who shows the poet how to "purge," "confesse," and "strive"; stanza 3 is of the Spirit, who enriches "heart" (of God = living), "mouth" (of Son = speaking), "hands" (of Spirit = enabling), with "faith," "hope," and "charity" (complemented by "run," "rise," and "rest"), each virtue pointing to a function of the three-in-one and one-in-three of the Trinity. The poem as a whole reminds us of the mysterious work of its subject, but as if to digest the Athanasian Creed.

In her complex analysis of this poem, Sibyl Lutz Severance argues that Herbert has organized "Trinitie Sunday" around ten groups of three—ten representing God's fullness and a return to unity. Thus the three stanzas form together one set or group, and the three lines of each stanza add three more discrete groups. The verbs of the first stanza recount God's grace to man, a fifth group, with the accompanying nouns forming a sixth group. The second stanza introduces a seventh set of confession, purgation, and dedication, with sets of triple nouns in lines 7 and 8 and the triple verbs of line 9 completing the ten groups. Such painstaking care in planning this poem is no accident;

for Herbert is demanding that the particular points of his metaphysical wit lead to an altogether witty structure in order to become one with it.[7]

A recurrent theme in Herbert's *The Temple* concerns his calling, his vocation as a priest—and as a poet. "Aaron" unfolds Herbert's ripest thoughts on the meaning of the true priest's office:

Holinesse on the head,
Light and perfections on the breast,
Harmonious bells below, raising the dead
To leade them unto life and rest:
Thus are true Aarons drest.   5

Profanenesse in my head,
Defects and darknesse in my breast,
A noise of passions ringing me for dead
Unto a place where is no rest:
Poore priest thus am I drest.   10

Onely another head
I have, another heart and breast,
Another musick, making live not dead,
Without whom I could have no rest:
In him I am well drest.   15

Christ is my onely head,
My alone onely heart and breast,
My onely musick, striking me ev'n dead;
That to the old man I may rest,
And be in him new drest.   20

So holy in my head,
Perfect and light in my deare breast,
My doctrine tun'd by Christ, (who is not dead,

---

7. See "Numerological Structures in *The Temple*," in *"Too Rich to Clothe the Sunne"*: *Essays on George Herbert*, ed. Claude J. Summers and Ted-Larry Pebworth (Pittsburgh: University of Pittsburgh Press, 1980), 231–32. Herbert, of course, wrote many poems with similar ingenuity, in which a specific occasion becomes the object and the form of the verse. "The Collar" is another example, which, in declaring (or having demanded) structural freedom discovers constraint; in supposing that worship is spontaneous, the poet recognizes the inevitable pattern of devotion, and in avoiding the "calling" of God he comes to hear it more clearly.

But lives in me while I do rest)
          Come people; Aaron's drest.   25

The poem is based, of course, on the dressing of Aaron (Exod. 28), the first priest, who is the Old Testament *type* of the priest of the New Covenant, or Christ himself, in whom the old man dies so that the new one may live. The metaphysical—and structural wit—of the poem is complex yet transparent. The name *Aaron* has five letters, and the poem has five stanzas, each of five lines. There are only two rhymes in each stanza, based on five words: *head-dead, breast-rest-drest*. Thus the first line of each stanza focuses on head, the second on breast, and so on, while the first stanza emphasizes a function of the head (or mind, seat of intellect), and the second stanza one of the breast (or heart, source of love and the affections). The third stanza is the pivotal one, in which living and dying explicitly meet; the fourth stanza looks for rest, and the final stanza describes the achievement of the whole poem—the dressing of Aaron in the doctrine of Christ, wherein believers may dwell. The poem also depends upon the music of Aaron's robe, with its hem made of alternating pomegranates and bells of gold: "A golden bell and a pomegranate, a golden bell and a pomegranate, upon the hem of the robe round about . . . and his sound shall be heard when he goeth in unto the holy place before the Lord, and when he cometh out, that he die not" (Exod. 28:34–35). The long third line of each stanza rings in memory of Aaron. Thus Herbert blends literal action into ethical movement, historical incident into spiritual consciousness, conviction into conversion in his temple of wit.

Herbert, who would be dressed and tuned by Christ, wrote of his own vocation in "Aaron"; in "Man" he extends this calling to all of us. The one poem, through its typological figure of Aaron, is pointing to the new priesthood; the other is a more general reflection on the whole creation and mankind's relationship to it. "Man" is thus a celebration of all God's round world, which includes man at the center, the principal creature through whom earth and heaven meet. Like "Aaron," "Man" also depends upon symmetry, balance, and correspondence, its subject being mirrored through its form; for Herbert is again molding verbal patterns against symbolic structures that sustain his whole poetic enterprise.

We have seen symmetries in "Aaron," and we can see still more in "Man." "Aaron" is built on a deftly contrived metrical and stanzaic pattern, in which each stanza is a typological pointer, the lines expanding—from six to eight to ten syllables—then contracting—to eight and six syllables—so that the middle line is always climactic, magnetically drawing the two before and the two that follow. We may see a similar scheme at work in "Man":

My God, I heard this day,
That none doth build a stately habitation,
But he that means to dwell therein.
What house more stately hath there been,
Or can be, then is Man? to whose creation   5
All things are in decay.

For Man is ev'ry thing,
And more: He is a tree, yet bears more fruit;
A beast, yet is, or should be more:
Reason and speech we onely bring.   10
Parrats may thank us, if they are not mute,
They go upon the score.

Man is all symmetrie,
Full of proportions, one limbe to another,
And all to all the world besides: 15
Each part may call the furthest, brother:
For head with foot hath private amitie,
And both with moons and tides.

Nothing hath got so farre,
But Man hath caught and kept it, as his prey.   20
His eyes dismount the highest starre:
He is in little all the sphere.
Herbs gladly cure our flesh; because that they
Finde their acquaintance there.

For us the windes do blow,   25
The earth doth rest, heav'n move, and fountains flow.
Nothing we see, but means our good,
As our delight, or as our treasure:
The whole is, either our cupboard of food,
Or cabinet of pleasure.   30

The starres have us to bed;
Night draws the curtain, which the sunne withdraws;

Musick and light attend our head.
All things unto our flesh are kinde
In their descent and being; to our minde   35
In their ascent and cause.

Each thing is full of dutie:
Waters united are our navigation;
Distinguished, our habitation;
Below, our drink; above, our meat;   40
Both are our cleanlinesse. Hath one such beautie?
Then how are all things neat?

More servants wait on Man,
Then he'l take notice of: in ev'ry path
He treads down that which doth befriend him,   45
When sicknesse makes him pale and wan.
Oh mightie love! Man is one world, and hath
Another to attend him.

Since then, my God, thou hast
So brave a Palace built; O dwell in it,   50
That it may dwell with thee at last!
Till then, afford us so much wit;
That, as the world serves us, we may serve thee,
And both thy servants be.

We catch Herbert, as so often, in a conversation or in an activity. Here the first line sets the tone for the rest of the poem, and it establishes also the pattern that will not change: the six-line stanza is easily divided into two parts; it grows suddenly from three to five syllables, then shrinks to four. The second half of the stanza repeats this pattern in reverse, thus mirroring the first half—four to five to three. While "Aaron" is balanced around a pivotal line and a middle stanza, helping us to see the linear movement of its typology, "Man" is designed to show the elaborate circle of reciprocity enjoyed by creation. Thus each stanza is a whole in two parts, and the total poem of nine stanzas teaches us spherical mathematics: the first four stanzas are one hemisphere, the fifth stanza is a fixed center, and the final four stanzas are another hemisphere. "Man is all symmetrie," Herbert says; and this poem is designed to prove that idea.

The central fifth stanza brings together the winds of earth and heaven that comfort us and support "our cupboard of food, / Or cabinet of pleasure" (ll. 29–30). Man's terrestrial habitation is the subject of stanzas 1–4, his celestial home of stanzas 6–9. This bilateralism is further emphasized by the outer correspondences, that is, stanza 1 is answered by stanza 9 (and the reverse): "What house more stately" is a brave palace for the servants of God who maintain the building of his creation. Likewise, stanzas 2 and 8 are joined by theme and diction: "For Man is ev'ry thing" (l. 7) who seeks to know that he is "one world, and hath / Another to attend him" (ll. 47–48). Man's "proportions" in stanza 3 have their correspondence in the ordered world where all things are "neat" (l. 42). Stanzas 4 and 6, finally, complete another, inner circle, with the one describing man's eyes that "dismount the highest starre" (l. 21), the other comfortably declaring that "The starres have us to bed" (l. 31). Thus there is in "Man" one action that moves outward—of microcosmic man in the world—and a second and simultaneous action that moves inward—of God's creative urgency. With every earthly image, there is a corresponding heavenly one; and with every ascending of man to God, there is a concurrent descending of God to man. Through its concentering circles of complementary stanzas and its correspondent verbal design, the poem becomes the witty structure it describes. "Afford us so much wit" to dwell in this house, Herbert gently urges (l. 52); in that knowledge is the capacity of true servanthood.

For his mastery of witty poetical structures, Milton has been insufficiently appreciated; yet, like Herbert's witty architecture, Milton's is most perfectly and subtly managed: he is often a metaphysical poet in the richest sense. His structural wit calls upon both verbal and nonverbal or formal designs and displays itself in many ways and places. To begin with a well-known example of verbal design, we may recall the metaphysical point associated with his use of *fall* in the Father's speech from book 3 of *Paradise Lost* (ll. 8–134). As this long verse paragraph develops, the words *fall* and *fell* plus their auditory cognates *fault* and *false* are sounded out eleven times with increasing frequency. The same design is, of course, climactic in *Paradise Regained* (4.561–81) when the narrator describes the fall of Satan by repeating *fall* and *fell* seven times (in total) as those words tumble down through their verse paragraph. It is not necessary for Satan to fall in order to elicit such verbal wit; when the arch fiend staggers backward in book 6 of *Paradise Lost*, he is subject to combined verbal and prosodic critiques, and the ten metrical feet (at lines 193–95) evidently imitate his ten backward paces:

> ten paces huge
> He back recoil'd; the tenth on bended knee
> His massy Spear upstay'd.[8]

Satan is the recipient of further witty verbal designs when Milton devises an acrostic in 9.510–14 in order to name and describe Satan's approach to Eve, so that the name "S-A-T-A-N" accompanies the description of the serpent.[9] Milton's wit is often highly sophisticated, even becoming abstract when, as we shall see in three important illustrations, metaphysical wit serves entire structures.

"At a Solemn Music," first of all, is about harmony, or the fashion in which we who are bound on earth may respond to God's celestial consort. Milton's aim is to reconcile this world's music with that heavenly world's song. The poem naturally moves through a scale, from low to high, but tuned concordantly, "In perfect diapason" (l. 23). To illustrate this harmony, Milton divides his poem into three octaves: the first eight lines of "verse" lead into the second eight lines, where "Jubilee" (l. 9) is rhymed with "everlastingly" (l. 17) to begin the final octave "with undiscording voice" (l. 18). "Disproportion'd sin" ruins "natures chime" with its "harsh din" and spoils the concord toward which we should incline. "Diapason" means complete harmony, and it signifies also "the consonance of the highest and lowest notes of the musical scale" (*OED*). We see, therefore, that Milton has constructed a diapason in verse while metaphorically describing it; and he ends this consort of well-assembled wit with a four-line prayer that God will keep us united in song "To live with him, and sing in endless morn of light" (l. 28).

8. According to James Whaler, "The exact number of backward paces of recoil is paralleled and measured by the number of metric beats in the term that tells it" (*Counterpoint and Symbol: An Inquiry into the Rhythm of Milton's Epic Style* [Copenhagen: Rosenkilde and Bagger, 1956], 100). All quotations of Milton are from *John Milton: Complete Poems and Major Prose*, ed. Merritt Y. Hughes (New York: Odyssey Press, 1957).

9. P. J. Klemp first noticed this acrostic: "Milton has fused form and content to produce an acrostic which acts in a way as a gloss upon the text. And this is no display of 'false wit.' The acrostic appears at a very dramatic moment in the narrative and is perfectly suited to its context" ("'Now Hid, Now Seen': An Acrostic in *Paradise Lost*," *Milton Quarterly* 11 [1977]: 91).

In the second instance, Milton employs the sonnet form as a mode of perception that controls his verbal meanings and shows the harmony and interdependence among all created things and their creator. Somewhat unexpectedly, his symbolic use of the sonnet as a fully metaphysical and structural principle of love and order occurs in unrhymed form, as Uriel, in response to a request for directions to earth, manages to summarize the creation of the universe to a disguised Satan at the end of book 3 of *Paradise Lost:*[10]

> Fair Angel, thy desire which tends to know
> The works of God, thereby to glorify   695
> The great Work-Master, leads to no excess
> That reaches blame, but rather merits praise
> The more it seems excess, that led thee hither
> From thy Empyreal Mansion thus alone,
> To witness with thine eyes what some perhaps   700
> Contented with report hear only in Heav'n:
> For wonderful indeed are all his works,
> Pleasant to know, and worthiest to be all
> Had in remembrance always with delight;
> But what created mind can comprehend   705
> Thir number, or the wisdom infinite
> That brought them forth, but hid thir causes deep.
> I saw when at his Word the formless Mass,
> This world's material mould, came to a heap:
> Confusion heard his voice, and wild uproar   710
> Stood rul'd, stood vast infinitude confin'd;
> Till at his second bidding darkness fled,
> Light shone, and order from disorder sprung:
> Swift to thir several Quarters hasted then
> The cumbrous Elements, Earth, Flood, Air, Fire,   715
> And this Ethereal quintessence of Heav'n
> Flew upward, spirited with various forms,
> That roll'd orbicular, and turn'd to Stars
> Numberless, as thou seest, and how they move;
> Each had his place appointed, each his course,   720

10. See Lee M. Johnson, "Milton's Blank Verse Sonnets," *Milton Studies* 5 (1973): 146–47. The same essay (pp. 129–53) provides interpretations of many other unrhymed sonnets in *Paradise Lost, Paradise Regained,* and *Samson Agonistes* without, however, drawing attention, as is being done here, to their role in establishing Miltonic structural wit.

The rest in circuit walls this Universe.
Look downward on that Globe whose hither side
With light from hence, though but reflected, shines;
That place is Earth the seat of Man, that light
His day, which else as th' other Hemisphere   725
Night would invade, but there the neighboring Moon
(So call that opposite fair Star) her aid
Timely interposes, and her monthly round
Still ending, still renewing through mid Heav'n,
With borrow'd light her countenance triform   730
Hence fills and empties to enlighten the Earth,
And in her pale dominion checks the night.
That spot to which I point is *Paradise*,
Adam's abode, those lofty shades his Bow'r.
Thy way thou canst not miss, me mine requires.   735

Never, perhaps, has a set of directions been graced with such elegant wit. Uriel's forty-two-line speech divides into three fourteen-line sections, creating an unrhymed triple sonnet in book 3, just as the six days of creation and the seventh of rest are appropriately placed in book 7. Each of Uriel's consecutive sonnets reveals an Italian or Petrarchan form: "Heav'n" appears prominently at the ends of lines 701, 716, and 729 to mark the divisions between octaves and sestets. As is characteristic of Milton's rhymed sonnets, which progress from temporal to timeless conditions as ontological contexts shift and expand from octaves to sestets, so here, in Uriel's triple blank-verse sonnet, the physical works of creation are linked to their timeless spiritual source. In the first of his sonnets (ll. 694–707), Uriel notes in the octave that the "works of God" cannot be praised too much, because, as he notes in the sestet, the "wisdom infinite / That brought them forth" is unlimited. The second sonnet (ll. 708–21) shows, in its octave, how God's "second bidding" evokes the "cumbrous Elements, Earth, Flood, Air, Fire," whereas the sestet turns to the spirit, "this Ethereal quintessence of Heav'n" and to the symbolic perfection of its "orbicular" imagery. The third and final sonnet (ll. 722–35) celebrates the completed triumph of light over darkness through the harmonious relationships among the sun, moon, and earth; the latter, with its "*Paradise, / Adam's* abode" represents the indwelling perfection of spirit in matter at the climax of the sestet. Uriel's triple sonnet thus moves from the deific idea of creativity to the fullness of its expression in the original Paradise; as it does so, it suggests the interdependence among all things spiritual and material in their attainment of an orderly scale of creation. The language, imagery, and increasing detail of Uriel's speech perfectly exemplify the symbolism of Milton's sonnet form. The interactions of matter and spirit, of octaves and sestets, and the metaphysical vision of a profound wit express, through poetic structures, a symbolic analogy to the divine love and creativity that lie at the heart of *Paradise Lost*.

Finally, in Adam and Eve's magnificent Morning Hymn in book 5, we see ideally displayed a witty structure that subsumes metaphysical wit and nearly conceals itself:

> These are thy glorious works, Parent of good,
> Almighty, thine this universal Frame,
> Thus wondrous fair; thyself how wondrous then!   155
> Unspeakable, who sit'st above these Heavens
> To us invisible or dimly seen
> In these thy lowest works, yet these declare
> Thy goodness beyond thought, and Power Divine:
> Speak yee who best can tell, ye Sons of Light,   160
> Angels, for yee behold him, and with songs
> And choral symphonies, Day without Night,
> Circle his Throne rejoicing, yee in Heav'n;
> On Earth join all ye Creatures to extol
> Him first, him last, him midst, and without end.   165
> Fairest of Stars, last in the train of Night,
> If better thou belong not to the dawn,
> Sure pledge of day, that crown'st the smiling Morn
> With thy bright Circlet, praise him in thy Sphere
> While day arises, that sweet hour of Prime.   170
> Thou Sun, of this great World both Eye and Soul,
> Acknowledge him thy Greater, sound his praise
> In thy eternal course, both when thou climb'st,
> And when high Noon hast gain'd, and when thou fall'st.
> Moon, that now meet'st the orient Sun, now fli'st   175
> With the fixt Stars, fixt in thir Orb that flies,
> And yee five other wand'ring Fires that move
> In mystic Dance not without Song, resound
> His praise, who out of Darkness call'd up Light.

Air, and ye Elements the eldest birth   180
Of Nature's Womb, that in quaternion run
Perpetual Circle, multiform, and mix
And nourish all things, let your ceaseless change
Vary to our great Maker still new praise.
Ye Mists and Exhalations that now rise   185
From Hill or steaming Lake, dusky or grey,
Till the Sun paint your fleecy skirts with Gold,
In honor to the World's great Author rise,
Whether to deck with Clouds th'uncolor'd sky,
Or wet the thirsty Earth with falling showers,   190
Rising or falling still advance his praise.
His praise ye Winds, that from four Quarters blow,
Breathe soft or loud; and wave your tops, ye Pines,
With every Plant, in sign of Worship wave.
Fountains and yee, that warble, as ye flow,   195
Melodious murmurs, warbling tune his praise.
Join voices all ye living Souls; ye Birds,
That singing up to Heaven Gate ascend,
Bear on your wings and in your notes his praise;
Yee that in Waters glide, and yee that walk   200
The Earth, and stately tread, or lowly creep;
Witness if I be silent, Morn or Even,
To Hill, or Valley, Fountain, or fresh shade
Made vocal by my Song, and taught his praise.
Hail universal Lord, be bounteous still   205
To give us only good; and if the night
Have gathered aught of evil or conceal'd,
Disperse it, as now light dispels the dark.

The hymn is offered as if it might be an appropriate canticle—this one recalling especially the Benedicite, Omnia Opera (or the apocryphal Song of the Three Children in the Book of Daniel), the hymn appointed for Morning Prayer in the Book of Common Prayer as an alternative to the Te Deum: "O all ye Works of the Lord, bless ye the Lord: praise him, and magnify him for ever." Milton also borrows phrases from Psalm 148. In spite of the disclaimer preceding the hymn that it is "unmeditated" or "prompt eloquence" (5.149), this lyric has an admirable balance and finely wrought shape. This Morning

Hymn (the evening is said to be the other time for such song) is carefully, symmetrically, and wittily planned.[11] Adam and Eve praise God in the first seven lines, even as they petition him in the final four; thus they call on the angels, the "Sons of Light," for aid in their song. Forty-five lines (160–204) describe different orders of creation. These lines are balanced in two sections of twenty lines each (160–79, 185–204), separated by a middle section of five lines (180–84). The first section addresses the celestial universe, the middle section points to the elements of creation, and the last section provides more praise that rises from the earth. The middle section actually begins at the center of the passage, twenty-eight lines from the beginning and the same number from the end; but if we count from the eighth line, where this forty-five-line passage begins, we reach "Perpetual Circle" (182), the actual center of the passage.

The imagery throughout the whole hymn depends upon circles—the sphere, the circlet, the orb—as befits its circular design and symmetry, thereby attaining a perfect and metaphysically witty union of image and form. In this respect, the Morning Hymn represents an advance over Uriel's reference, in the second of his sonnets discussed above, to "orbicular" forms, which present an image without a corresponding structural exemplification. To all the Morning Hymn's manifestations of circular perfection, worship is rising, joining in ascent to "his praise," a notable phrase, occurring eight times, that spells out the motif of the song. This lyric, as we may surely style it, also invokes various kinds of light that put the end to all darkness: sun, eye and soul, noon, stars and moon, fires, sky. Finally, in the concluding four-line section, God is asked to disperse the brooding night, "as now light dispels the dark"; with "his praise" Adam and Eve and all of creation sing gloriously and melodiously, in words of consummate art and skill.

11. For a discussion of the Morning Hymn in relation to the theme of innocence, see Lee M. Johnson, "Language and the Illusion of Innocence in *Paradise Lost*," in *Of Poetry and Politics: New Essays on Milton and His World* (Binghamton, N.Y.: Medieval and Renaissance Texts and Studies, 1994), 47–48. See also Kathleen M. Swaim, who discusses the fundamental connections among the Morning Hymn, the Psalter, and the Book of Common Prayer in "The Morning Hymn of Praise in Book 5 of *Paradise Lost*," *Milton Quarterly* 22 (1988): 7–16. In another context, P. G. Stanwood describes the Morning Hymn (and Herbert's "Trinitie Sunday") as liturgical offerings in "Liturgy, Worship, and the Sons of Light," in *New Perspectives on the Seventeenth-Century English Religious Lyric*, ed. John R. Roberts (Columbia: University of Missouri Press, 1994), 105–23.

Milton's marvelous lyric is the manifestation of true prayer in a religious setting that brings forth abundance and exuberance. Yet this "spontaneous" song, which is of course not spontaneous at all, becomes memorable because of its systematic, witty ordering. Milton neatly regulates and organizes the worship of the unfallen Adam and Eve, instructed and accompanied by the Sons of Light. Adam and Eve have yet to know about formal, structured prayer, but Milton is not so innocent; for he is quite conscious of the shape and the rightness of their song.

George Herbert asked the question that stands as the eponymous motto of this essay. His own answer is characteristically ambivalent, but we may respond on his behalf, and for the most part affirmatively. Indeed, he himself often builds elaborate mansions out of conventional materials, which yet, paradoxically, remain coherent and homelike. Herbert's genius, like Milton's, lies to a large extent in that uncommon ability of so many seventeenth-century poets to transmute metaphysical wit into proportioned and habitable dwellings, the "Work of no Forrain *Architect*." We have hoped to show that mere ingenuity may describe metaphorical wit, but that metaphysical wit seeks ever wider significance in its comparisons. Thus Herbert frequently designs whole poems that use to large advantage discrete details of language and even the mapping of words on the page. Milton's effects are similar, but often much larger and more ambitious—befitting, perhaps, his capacious epic. The complexity of his plans has always called forth admiration; to follow his way along the winding metaphysical stair is to experience yet more of the wonder of the poet who leaves witty structures everywhere.

Erna Kelly

Women's Wit

Pierre Le Moyne, a French Jesuit, whose *Gallery of Heroick Women* was translated into English in 1652, wrote that "there is nothing, which the Understanding of Women may not attain"; "Wit may be as strong and Reason as vigorous in the Head of a woman, as in that of a Man." However, many of the century's prose tracts concerning women suggest Le Moyne was unusual in his beliefs. For example, Daniel Tuvill in *Asylum Veneris, or A Sanctuary for Ladies* argued, "Learning in the breast of a woman, is [like] . . . a sword in the hands of a Mad man, which knoweth not how to rule as reason shall inform him. . . . The pen must be forbidden them." If women wish to express themselves they should use "needles"; that is, after all, how Philomel expressed herself. While his words are not as harsh as Tuvill's, the opening lines of *The Ladies New-Year's-Gift: or, Advice to a Daughter* show that George Saville, Marquis of Halifax, likewise assumed men were women's superiors in reasoning ability: "You must first lay it down for a foundation in general, that . . . men, who were to be the law-givers, had the larger share of reason bestowed upon them." In his character sketch of "A Wife," Sir Thomas Overbury simply noted, "Books are a part of a man's prerogative."[1]

1. Le Moyne, *The Gallery of Heroick Women*, trans. Marquise of Winchester, 1652, in Margaret Ezell, *The Patriarch's Wife: Literary Evidence and the History of the Family* (Chapel Hill: University of North Carolina Press, 1987), 44–45; Tuvill, *Asylum Veneris* (London: Printed by Edward Griffin, 1616), 87–88; Saville, *The Lady's New-Year's-Gift* (London, 1688); Overbury, "A Wife," in *The Overburian Characters*, ed. W. J. Paylor (Oxford: Basil Blackwell, 1936), cited in Angeline Goreau, *The Whole Duty of a Woman* (New York: Doubleday, 1985), 45, 1.

Just as women in general had an occasional advocate like Le Moyne, individual female writers also had some support: for example, Anne Bradstreet's brother-in-law published her poems, Margaret Cavendish's husband wrote admiring prefaces for her works, and Dryden included Aphra Behn's version of "Oenone to Paris" in his edition of *Ovid's Epistles.* Yet even Dryden, who James Winn demonstrates had good rapport with women writers, criticized the sexual explicitness of Behn's writing, and Anne Finch concurred, concluding that Behn "a little too loosely writ."[2] While attacks on female reason as well as criticism of individuals hurt women writers as a whole, perhaps even more damaging, because of its insidious nature, was the hostility embedded in commendatory verses.

Seventeenth-century audiences expected hyperbolic praise in the verses that introduced most volumes of poetry, and at times commendatory verses written for female writers like Bradstreet and Behn live up to this expectation. For example, Bradstreet's poetry is a "Golden splendent *STAR*,"[3] shining like the sun (528) or a moon eclipsing the sun with "bright silver," making "his gold looke dim" (C. B., 529). Behn is "The Ages Glory" (G. J.);[4] her muse, "Godlike" (125); predictably her "wondrous Work" (9) will outlast "Pyramids, . . . Monuments . . . / Marble Tombs" (135) and "mount the Skies" (10) as a constellation, not only hearkening back to Milton's and Jonson's praise of Shakespeare but, in the constellation metaphor, also punning on Behn's literary name, Astrea.

2. For Dryden's relationship with female writers, see esp. chap. 7 of *"When Beauty Fires the Blood"* (Ann Arbor: University of Michigan Press, 1992). For Dryden's criticism of Behn, see letter 69 in *The Letters of John Dryden,* ed. Charles E. Ward (Durham: Duke University Press, 1942), 127. For Finch's criticism of Behn, see "The Circuit of Apollo," l. 14, in *The Meridian Anthology of Early Women Writers,* ed. Katharine Rogers and William McCarthy (New York: Meridian, 1987), 94.

3. N. H., "In praise of the Author," in *The Complete Works of Anne Bradstreet,* ed. Joseph McElrath Jr. and Allan Robb (Boston: Twayne, 1981), 530. All quotations from commendatory writings for Bradstreet are from this edition and volume and indicated by page number in the text; author's name or initials will be included when a page contains several poems. Quotations from Bradstreet's "The Prologue" are also from this edition and indicated by stanza number in the text.

4. *The Works of Aphra Behn,* ed. Montague Summers, 6 vols. (New York: Benjamin Bloom, 1915, 1967), 6:9. All quotations from commendatory poems for Behn are from this edition and indicated by page number in the text; author's name or initials will be included when a page contains several poems. All quotations from Behn's poetry are also from this edition and indicated by stanza number in the text.

Frequently, however, commendatory verses written for female poets undercut their very nature: they are often ambivalent, sometimes damn with faint praise, and occasionally even display outright hostility. In fact, it is difficult to find commendations of women's poetry that do not undermine their praise by calling attention to the remarkableness of the poet's achievement given her sex. For example, in "To my deare Sister," John Woodbridge uses a pun that relies on a contrast between Bradstreet's volume and typical "woman's work": "What you have done, the Sun shall witnesse beare, / That for a womans Worke 'tis very rare" (528). Furthermore, although he claims that Bradstreet's "In honour of . . . Queen Elizabeth" has, in his eyes, "Acquitted" female writers, Woodbridge minimizes the poem by calling it "*Eliza's* ditty" (528). The verses signed by H. S. begin with surprise that Bradstreet would "e're aspire" (530) to write about historical events, thus not only questioning the appropriateness of epic poetry for female writers but also emphasizing aspiration over actual achievement. R. Q. takes the others' ambivalence a step further; his poem is overtly hostile. In mock-heroic lines, he portrays women writers as rebels who "vent their plot in Verses." Their rebellion, however, does not succeed: they will never escape their nature and can never be taken seriously, for "they seldome rise till ten a clock" (529).

Likewise, in the poems commending Behn's verse, gender is almost always an issue. One poem opens with "Thou Wonder of thy Sex!" (9). Charles Cotton tells Behn that her lines are as "Soft, as . . . [her] Sex; and Smooth, as Beauty's Face" (6); John Cooper finds "Her Face's Beauty's copy'd in her style" (118); and T. C. describes her poetry in terms of a seductive woman:

> We yield our selves to the first beauteous Foe;
> The easie softness of thy thoughts surprise,
> And this new way Love steals into our Eyes;
> Thy gliding Verse comes on us unawares.
>
> (121)

No verses commend Cavendish's volume; however, even its single prose commendation, an epistle by Cavendish's friend and onetime maid Elizabeth Toppe, does not ignore the issue of gender: it begins, "*You are . . . the first English Poet of your Sex.*"[5]

---

5. Margaret Cavendish, *Poems and Fancies* (1653; rpt. Menston, Yorkshire: Scolar Press, 1972), A5v. Unless otherwise noted, all quotations from Cavendish's prose and poetry are from this edition and indicated by page or line number in the text.

As the commendatory poems demonstrate, poets and readers alike were keenly aware of gender. When it did not create outright hostility, awareness of gender often created awkwardness for female poets, especially in a genre such as amatory verse with its traditional male speaker and silent female object of desire or in a genre such as elegy with its traditional configuration of male poet and female muse.[6] Awareness of gender could also lead to another problem for women writers: stances that created interesting tensions if the poet was male could sound bland when voiced by a female. As Dorothy Mermin points out, "Spiritual calms forged in despite of passion are less arresting when sexuality is apparently out of the question, and women's renunciations of worldly ambition go smoothly with the grain of social expectation, not interestingly against it."[7]

Women poets dealt with the difficulties and sometimes outright hostility produced by gender awareness in a number of ways. At times they abandoned or avoided problematic genres. Bradstreet, for example, abandoned both the formal elegy and the epic. Sometimes they retained the conventions of a problematic genre but applied them to an unproblematic topic or in a manner that circumvented "uncomfortable" implications. Katherine Philips used this approach, grafting the conventions of amatory verse on poems about friendship. As Arlene Stiebel points out, because figurative language conceals as well as reveals, readers can ignore the poems' lesbian aspects and see them instead as "asexual representations of well-known literary conventions," exempting Philips "from social condemnation" but unfortunately also reinforcing heterosexual privilege.[8] A less significant yet still unfortunate result of such a reading is the blandness that Mermin has observed. A third strategy female poets used to deal with gender awareness was self-effacement, deprecating their poetic skills to ameliorate the discomfort readers felt when the traditional formula of poet equals male was disrupted.[9] However, women did not always deal with

---

6. See Dorothy Mermin, "Women Becoming Poets: Katherine Philips, Aphra Behn, Anne Finch," *ELH* 57 (1990): 335–55; and Timothy Sweet, "Gender, Genre, and Subjectivity in Anne Bradstreet's Elegies," *Early American Literature* 23 (1988): 152–74.

7. "Women Becoming Poets," 349.

8. "Not Since Sappho: The Erotic in Poems of Katherine Philips and Aphra Behn," *Journal of Homosexuality* 23 (1992): 155, 153, 162.

9. On the frequency and intensity of women's apologies see Mermin, "Women Becoming Poets," 338–40; Goreau, *Whole Duty of a Woman*, 8; Sylvia Brown, "Margaret Cavendish: Strategies Rhetorical and Philosophical against the Charge of Wantonness, Or Her

gender awareness through avoidance, disguise, or apology. Finding their poems received with ambivalence and hostility, female poets used wit to prove the unfairness of this reception as well as to lessen the likelihood of future attacks. Their wit provides ample evidence that Le Moyne's statements were accurate.

Among poems written by seventeenth-century women, three types seem to have provided especially favorable opportunities for the display of their wit: poems about poetry, poems using metaphors taken from activities tradition-ally associated with women (such as cooking and attention to dress), and amatory verse. The characteristic that makes them particularly suitable for a display of women's wit is the high degree of gender awareness that their conventions and topics provoked. Because they were less safe than poems that disguise or apologize, amatory verse and poems about female poetic skill create the interesting tensions that Mermin notes are often missing from poems that deal with safer topics. These poems are natural sites for the unexpected reversals—the paradoxes, ironies, and unusual comparisons—that are at the heart of wit. Likewise, seemingly safe areas, for example "women's work," become unsafe when written about, because women's work was not a conventional poetic topic nor a traditional source of figurative language. Precisely because these genres and topics went against the grain, women who dared to use them created poems made interesting by ironic wit forged from inherent contradictions, "Wit . . . as strong . . . as that of a Man," but a wit, I would add, that is also distinctly their own.

Women's poems about poetry may initially seem apologetic, yet closer inspection usually reveals quite the contrary. These works not only display wit but also frequently exhibit anger. Their wit shows that attacks upon women's intelligence were unwarranted; it also makes the expression of so "unwom-anly" an emotion as anger more acceptable. It calls attention away from the message to the ingenuity of its presentation, perhaps before the reader can become too angered by the message. Furthermore, the doubleness of many witty devices as well as the humor they create make it impossible to pin the poet down. The poet in effect says with a smile, "I didn't really mean this—or did I? You will never know."

Excuses for Writing So Much," *Critical Matrix: Princeton Working Papers in Women's Studies* 6 (1991): 20–45; Claudia Limbert, "Katherine Philips: Controlling a Life and Reputation," *South Atlantic Review* 56 (1991): 27–42.

At first glance, "The Prologue" to Bradstreet's *The Tenth Muse, Lately Sprung Up in America* seems to beg critics to spare the poems that follow. Bradstreet apparently thinks that doing the critics' job for them will deflect their disparagement, so she claims her pen is "mean" (st. 1); her brain "weake" (st. 4); and her "lowly lines . . . will make" theirs "but more to shine" (st. 8). The reason for such extreme self-effacement becomes clear in stanza 5, which describes the reception a female writer might expect:

> I am obnoxious to each carping tongue,
> Who sayes, my hand a needle better fits,
> A Poets Pen, all scorne, I should thus wrong;
> For such despight they cast on female wits:
> If what I doe prove well, it wo'nt advance,
> They'l say its stolne, or else, it was by chance.

Voicing these thoughts appears to give Bradstreet the courage to argue against such censure in the following stanza. There she suggests, although indirectly, that her male contemporaries emulate "the antick *Greeks*" who treated women in a manner "far more milde": "Else of our sex why feigned they those nine / And poesy made *Calliope's* owne childe?" (st. 7). Immediately, though, she recognizes the flaw in her argument. Hostile readers, seizing the word "feigned," will "full soone untye" her "weake knot," countering with "The *Greeks* did nought, but play the foole and lye" (st. 6). Disheartened, she backs down, resigning herself to the status quo—"Let *Greeks* be *Greeks,* and women what they are / Men have precedency and still excel"—and continues in this vein, presumably hoping to predispose critics favorably toward the stanza's last line: "Yet grant some small acknowledgment of ours" (st. 7). Concluding the poem, Bradstreet adds one more stanza in praise of male poets and caps it with a self-effacing final couplet.

However, the mixed diction and weak rhyme of couplets such as "And this to mend, alas, no Art is able, / 'Cause Nature made it so irreparable" invite the reader to invert the poem's self-effacing tone in order to hear the protest just beneath its surface. The hyperbole of the previous line—"My foolish, broken, blemish'd Muse so sings"—does the same. Furthermore, the halting effect the line achieves through the use of *b, f, k,* and *d* in its adjectives, making Bradstreet's muse indeed seem broken, blemished, and foolish, proves she is not at all the unskilled poet she pretends to be. Throughout the poem Bradstreet playfully undercuts her feigned humility and overturns "maxime's" (st. 4) that keep women in their place. For example, after protesting that she cannot speak like "that . . . sweet tongu'd *Greek*" she presents the reader with perfectly metrical lines, "fluent" as anything Demosthenes might utter (st. 4). Furthermore, once the reader is tipped off to the ironic tone of the poem by lines like those cited above, the stanza becomes capable of sustaining, in addition to a literal meaning and its ironic reversal, a third level of meaning, again ironic but sadly so. It is lamentably true that unlike Demosthenes, who improved his speech through practice, "Art" will not help Bradstreet "speake . . . more plaine" (st. 4). Instead, as her poem demonstrates, if she wishes to practice her art, she had better veil her anger and belie her talent. While a protest, even if veiled, might relieve some of the pain that anticipating a hostile reception creates, unlike Demosthenes, who "By Art" is afforded "A full requitall of his striving paine," art or poetry never allows female poets to escape completely their suffering (st. 4). Instead, it continually reminds them of those who prefer that they create needlework rather than literary works.

The poem's irony also casts a new light on the "Preheminence" claimed for men in stanza 7. It begins, "Let *Greeks* be *Greeks*." Yet what are Greeks? Liars, according to the poet-critics of stanza 6, but "milde" or "sweet tongu'd" like Demosthenes, according to the speaker of the poem. Contemporary males, on the other hand, as stanza 5 shows, can be "carping" creatures. Although the primary meaning of carping is censuring, the *OED* points to possible deriva-tion from an Old Norse verb that meant to brag. Certainly, bragging departs from the truth as much as does feigning the existence of muses. The *OED* also lists chattering as a possible seventeenth-century meaning for carping. Cen-suring, bragging, and chattering are neither sweet nor mild, nor particularly poetic. In comparison to the Greeks, the "precedency" of contemporary male poet-critics becomes ridiculous. Censuring, bragging, and chattering also look forward to the eighth and last stanza's mock-heroic opening lines: "And oh ye highflown quills, that soare the skies, / And ever with your prey, still catch your praise." Hardly noble, these chattering bird-poets brag or elevate their own stature by censuring or preying upon female poets. If an appetite for the "Bayes" results in such gluttony, Bradstreet will settle for a humble but "whol-some Parsely wreath" (st. 8).

Unlike Bradstreet's mock self-deprecation, the self-deprecation in Caven-dish's defenses of her writing apparently was often meant to be taken seriously.

Cavendish may have been more anxious about her literary reception than were other female poets of her age: many of her books contain close to a half dozen prefaces. At times, however, even Cavendish provides a witty counterattack. In a preface to *Poems and Fancies*, while allowing for a negative reception, Cavendish also builds in an attack on any reader who gives her such a reception.

> If you dislike, and rise to go away,
> Pray do not Scoff, and tell what I did say,
> But if you do, the matter is not great,
> For tis but foolish words you can repeat.
>
> (A6v)

The fear of censure displayed in the first two lines is dealt with in the third. "The matter is not great" could imply slight content and thus the conventional use of self-effacement to ward off an attack; it could also imply authorial indifference, affording Cavendish the safety of detachment. It supports a third meaning as well: *pia mater*, or the membrane covering the brain.[10] If the *pia mater* is small, so must be the brain it covers, hence scoffers' inability to comprehend Cavendish's poetry. Furthermore, because of limited mental capacity, scoffers will remember only a small amount of her text or "matter": they are capable of recognizing and repeating only "foolish words," and her text, Cavendish implies, contains chiefly or solely wise words.

Cavendish's belief in her own mental capacity often manifests itself in concern over being read correctly. For example, earlier in the same preface she writes, "I desire all that are not quick in apprehending, or will not trouble themselves with such small things as *Atomes*, to skip this part of my *Book*, and view the *other*" (A6v). Again she builds in multiple meanings. The phrase "small things" functions not only literally as a description of atoms but also ironically, since a theory of atoms is by no means a small or trivial concept. Cavendish concludes the preface with an even more emphatic verse warning:

> *Pray do not censure all you do not know,*
> *But let my Atomes to the Learned go,*
> *If you judge, and understand not, you may take*
> *For Non-sense that which learning Sense will make.*

10. I wish to thank D. D. C. Chambers for his suggestion that "matter" might be read as *pia mater*.

> *But I may say, as* Some *have said before,*
> *I'm not bound to fetch you* Wit *from* Natures Store.
>
> (A6v)

Would-be critics too dull to grasp the irony of earlier lines might be intimidated into keeping still by these lines, which state clearly that censurers risk being dismissed both as ignorant and as dim-witted. Cavendish turns potential comments on her lack of ability as a writer into evidence of her critics' lack of ability; in censuring readers, she reminds them that the reader-writer contract has two parties. The humor here is based on the exaggerated last line; one can almost see Cavendish throwing up her arms in exasperation as she implies that fitting scientific ideas into pleasant lines of verse has been labor enough and wonders how critics can expect her to refit their brains as well.

In addition to opening *Poems and Fancies* with poems that defend the volume, Cavendish also devotes the volume's last three pages to the same cause. In one of the concluding poems she uses clothing as the central metaphor. The poem itself is proof that contrary to its opening line Cavendish does not "*Language* want, to dress" her "*Fancies* in" (l. 1). Her fancies are, as she says, the poem's content or "Soul" (l. 17); however, by using the word "Fancies" in close connection with metaphors such as "Silver Lace" (ll. 3, 10), "rich Hood" (l. 9), and "Bravery" (l. 5), Cavendish makes the word's meaning oscillate in the reader's mind between her primary meaning, content, and another meaning of the word, trivial sartorial touches. Although the poem initially appears to apologize for a lack of skill, it actually rebukes any reader who is taken by stylistically "glittering Shews" (l. 8). Near the poem's conclusion, Cavendish once more displays her capacity for wit by adding yet another possible meaning to "Fancy." In the event she has not shamed her readers into accepting her "Language" because it eschews excessive ornament, or fancies, she makes the following plea: "Be just, let Fancy have the upper place, / And then my *Verses* may perchance finde grace" (ll. 19–20). These lines can work two ways. They can simply reinforce what has been said, that is, rank content higher than style, or they can be read in the following manner: if you are unable to put content above style, let your fancy (that is, imagination)[11] rule you and imagine that this is good poetry.

---

11. Based on a reading of Cavendish's prose works as well as her poetry, I believe by "fancy" she usually means imagination or a combination of imagination with reasoning, especially in making witty comparisons.

In poems about poetry, women poets in the seventeenth century used wit to prove they should be accepted as poets. Yet they were realistic about the prejudice they needed to overcome to gain this acceptance. If wit was not always enough to make their writing (both the product and the act) acceptable, then at least it enabled them to voice their annoyance over exclusion as Cavendish does in "I *Language* want." Like many of her contemporaries, Cavendish takes images for her poems from activities typically associated with women. By using these images as metaphors for atypical activities such as reading and writing, female poets were able to reexamine the common understanding both of typical and of atypical female activities. However, the wit of these comparisons is often as subversive as it is illuminating, as Cavendish's poem demonstrates. Turning stereotypical female attachment to clothing into an attack on readers who are excessively attached to verbal ornament, Cavendish uses wit not only to question the stereotype but also to exhibit her poetic skill, as well as to express anger, or at least annoyance, with having to prove it.

In "*Natures* Cook," Cavendish again uses an activity typically associated with women. The poem opens with an assertion: "*Death* is the *Cook* of *Nature*; and we find / *Meat* drest severall waies to please her *Mind*." The poem then shifts to proving its opening assertion, Death's versatility as a cook, by listing a large number of Death's grotesquely humorous cooking techniques:

> Some *Meates shee* rosts with *Feavers, burning hot*,
> And some *shee* boils with *Dropsies* in a *Pot*.
> Some for *Gelly* consuming by degrees,
> And some with *Ulcers*, Gravie out to squeese.
>
> (ll. 3–6)

The catalog of grim but apt recipes continues—flesh pickled "in the *Sea*," "*Brawne* . . . sous'd . . . in *Wine*," tongue dried "with *Smoake* from *stomacks* ill," "*Blood-puddings*" from cut "*Throats*"—until nearly two dozen have been set down (ll. 9, 10, 21, 23). Although Virginia Woolf complained about Cavendish's capacity for comparisons—"She similised, energetically . . . eternally"—this talent enabled Cavendish to produce a marvelous tour de force.[12]

By associating cooking with so universal a concern as death, this poem elevates "women's work" to a metaphysical level, while simultaneously demot-

---

12. *The Common Reader* (New York: Putnam, 1910), 77.

ing the great leveler, Death. However, unlike Donne, who in the Holy Sonnet beginning "Death be not proud" allows Death to posture as a great foe before cutting him down, Cavendish makes Death a menial worker from the beginning. Starting from a low position, Death is further undercut as Cavendish shows that despite Death's inventiveness and thrift, she is a terrible cook. Her dishes are extremely unappetizing: "a *French Fricasse*" of "*Pox*" chopped with "*Flesh*, and *Bones*," "*Braines* drest with *Apoplexy*" or swimming in "*Sauce of Megrimes*," or "*A Hodge-Podge of Diseases*" stewed in "*Sweat*" (ll. 11–12, 20–21, 17–18). In fact, Death's cooking is so bad it kills. In demoting death, Cavendish, like Donne, promotes herself as a poet, but unlike Donne's Death, Cavendish's Death, personified as a female, is not vanquished. Instead, she continues concocting new ways to cook carcasses: women's work is never done. Perhaps Cavendish intended a further irony. She claimed to have very little culinary skill herself; she also probably had very little interest in acquiring further skill in this area. Her prefaces, her autobiography, and many of the asides within her works show her main ambition was fame. For example, she dedicates *The World's Olio* "to Fortune," for "if Fortune please . . . she may place my Book in Fames high Tow'r"; in *Poems and Fancies* she writes, "all I desire is *Fame*" (A3), and midway through *The Blazing World* she exclaims, "I'd rather die in the adventure of noble achievements than live in obscure and sluggish security; since by one, I may live in a glorious Fame; and by the other I am buried in oblivion."[13] A woman, and thus barred from political and military avenues, she turned to writing as a means to the fame and consequent immortality she craved. Perhaps she saw writing as a kind of cooking of the mind. While "*Natures* Cook" may not be a work of conventional beauty, like a pieced quilt it displays ingenuity and the will to make the best out of scraps, in this instance the scraps of activity and power allowed women. The hostility conveyed by the grotesque dishes and the message that cooking can kill may reflect a conscious resentment toward the limitations put on women. Female poets in the seventeenth century use wit not only to bring recognition to "women's work" but also to reexamine it; they use it to subvert as well as to elevate what has been traditionally expected of them.

In poetry of this period women also use wit to subvert the imagery males

---

13. *The World's Olio* (London: J. Martin and J. Allestrye, 1655), 1; *The Description of a New World Called the Blazing World* (London: A. Maxwell, 1668), 49.

traditionally used to describe females, challenging the unrealistic views of women that this imagery promoted. Cavendish's stance in the final poem in *Poems and Fancies*, at first, appears to be quite meek:

> A *Poet* I am neither *borne*, nor bred,
> But to a *witty Poet* married
> *Whose Braine* is *Fresh*, and *Pleasant*, as the Spring,
> Where *Fancies* grow, and where the *Muses* sing.
> There of I leane my Head, and *list'ning* harke,
> To heare *his words*, and all his *Fancies* mark;
> And from that *Garden Flowers* of *Fancies* take,
> Whereof a *Posie* up in *Verse* I make.
> Thus I, that have no *Garden* of mine owne,
> There gather *Flowers* that are *newly blowne*.

Certainly, this poem is a genuine tribute to Cavendish's husband, just one of many throughout her volumes of prose and verse. However, it is also subversive. It subverts its own thesis as well as male poetical convention: it takes some poetic skill to sustain the garden metaphor for the entire poem; it also takes some wit to take the time-honored comparison of a woman's face to a garden[14] and place that garden in the male mind, which after all, is where it always has been. Cavendish's wit allows her to be simultaneously the woman men want her to be as well as a woman with a mind of her own, one who questions male myths about female beauty.

Aphra Behn, on the other hand, seldom tries to have it both ways, that is, be the woman men want as well as the woman she wants to be. Her amatory poems concede little to the male imagination and the male ego, often questioning traditional male images of women, love, and even lovemaking. In "*In Imitation of* Horace," Behn exercises subversive wit by using imagery traditionally associated with females to describe a male; in doing so, she creates the interesting tensions Mermin finds lacking in some women's poems. Only one or two phrases in Behn's opening stanza hint that her poem may not address a beautiful woman:

---

14. See especially Thomas Campion's "There is a Garden in Her Face." See also Spenser's "Epithalamion," ll. 173–74; Jonson's "A Celebration of Charis," st. 5; Herrick's "Cherry-Ripe"; Lovelace's "To Lucasta. The Rose" and "A Black Patch on Lucasta's Face," ll. 3–4.

What mean those Amorous Curles of Jet?
  For what heart-Ravisht Maid
Dost thou thy Hair in order set,
  Thy Wanton Tresses Braid?
And thy vast Store of Beauties open lay,
That the deluded Fancy leads astray.

"Curles of Jet" rather than conventional golden tresses may hint that some-thing is awry, but the motivation for the coiffure—a "heart-Ravisht Maid—is the only solid clue. Because the remaining lines of the stanza are replete with phrases like "Wanton Tresses" and "Beauties open lay," phrases that strongly suggest female sexuality, these lines lull readers back into envisioning a con-ventional address to a woman; so does the opening line of the next stanza: "For pitty hide thy Starry eyes." However, the tension returns in the next line as Behn describes the "Languishments" of those eyes; this is not a haughty Petrarchan lady. This object of desire desires as well. Furthermore, although Behn rapidly returns to conventions for addressing a woman by claiming these eyes will transform the speaker into a "Slave that dyes," the expected death, from unrequited love, is replaced with quite another kind, death from requited love or "Excess . . . Joy," in other words sexual consummation. Not until the third stanza with its direct address to the "Charming Youth" does Behn dispel the confusion that she creates. Her withholding of this informa-tion until the middle of the poem may have been calculated not only to delight readers through surprise but also to gain acceptance for her role reversal. The pleasure readers may feel in finally finding the key to the puzzle might predispose them to accept a new formula for amorous verse: female speaker and male object of desire. However, as the editors of an anthology of seventeenth-century women's verse point out, Behn's reversal of roles does not mean that she takes "a male view of sex"; instead, she transforms "the emphasis and tone, using only Horace's initial idea to construct a new kind of erotic poem," one that emphasizes women's vulnerability.[15]

In the original poem, Pyrrha is scolded for seducing young men; in Behn's poem the young man is not scolded but begged to restrain his seductive glances and sighs. Furthermore, unlike the women of many male poems,

15. *Kissing the Rod: An Anthology of Seventeenth-Century Women's Verse*, ed. Germaine Greer et al. (London: Virago Press, 1988), 249.

beauties who torment men with their inaccessibility, Behn's beautiful youth, a suitor as well as an object of desire, is quite available, in fact, too available. While male poets often rail against the object of their desire for denying them access, Behn's speaker pleads, "Cease, Cease, with Sighs to warm my Soul, / Or press me with thy Hand" (st. 4). Satisfying desire has negative conse-quences for a woman. One could say that in consummating a heterosexual relationship, men attain the object of their desire, while women yield to their desire. Men gain control; women, because they become emotionally involved, lose control. Like the speakers of many male amatory verses, Behn's speaker is faced with a difficult situation. Although her situation is different from the male speaker's situation, it is equally difficult; however, unlike male poets, Behn does not place undue blame on the object of desire. In male amorous verse, the female is usually portrayed as fully aware of the power she so cruelly wields; the intensity of her power is often conveyed in images of fire and light and her callousness, in images of hardness, coldness, and silence. Behn, on the other hand, although she uses the traditional images of lightning and fire, softens them into a "tender force" (st. 4), making the object of desire quite human. Unlike the distant, silent woman of Petrarchan poems, Behn's youth speaks "Words of Melting Love." Far from coldly calculating, the youth is merely "fond," foolishly underestimating his ability to harm the speaker: "she that hears thy voice and sees thy Eyes / With too much Pleasure, too much Softness dies" (st. 3). Behn's emphasis on women's vulnerability in this poem is consistent with that of her other lyrics. It is not that Behn depicts women as without sexual desire; in this area the women in her lyrics are men's equals. This is true not only of the woman in the Horatian imitation but also of the women in "The Disappointment," "The Willing Mistress," "To Alexis," and "The Golden Age." However, the consequences of giving into or even dis-playing desire make women more vulnerable than men.

Although "The Disappointment" treats humorously its central situation (male impotence resulting from a woman overtly acknowledging her desire), vulnerability is again an important concern—male vulnerability certainly, but female as well. Attending as it does to the woman's point of view, Behn's poem reexamines and helps redefine sexual relations between men and women. Richard Quaintance has examined ten "imperfect enjoyment" poems written between 1577 and 1682 and concludes that, with the exception of Behn's poem, all the poems' narrators take the male point of view; thus, he sees

Behn's poem as transforming the genre.[16] Behn's Chloris is depicted typically enough at first, with traditional brighter-than-the-sun eyes, which ensnare Lysander. She follows the male script for female behavior scrupulously, indirectly assenting to his attentions with silence and lack of protest, until she mistakenly assents more directly by placing her hands on his chest "not to put him back design'd / Rather to draw 'em on inclin'd" (st. 2). Nothing she can do after this will reverse the situation, although she tries resuming the expected script, even feigning resistance this time. Both Chloris and Lysander feel shame at different moments; in fact, the word *shame* becomes almost a chorus within the poem. Yet by the poem's conclusion he has transformed his shame or vulnerability into rage; she remains somewhat vulnerable as the object of his rage.

The wit in Behn's erotic love lyrics comes, in large part, from the unexpected reversals that occur when the situation is seen from a woman's point of view. Even though Behn uses her revisions to acknowledge poignantly the female vulnerability that male poets shrug off, she also manages to make her readers laugh at both male and female reactions to a reversed situation. Using exaggeration and surprise, she builds up in the reader an expectation that mirrors that of the lovers with line after line of erotic description:

> His burning trembling Hand he prest
> Upon her swelling Snowy Brest
> . . . .
> His daring Hand that Altar seiz'd
> Where Gods of Love do sacrifice:
> That Awful Throne, that Paradice
> Where Rage is calm'd, and Anger pleas'd.
>   (sts. 4–5)

Chloris lies "breathless . . . / Her soft Eyes . . . cast[ing] a Humid Light" as Lysander, "Mad to possess," throws himself "On the Defenceless Lovely Maid" (sts. 6, 8). However, Behn suddenly pulls the rug out from under the couple and the reader: a deity "envying" Lysander has conspired "To snatch his Power" (st. 8). The comedy continues when Chloris, wondering why Ly-

16. "French Sources of the Restoration 'Imperfect Enjoyment' Poem," *Philological Quarterly* 42 (1963): 190–99. See also Judith Kegan Gardiner, "Aphra Behn: Sexuality and Self-respect," *Women's Studies* 7 (1980): 74.

sander's advances have stopped, reaches for him "beneath the verdant Leaves" and finds instead what feels like "a Snake" (st. 11). Behn playfully fuses the stereotypical female response to snakes with the stock situation of a frightened maid fleeing a pursuing lover, twisting it into the flight of an embarrassed, disappointed nymph. The irony of the situation is reinforced ten lines later in a mock-heroic comparison of Chloris to Daphne fleeing Apollo. Lysander, no god, poses little threat to Chloris; he can only rage at his all too human inability to fulfill the expectations his advances had promised. We may feel it unfortunate that Chloris eventually becomes the object of Lysander's rage, but at the same time we laugh because she is safely out of reach and his empty blustering is a cheap substitute for his temporary loss of sexual power.

If Behn shows her wit or cleverness by using a male-dominated genre to gain recognition for a female point of view, delighting readers through unexpected variations on stock poetic themes, she also shows her wit by embedding in the new contexts lines that appear to echo those of well-known male poets. For example, when Behn's lovers kiss in "The Disappointment," "Their Bodies, as their Souls, are joyn'd" (st. 6). However, the narrator is a bit too hasty, and a concept that was serious in "The Extasie" becomes humorous in Behn's poem: struggle as they might, it is their lips alone that her lovers are able to join; consequently, they will never achieve the "Transports" promised in Behn's next line or Donne's title. In "The Golden Age," Behn echoes the first nine lines of "The Canonization":

> Be gone, and make thy Fam'd resort
>   To Princes Pallaces;
> Go Deal and Chaffer in the Trading Court,
> That busie Market for Phantastick Things;
> Be gone and interrupt the short Retreat
>   Of the Illustrious and the Great;
>   Go break the Politians sleep,
>   Disturb the Gay Ambitious Fool,
> That longs for Scepters, Crowns, and Rule.
>   (st. 9)

"The Golden Age" also bears some resemblance to Carew's "A Rapture" and Lovelace's "Love made in the first age." All three belong to the "Perswasions to enjoy" genre, using delicious descriptions of lovemaking to entice. Behn, like Carew, uses wit to expose the dishonor inherent in "Honour," and like Lovelace does not make her purpose apparent until near the end of the poem. However, the similarities end here.

Carew's and Lovelace's poems are aggressive. For example, Carew begins, "I Will enjoy thee now my *Celia,* come,"[17] and although Lovelace like Behn does not address his mistress until he has completed his edenic description, his purpose is not merely to make her long for fulfillment. It is, in fact, coupled with an unexpected desire for revenge: "Now, *CHLORIS!* miserably crave, / The offer'd blisse you would not have."[18] His hostility continues as he vows to deny her "evermore," presumably masturbating as he cuts her off. Behn's poem is neither as aggressive nor ultimately as bitter. Although Lovelace and Carew claim a woman has much to gain by giving in, they write from an almost exclusively male-centered perspective. Eugene Cunnar finds that most seventeenth-century male poets who used the Golden Age myth "really did not promise the woman equality nor did they voice any real concerns about woman's desire."[19]

Lovelace seems at first to give women the constancy they want but then undercuts it. Faith remains unbroken in Lovelace's golden age because vows hold only up to the point of sexual consummation: "Their Troth seal'd with a Clasp and Kisse, / Lasted untill that extreem day, / In which they smil'd their Souls away" (ll. 33–35). Although "extreem day" and "smil'd their Souls away" might be interpreted as death, given the context of the poem—an edenic scene of perpetual spring, perpetual renewal—this interpretation is questionable. Rather than refer to an actual death, the phrase "smil'd their Souls away" more likely refers to the figurative death of intercourse. The "extreem day" then becomes the moment of consummation. If women desire

---

17. *The Poems of Thomas Carew,* ed. Rhodes Dunlap (Oxford: Clarendon Press, 1949); all quotations from Carew's poems are from this edition and indicated by line number in the text.

18. *The Poems of Richard Lovelace,* ed. C. H. Wilkinson (Oxford: Clarendon Press, 1930), ll. 55–56; all quotations from Lovelace's poems are from this edition and indicated by line number in the text.

19. "Fantasizing a Sexual Golden Age in Seventeenth-Century Poetry," in *Renaissance Discourses of Desire,* ed. Claude J. Summers and Ted-Larry Pebworth (Columbia: University of Missouri Press, 1993), 205.

faithfulness, they are given it in Lovelace's paradise, but in terms acceptable to males—that is, terms that stipulate males may roam freely as soon as the courtship is sexually consummated. Lines such as "Lasses like *Autumne* Plums did drop, / And Lads, indifferently did crop / A Flower, and a Maiden-head" (16–18) reinforce this point of view. As Achsah Guibbory notes, these lines also point to the traditional association of woman with nature and the corollary belief that like nature, woman exists for man's benefit: "the ideal sexual order" is one "in which the man is free and active, the woman passive and submissive."[20] I would add that the imagery of these lines further reinforces women's subservience by their emphasis on downward movement. Configured as plums, women "drop" to a lower position, and although "crop" means gather, it also means to cut off. Cut off from their stems, women and flowers fall down. Beneath men, these lines tell the reader, is where women belong.

Although Carew points out that Honor cheats women as well as men, causing "greedy men" to "empale free woman" within "private armes" (ll. 19–20), like Lovelace, he writes his poem mainly from a male point of view. Very little in the poem points explicitly to the pleasures Celia will gain in the unenclosed commons of his paradise. Instead, Carew devotes most of "A Rapture" to describing the speaker's enjoyment of Celia. The descriptions are as aggressive as the poem's opening line: he will "rifle all the sweets," "seize the Rose-buds," and imprint "A tract for lovers" on Celia's body (ll. 59, 63, 71). All of Celia's actions, on the other hand, are dictated by him:

> My Rudder, with thy bold hand, like a tryde,
> And skilfull Pilot, thou shalt steere, and guide
> My Bark into Loves channell, where it shall
> Dance, as the bounding waves doe rise or fall:
> Then shall thy circling armes, embrace and clip
> My willing bodie.
>
> (ll. 87–92)

Behn, on the other hand, makes Honor's cheat apply more evenly to both sexes.

In Behn's poem the male and female benefits are more convincingly inter-

---

20. "Sexual Politics/Political Sex: Seventeenth-Century Love Poetry," in *Renaissance Discourses of Desire*, ed. Summers and Pebworth, 215.

dependent because what women want is given ample consideration. For example, like Lovelace's first age, Behn's golden age promotes fidelity, but not because a vow is held only until consummation. Fidelity thrives in Behn's eden because male appetite is naturally renewed within the same relationship: "Joyes . . . were everlasting, ever new / And every Vow inviolably true" (st. 7). In fact, when looking at the conditions of the golden age or the current age, Behn often points to their effect on women before she shows their effect on men. For example, in the golden age "Nymphs were free, no nice, coy disdain; / Deny'd their Joyes, or gave the Lover pain" (st. 6). Later in the poem Behn begins a survey of the current age with the following lines: "Oh cursed Honour! thou who first didst damn, / A Woman to the Sin of shame" (st. 8). The remainder of the stanza traces specific consequences of honor and shame. Threatened by shame, women confine their "Gust" behind a screen of haughtiness, their hair behind an "Envious Net." While this is obviously to the male's disadvantage, it is expressed as a loss for women. Although the poem's final fourteen lines urge Sylvia to enjoy herself while she may, until this point this poem feels different from male carpe diem poems. As Guibbory suggests, this is, in part, a result of Behn's infusing nature with "a kind of peaceful, soft sensuality."[21] Lovelace, I would argue does likewise, but to a much lesser degree. Giving female desire as much attention as male desire is also a mark of how the atmosphere found in Behn's poem compares with that of the male carpe diem poems. Ironically, because it understands the female point of view better, Behn's poem might have had better success at seduction than theirs did.

Whether Behn intended "The Golden Age" to be no more than a witty exercise or also had a particular Sylvia in mind is unclear. However, she seems to have at least considered the possibility of a female lover in "*To the fair Clarinda, who made Love to me, imagin'd more than Woman.*"[22] Behn uses her wit to carve out a new understanding of one-half of the population's experience in sexual relations, or at least to expose that experience to a wider

21. Ibid., 217–18.
22. On the lesbian aspects of this poem as well as several other poems by Behn, see Arlene Stiebel, "Subversive Sexuality: Masking the Erotic in Poems by Katherine Philips and Aphra Behn," in *Renaissance Discourses of Desire*, ed. Summers and Pebworth, 232–35; see also Bernard Duyfhiuzen, "'That Which I Dare Not Name': Aphra Behn's 'The Willing Mistress,'" *ELH* 58 (1991): 63–82.

audience. First, she asserts that women's sexual desire exists independent of male endeavors to excite it. She then exposes the consequences for women if they attempt to satisfy their desire. They do not obtain the bliss male poets promise, or if they do, it is brief; the ultimate consequence for women is usually abandonment. Furthermore, as "The Disappointment" demonstrates, if women are too expressive in making their desire known, there is no bliss at all. In either case the result is shame for the woman. However, Behn's poems also point out ways for women to deal with these consequences. They can plead with men to forgo their suits, they can love two men at the same time (see "On her Loving Two Equally"), they can daydream about a golden age, they can love a woman, or they can mitigate the consequences somewhat by writing witty poems about the situation.

Not having to fight sexual bias against their inclusion in the world of letters, male poets in the seventeenth century did not need to call attention to their wit in order to gain a place among their peers nearly as much as did their female counterparts. For example, I know of no instance of a male poet wittily defending his right to write regardless of his sex. And although male poets used wit to analyze their experience and challenge behavioral norms, they had a number of behavioral codes from which to choose. Given fewer approved behaviors, women poets frequently used wit to reexamine male descriptions of and prescriptions for women's experience. Their wit is often subversive, whether used to gain entrance to the male world of letters, to reexamine women's experience, or to question male perceptions of sexuality. But it is also constructive. While female poets used wit to break down barriers and commonly held perceptions, they also used it to refigure female experience, often elevating this experience and consequently themselves.

Jim Ellis

The Wit of Circumcision,
the Circumcision of Wit

In "A Litany" Donne wrote of Christ's experience of bodily torment on the cross as "that bitter agonie / Which is still the agonie of pious wits" (ll. 163–64). In "Sospetto d'Herode" Crashaw wrote of "the knotty riddles" of Christ's incarnation, among which is the circumcision, and wondered why "the unblemisht Lambe, blessed for ever / Should take the marke of sin, and paine of sence" (24.5–6).[1] The body of Christ in seventeenth-century religious poetry is often a site of both aesthetic and theological difficulty, but perhaps nowhere is this so acute as in poems on the topos of Christ's circumcision. The event was memorialized surprisingly frequently: Herrick wrote three songs on the circumcision; Crashaw treated the event in poem and song three times, Milton once, Quarles twice; and both Donne and Lancelot Andrewes discussed the circumcision in a number of sermons. Treatments of the event inevitably circle around to a demand that the reader circumcise the foreskin of his or her heart, an operation that I will be calling a circumcision of wit. What the poetry often simultaneously calls for and enacts is a particular way of reading the body of Christ, and subsequently our own bodies. Just as Christ's circumcision marks the divide between the order of law and the order of grace (which become, in effect, two orders of law), it will also be seen

1. *John Donne: The Divine Poems*, ed. Helen Gardner (Oxford: Clarendon Press, 1952), 16–26; all references to the poetry of Crashaw are from *The Poems of Richard Crashaw*, ed. L. C. Martin (Oxford: Clarendon Press, 1957).

to divide two hermeneutic regimes. The reading strategy that follows after Christ's circumcision, that which employs a circumcised wit, functions as the literal circumcision did to mark out a community and to demonstrate submission to the law. After discussing this circumcised wit in relation to the poetry of the circumcision, I will suggest that this form of wit is historically linked both to the emergence of the individual during this period and to the escalating challenges to both religious and political communities that culminated in the English civil war.

The poems dealing with the circumcision are, as a group, somewhat foreign to the modern reader. In spite of their "authorization" by the observation of the day of Christ's circumcision in the Book of Common Prayer, there is nonetheless something unseemly about them. Herrick's "To his Saviour. The New yeers gift" is a good example:

> That little prettie bleeding part
> Of Foreskin send to me:
> And Ile returne a bleeding Heart,
> For New-yeers gift to thee.
>   (ll. 1–4)[2]

Although we might expect this sort of imagery from Crashaw, it is a little surprising in Herrick: the exchange of the uncomfortably literally portrayed foreskin for the metaphorically circumcised heart, couched in terms of a traditional New Year's exchange of gifts, is mildly grotesque.

One is reminded of Hobbes's comment that "where Wit is wanting, it is not Fancy that is wanting, but Discretion. Judgement without Fancy is Wit, but Fancy without Judgement not." Hobbes designates Fancy as the capacity to see similarity where others do not, which has traditionally been identified as one of the primary characteristics of metaphysical wit: those difficult but sparkling metaphors. Hobbes, however, along with more philosophically inclined critics, stresses that the main component of wit is judgment or discretion. Although by "discretion" Hobbes means primarily "*Distinguishing,* and *Discerning,* and *Judging* between thing and thing," discretion carries with it the secondary meaning of tactfulness or appropriateness. Discretion must

---

2. All references to the poetry of Herrick are from *The Poetical Works of Robert Herrick,* ed. L. C. Martin (Oxford: Clarendon Press, 1956).

account for "Time, Place, and Persons": it is fine for a poet to "play with the sounds, and aequivocall significations of words," but in a sermon "there is no Gingling of words that will not be accounted folly."[3] According to Hobbes, then, wit is a double perception of similarity and difference, tempered by the knowledge of what is acceptable to the community. Beyond the superficial notion of wit as a sense of occasion it is important to recognize the way in which wit, in order to function as wit, simultaneously demands and enacts a community among its listeners. Wit depends upon and creates a shared inter-pretative strategy and a shared perception, and we will see an awareness of this in both the poetry and the sermons.

An example of what might be considered a different community of wit is discussed by Leo Steinberg, who documents the extraordinary interest of Renaissance painters in Christ's genitals. "Renaissance art," he notes, "pro-duced a large body of devotional imagery in which the genitalia of the Christ Child, or of the dead Christ, receive such demonstrative emphasis that one must recognize an *ostentatio genitalium* comparable to the canonic *ostentatio vulnerum*, the showing forth of the wounds." This emphasis, he argues, is not attributable solely, if at all, to desire for descriptive naturalism, or to the Renaissance's newfound interest in the human body. Portraying Christ's body always has theological ramifications, and just as no action of Christ was accidental, no aspect of the representation of his body is insignificant. Stein-berg argues instead that the prominence of Christ's genitals in religious art was possible only at a particular juncture in theological history, when the Church was free to emphasize the miracle of Christ's incarnation in the flesh, before an encroaching secularization took hold at the end of the Renaissance. It is then that the oblivion set in, so that by the eighteenth century, at least in painting, "the Circumcision of Christ, once the opening act of the Redemp-tion, had become merely bad taste."[4]

The paintings Steinberg documents, like Herrick's poem on the circumci-sion, are clearly products of a community with a different standard of discre-tion than ours. The strangeness of Herrick's poem is due not only to its subject

---

3. Thomas Hobbes, *Leviathan*, ed. C. B. Macpherson (London: Penguin, 1968), 137, 135, 137.

4. "The Sexuality of Christ in Renaissance Art and Modern Oblivion," *October* 25 (1983): 1, 72.

matter appearing to be in questionable taste but also more importantly to the hermeneutic strategy, the combination of fancy and judgment, that it employs and that it requires of its reader. The experience of Christ's body in this poem is somewhat complicated, in that we are asked to recognize both the physical suffering and the gift of joy that that suffering represents. Christ's literal circumcision is exchanged for Herrick's figuratively circumcised heart, and the incongruity of the exchange is made more obvious by the rhyme on "part" and "heart" and the repetition of "bleeding," which paradoxically force us to consider the similarity of the two terms of exchange. Implicit in this poem is a progression from a literal to a figurative reading strategy, or rather the exchange of one for the other.

Both this progression and the chiastic structure of the exchange are present in Francis Quarles's very odd poem "Of our Saviours Circumcision, or New-yeares day." In this work Quarles contrasts Christ with Ziska, the pagan general who wanted his skin made into a drum in the vain belief that the very sound of it would frighten the enemy. Quarles says of Christ's foreskin,

> this small peece of skin was such a spell
> It scar'd the sootie Regiments of Hell.
> It made the infernall Legions retreit
> And did indeed what *Zisca* but conceit.
>
> (ll. 7–10)[5]

The comparison here, as in the Herrick poem, is between two different orders of wit. Ziska, with his lack of sophistication, mistakenly conceits that his skin will be literally effective. Christ's foreskin is asserted to have a literal efficacy, which is to say, an efficacy that it has only metonymically, or perhaps literally has in its capacity as metonym. Does the foreskin harrow hell or not? What causes the dilemma here is the strong emphasis Quarles puts on the foreskin's actually doing something—the "did indeed" as opposed to the vain "conceit" of Ziska's action—which troubles our usual notion of what it means to act. We are faced either with considering that Quarles is discussing a heretofore unrecorded episode of history or adopting another, less literal way of reading,

5. Francis Quarles, *Hosanna or Divine Poems on the Passion of Christ and Threnodes,* ed. John Horden (Liverpool: Liverpool University Press, 1960), 9.

an alternative that his description of the foreskin as a "spell," and thus perhaps as primarily a signifying phenomenon, may point us toward.

The progression found in the poems from one form of wit to another is also discussed by Donne. In his sermon on Phil. 3:2,[6] Donne praises the wit of Holy Writ, saying, "This is one of those places of Scripture, which afford an argument for *that*, which I finde often occasion to say, That there are not so *eloquent* books in the world, as the *Scriptures*." The text in question reads: "beware the concision: for we are the circumcision." Donne remarks that "Saint *Paul* embraces here, that elegancy of language familiar to the holy Ghost, They pretend *Circumcision*, they intend *Concision*; there is a certaine elegant and holy delicacy, a certain holy *juvenility* in Saint *Pauls* choosing these words of this musicall cadence and agnomination, *Circumcision* and *Concision*." The argument of this sermon depends upon the play between these two words and the different reading styles that Donne will associate with these two terms: after Christ, he argues, we are no longer to read circumcision literally. To do so implies a concision, a tearing apart or cutting up, a mutilation of the flesh that God no longer requires of us. The play between these two words depends upon the apparent paradox that the same physical act could be denoted by two different words with two different implications depending on whether this act takes place before or after Christ. Similarly, Donne plays on the fact that the word *circumcision* denotes either a physical act or a spiritual condition, again depending on whether one is reading B.C. or A.D. After Christ, the Jews are not circumcised: "We are the circumcised," says Paul, not the Jews, because we understand that circumcision involves the heart, not the penis.

Donne, in a New Year's Day sermon,[7] implies that God instituted the practice because the Jews were naive readers: "The Jew was but in an infancy, in a minority, and God did not looke for so strong a proceeding from the *Jew*, as from *us*, but led him by the armes, by the helpe of *Ceremonies* and *Figures*, and accordingly required but a *Circumcision* in *one* part of the body." The effect of Christ's actions is to make it incumbent upon us to become more sophisticated readers than the Jews, to learn to read, in effect, metaphysically.

6. *The Sermons of John Donne*, ed. Evelyn M. Simpson and George R. Potter, 10 vols. (Los Angeles: University of California Press, 1953–1962), 10:103–18.

7. Ibid., 6:186–204.

For by the end of the sermon on Phil. 3:2, it is the whole body that is rebellious, and the entire body that must be circumcised, because it is from the body that all our reasons for disobeying God come. A circumcised wit does not listen to the body, or rather learns to read it metaphysically as, for example, the rabbis must when faced with the task of circumcising Christ: "Ye must not be more pitifull then wise," Herrick counsels the Priest in "The New-yeeres Gift, or Circumcisions Song,"

> For, now unlesse ye see Him bleed,
> Which makes the Bapti'me; 'tis decreed,
> The Birth is fruitlesse.

> (ll. 17–19)

The priests must resist the promptings of pity that arise from their bodies, like the objections that Donne imagines Abraham having to God's command. Only by conquering the body (through learning to read correctly) will the priests conquer death: in this case, by enabling Christ to save us from death. The dilemma that the priests face in performing the ritual is the dilemma that Donne puts all of us in: only by changing our relation to the body will we conquer our own deaths, and the way to do this is by learning to read with metaphysical wit.

The event of Christ's circumcision is intimately concerned with significa-tion, and different types of reading. Corresponding to the two orders of law in the Bible are two laws of reading, the second of which no longer requires us to bear the signature of Abraham on the flesh. Donne notes in the New Year's Day sermon that the meaning of physical circumcision is in a way exhausted by Christ's circumcision: "upon this *Day* it was perfected and consummated in the person of *Christ Jesus.*" It is necessary that Christ undergo circumcision, in order to demonstrate the truth of the prefiguration and prophecy of the Old Testament, and to make possible typological readings in the present. Donne argues, "The Jewish Circumcision were an absurd and unreasonable thing, if it did not intimate and figure the Circumcision of the heart." Christ through this act thus institutes or allows a form of reading based on typology by consummating the act, exhausting its power of signification, and initiating a new scheme of figuration. Our circumcision, a figurative or metaphysical one, is then both required and prefigured by Christ's.

This reading practice is demonstrated in the way we read Christ's body, and the way we must then read our own bodies. Crashaw's "On the still surviving markes of our Saviours wounds" illustrates this well:

> What ever story of their crueltie,
> Or Naile, or Thorne, or Speare have writ in Thee,
> Are in another sence
> Still legible;
> Sweet is the difference:
> Once I did spell
> Every red letter
> A wound of thine
> Now, (what is better)
> Balsome for mine.
>
> (ll. 1–10)

The poem is extraordinary for its emphasis on Christ's body as a text to be read and troubled over. The wounds are signifiers, "red letter[s]," which when read literally, yield a story of torment. A second reading, however, brings Crashaw a story of salvation. The difference between these two stories is effected precisely through the suffering the wounds recount, that is to say, through Christ's sacrifice. The two orders of reading represented here correspond to the two hermeneutic regimes that Donne discusses in his sermons on circumcision. Crashaw's way of reading the red letters of the body not as wounds but rather as signifiers of salvation mirrors Herrick's instructions to the priests regarding the promptings of their bodies. In both cases the first reading of the body is inadequate.

Although Crashaw states that he has learned to read the wounds differently, clearly Christ's suffering body retains a crucial importance in demonstrating that Christ was God incarnate, and that he really did suffer for our sins. In order to read Christ's wounds correctly one must be able to read these two orders simultaneously. Thomas F. Healy documents this simultaneity in another epigram by Crashaw, noting that the two reactions we have to the poem "remain distinct, but indivisible, intricately combined to allow a concentration neither wholly on the 'literal' nor on the 'symbolic' senses of the epigram."[8] Similarly, Christ's blood in the circumcision poems is always simultaneously something else: a balm, a gift, rubies. While the comparison of the

---

8. "Crashaw and the Sense of History" in *New Perspectives on the Life and Art of Richard Crashaw*, ed. John R. Roberts (Columbia: University of Missouri Press, 1990), 56.

blood to jewels is clearly metaphoric, the other terms have a more literal status: Christ's blood *is* a balm for sinners; the shedding of his blood *is* a gift to humans. The reading practice called for here is akin to a typological reading, in which both terms of the comparison retain their specificity, with body and soul standing in some relation of type and antetype.

The circumcision is itself figurative, and in turn inspires figuration. As an event it both initiates and represents Christ's suffering, thus playing a curious double role. The first shedding of the blood is generally seen to prefigure the last, which is what perhaps leads Crashaw and Herrick to compare the spurt-ing blood to buds that will later blossom. Crashaw says, "These purple buds of blooming death may bee, / Erst the full stature of a fatall tree" (ll. 15–16), thereby connecting the circumcision and the crucifixion. Herrick is more restrained in "The New-yeeres Gift, or Circumcisions Song":

> Spring Tulips up through all the yeere
> And from His sacred Bloud, here shed,
> May Roses grow, to crown his own deare Head.
> (ll. 21–23)

Although an apparently innocent image, the roses are also mildly sinister, prefiguring the crown of thorns that will later bloom with blood. This is, however, a perfectly reasonable connection for Herrick to make. Steinberg draws attention to what he calls the "blood hyphen" in Renaissance paintings of the crucifixion, a trickle of blood that leads from the wound in Christ's side to his crotch, thus joining the first and last shedding of his blood: "Linking beginning and end, the knife's cut to the gash of the lance, we trace a passage on the body of Christ from man to God; the sexual member broaching the mortal Passion, the breast yielding the gift of grace."[9] If there is a common motif in these poems, it is that this first shedding of the blood prefigures and guarantees the last. This is most gloriously described by Crashaw in "Our Lord in His Circumcision to his Father":

> Tast this, and as thou lik'st this lesser flood
> Expect a Sea, my heart shall make it good.

9. "Sexuality of Christ," 58.

> Thy wrath that wades heere now, e're long shall swim
> The flood-gate shall be set wide ope for him.
>
> (ll. 2–5)

What Crashaw's lines makes clear, as does his reference to "blooming death," is that the mark on the body is also a mark of coming death, but one through which death will be overcome. Christ's sacrifice represents a triumph over death and, implicitly, over the body and its corruption.

I have been arguing that the poetry of the circumcision calls for a changed reading practice, one that can be identified as a circumcised wit, that reads the body in a particular way. If, as Hobbes implies, wit is specific to the community in which it is found, we should perhaps look to the historical circumstances that may have produced the conditions necessary for reading this poetry. One continuous strain in seventeenth-century writings about the circumcision has to do with law, contract and community. From its origins, circumcision has worked both to demonstrate submission to the law and to establish membership in a community. The practice among Jews was initiated, says the Bible, by Abraham, who was circumcised at the age of ninety-nine. In Gen. 17:10–11 God says to Abraham, "This is my covenant, which you shall keep, between me and you and your descendants after you: Every male among you shall be circumcised. You shall be circumcised in the flesh of your foreskins, and it shall be a sign of the covenant between you and me." Calvin emphasizes above all else the status of the sacrament as a seal, comparing it to "the seals attached to government documents and other public acts." He sharply distinguishes the performance of a sacrament from the simple swearing of obedience, insisting that "a sacrament never lacks a preceding promise but is rather joined to it by way of appendix, to confirm and seal the promise itself, and to make it as it were more evident to us."[10] The force of Calvin's argument is to give the sacrament the status of a signature on a contract under which both parties have obligations.

It is in accordance with this covenant or contract that Christ is circumcised. In his sermon on Gal. 3:4–5, "When the fulnesse of time was come, God sent his Son, made of a woman, made under the law," Lancelot Andrewes stresses the importance of Christ demonstrating his obedience to the law. Andrewes reads the circumcision as "the signature of Abraham's Seed,"

---

10. John Calvin, *Institutes of the Christian Religion*, ed. and trans. Ford Lewis Battles (London: Collins, 1976), 87.

which is written on Christ's flesh. Christ voluntarily submits to the ritual, "That so He, keeping the Law, might recover backe the *chirographum contra nos*, the *handwriting that was against us*; and so set us free of the debt."[11] The legal language here is typical of discussions of circumcision: the reading from the Epistles for the Circumcision in the Book of Common Prayer, for example, quotes Rom. 4:14, which states of God's promise to Abraham's descendants that "if they which are of the law be heirs, faith is made void, and the promise made of none effect." Although the point being made is that the law has been superseded by grace, the language itself indicates that the issue is still to be considered within the framework of the law.

The kind of devotional poetry we are discussing often uses legal or commercial language as well, speaking of the circumcision in terms of a contract entered: in "Of our Saviours Circumcision, or New-yeares day," Quarles calls the foreskin a "pawn," for example, which

> were but laid
> For his Good-Frydayes earnest, when he paid
> For our Redemption blood in full summes.
> (ll. 11–13)

Milton in "Upon the Circumcision" writes that Christ will entirely satisfy "that great Cov'nant" (l. 21), which he "seals obedience first with wounding smart" (l. 25).[12] The circumcision acts as something of a guarantee that Christ will redeem man on the cross. This transaction prefigures another exchange, that which Herrick figures as an exchange of gifts at New Year's. Christ's undertaking of the contract is "the best New-yeares Gift to all," which we must requite by offering him our circumcised hearts in return. Christ submits to one law under which we stand condemned, in order to invalidate it and redeem us, and institutes a new law or contract that requires of us a different form of compliance.

If the terms of this contract require the circumcision of wit, which enjoins us to read the body and the world with a metaphysical wit, it makes sense to consider whether this form of reading is itself in some sense contractual.

11. *XCVI Sermons*, 5th ed. (London, 1661), 7.
12. *The Complete Poetry of John Milton*, ed. John T. Shawcross (New York: Doubleday/ Anchor, 1971), 156–57.

Unlike a literal reading—which, like a constative statement in J. L. Austin's terms, can be true or false—metaphysical wit operates in another hermeneutic regime, like Austin's performative statement. Wit is contractual or performative at least in the sense that it can only be enacted: the relations it makes are made in the reading process itself. The concord is established in discord only in the assertion of it, and this assertion depends upon our agreement to employ the same hermeneutic strategy, an agreement that is enacted precisely in the reading process. Apropos of Austin's comment on performative statements that "our word is our bond," we might note that it is at this time in history that verbal contracts became binding.[13]

Both historians and literary critics have documented an increasing interest in Renaissance England in the contract, in connection with the emerging market society, political or legal theory, or theology. Generally this interest is discussed in relation to the emergence of the individual in the early seventeenth century, who comes to be in Hobbes's writings the atom of society. C. B. Macpherson describes this theory as "possessive individualism," arguing,

> Its possessive quality is found in its conception of the individual as essentially the proprietor of his own person or capacities, owing nothing to society for them. . . . The relation of ownership, having become for more and more men the critically important relation determining their actual freedom and actual prospect of realizing their full potentialities was read back into the nature of the individual. The individual, it was thought, is free, inasmuch as he is proprietor of his person and capacities. . . . Society consists of relations of exchange between proprietors.[14]

Hobbes sees the contract as the basis of civil society, which is made up of individuals voluntarily entering into a contract with the sovereign. But if the

13. J. L. Austin, *How to Do Things with Words*, ed. J. O. Urmson and Marina Sbisa (Oxford: Oxford University Press, 1962), 10. Austin collapses the distinction between constative and performative statements by the end of this work, arguing that all statements are performative. The distinction, while ultimately false, is nonetheless useful for the present argument. On the verbal contract, see Christopher Hill, "Covenant Theology and the Concept of 'A Public Person,'" in *Power, Possessions, and Freedom: Essays in Honour of C. B. Macpherson*, ed. Alkis Kontos (Toronto: University of Toronto Press, 1979), 7.

14. *The Political Theory of Possessive Individualism: Hobbes to Locke* (Oxford: Clarendon Press, 1962), 3. On the contract in theology and its connection to contemporary legal theory, see Hill, "Covenant Theology." On the changes in contract law, see Alan Harding, *A Social History of English Law* (Harmondsworth: Penguin, 1966).

primary feature of the individual is proprietorship or ownership of self, it is perhaps necessary to ask who or what owns what or whom. It is clear enough that the emergence of this new form of subjectivity, the individual, must be accompanied by a new conception of the body: in this case, one of possession or ownership.

If an individual owns the body, the relation between individual and body must involve both estrangement and incarceration. "Possession" of the body would then involve both an ownership and an occupation, a formulation that captures the tense relationship that Robert Ellrodt locates in metaphysical poetry and its conception of the body of Christ. He argues that "true meta-physical poetry registers a particular kind of experience or perception. It follows out a sense of double natures simultaneously apprehended whose warrant is Christ's own nature, the union of man and God. We are body and soul together. Metaphysical wit seeks to hold in a tense equilibrium two orders of being which are irremediably distinct yet indissolubly bound together."[15] One often gets the sense in the writings of the metaphysical poets that Christ's suffering through the body is only a part of the much larger trial of his suffering of the body, suffering the ignominy of incarnation. The sense of suffering their own bodies is particularly strong in the poetry of Donne and Crashaw, although their relation to that suffering is portrayed rather differently by each. This relation to the body could bring us to an understanding of what it means to circumcise our hearts.

The heart often acts as a metonym for the body in both the poetry and the sermons we are discussing. Herrick's "Another New-yeeres Gift," for example, demands that we circumcise "hearts, and hands, lips, eares, and eyes" (l. 9). It is clear enough in Donne's discussion of the circumcision of the heart, or spiritual circumcision, in his New Year's Day sermon on Genesis, that it is the body which we must circumcise: "Briefly then, Spirituall Circumcision is to *walke in the spirit; for then,* saies the Apostle, *ye shall not fulfil the lusts of the flesh.*" Earlier in the sermon, Donne states the first reason for circumcision: "to reproach Mans rebellion to *God, God* hath left one part of Mans body, to rebell against him."[16] For the Jews, the stigmata on this most rebellious part

15. Quoted in A. J. Smith, *Metaphysical Wit* (Cambridge: Cambridge University Press, 1991), 6.
16. *Sermons,* 6:196, 192.

of the body reminds man of his affront to God. Insofar as the circumcision is a reminder of original sin, the circumcision of Christ is for such theologians as Saint Bernard an unnecessary defilement of Christ's sinless body,[17] something that constitutes one of the "knotty problems" of Christ's incarnation for Crashaw. After Christ's institution of the new law, the whole body is figured as rebellious—or more specifically, those promptings that arise from the senses or those desires that are typically associated with the world, the flesh, and the devil.

We should be more specific about the relation between the body and the soul, as the body, like subjectivity itself, is by no means historically stable. Although the poets seem to use the circumcision of the heart to refer to the body, it is nonetheless a spiritual rather than a physical circumcision. What must be circumcised is not the body, but those urgings or desires that come from the body and the senses. The circumcision then should be seen in connection to the relation between the soul and the body, or rather the way the soul reads the body, as demonstrated in the poems by Herrick and Crashaw. In his New Year's Day sermon on Gen. 17:24, Donne calls the promptings of the body affections, and although he sees these as the root of all sin, he does not say we must ignore them: "this Day Circumcise thy heart to him and all thy *senses,* and all thy *affections.* It is not an utter *destroying* of thy senses, and of thy affections, that is enjoyned thee; . . . captivate, subdue, change thy affections . . . change thy *choler* into *Zeale,* thy *amorousnesse* into *devotion,* change thy *wastfulnesse* into *Almes* to the poore, and then thou hast circumcised thy *affections* and mayest retaine them." The affections, says Donne, are retained: the implication is that it is not the body that is sinful and needs to be changed, but rather our relation to the body. The circumcision of the heart is thus somewhat different than the mortification of the body, as Frances P. Malpezzi would have it, and is instead an activity intimately concerned with reading.[18] The affection that becomes choler must be interpreted or read differently as zeal, an operation that seems to be an enactment of paradiastole, the conversion of a vice into a virtue by using a positive rather than a negative term to name it. The circumcision of the heart

---

17. Steinberg, "Sexuality of Christ," 52.

18. *Sermons,* 6:203–4; Malpezzi, "The Feast of the Circumcision: The Return to Sacred Time in Herrick's *Noble Numbers,*" *Notre Dame English Journal* 14 (1981): 29–40.

can be seen as a circumcision of wit, as Donne's treatment of it as a rhetorical matter, or a matter of reading, suggests. Here we might remember Hobbes's association of wit with judgment or discretion: what Donne is calling for is a wit that reads the body in the light of Christ's example.

Sin is for Donne the effect of the possession of a body, which he makes explicit in *Devotions Upon Emergent Occasions:* "*sinne* is the *root,* and the *fuell* of all *sicknesse,* and yet that which destroies both *body* & *soule,* is in *neither,* but in *both together;* It is in the *union* of the *body* and *soule;* and, O my God, could I *prevent* that, or can I *dissolve* that?"[19] The spiritual dilemma that Donne outlines seems to arise from anxieties connected with the new form of subjectivity that appeared within his lifetime, for which Hobbes would provide the first political theory. Anne Ferry's study of "inwardness" in Renaissance sonnets documents the changing attitude to the concept of individuality, which impinged upon reading and writing styles. Conservatives came out strongly against biblical interpretations that were not authorized by the church, either questioning or demonizing individual or "unlicenced" readings of the Bible. Individuality, argues Ferry, was seen as a questionable straying, something that could easily be aligned with sin and could certainly be situated in, or at the site of, the body. One of the effects of the circumcision of the heart or wit is thus a policing of individuality, by policing reading strategies that privilege the individual's interpretation over the community's. One could argue that Herbert's "Paradise," which as Michael C. Schoenfeldt convincingly argues enacts a circumcision, is about precisely this problematic. Whereas Schoenfeldt argues that the circumcision acts as a policing of "an aggressive male sexuality," it could also be read more generally as a policing of individuality, given the poem's emphasis on ordered rows, enclosures, and fears of "start[ing]"—that is, standing—out.[20] Donne's uneasy and divided attitude toward the individual is similar to that of Hobbes. In order to ward off anarchy, political or interpretative, the individuals who form the community must enter a contract transferring certain powers to the sovereign. For Donne this necessarily means that the individual must cede the final word on

19. *Devotions Upon Emergent Occasions,* ed. Anthony Raspa (Montreal: McGill-Queen's University Press, 1975), 118.

20. Ferry, *The "Inward" Language: Sonnets of Wyatt, Sidney, and Shakespeare and Donne* (Chicago: University of Chicago Press, 1983); Schoenfeldt, *Prayer and Power: George Herbert and Renaissance Courtship* (Chicago: University of Chicago Press, 1991), 247.

scriptural interpretation to the church. What is pared away in this particular circumcision is thus a dangerous individuality that threatens the community of believers.

It is not surprising then, that the real subject of Donne's sermon on Phil. 3:2, on concision and circumcision, is an attack on reformers in the church: "this is *Concision, Solutio continui,* a breaking of that which is intire, to break the peace of the Church, where we were baptized, by teaching otherwise then that Church teaches, in these things *De modo,* of the manner of expounding such or such articles of faith." Donne compares these reformers to the Philippians who advocated circumcision after the coming of Christ: "they pretend *Reformation,* but they intend *Destruction.*"[21] This form of misreading is the subject of Herrick's epigram "Upon Zelot":

> Is *Zelot* pure? he is: ye see he weares
> The signe of *Circumcision* in his eares.

Zelot, like the reformers Donne is preaching against, does not read correctly; rather, he is reading according to a contract that is no longer in effect: he mistakes the concision or the mutilation of his body for the true circumcision. This concision can further be read as a figuration of Zelot's own political misreadings: his advocacy of a concision of the Church that presumably led to his own concision. Herrick thus demonstrates the difference between the two terms, employing the form of reading that is initiated by Christ's completing and thus exhausting the original signification of circumcision.

Herrick's poem points us toward a consideration of the politics of religious verse in the seventeenth century, which can only be glanced at here. Differences in reading strategies were of course among the most fervently contested issues in the religious controversies of the Renaissance. But reading strategies are always dependent on or related to other issues such as the subject's relation to authority, to the community, and to the body. In the case of the devotional poetry I have discussed, the poets deal primarily with the question of how to read the body of Christ and our own bodies, but their elucidation of a circumcised wit inevitably speaks to more general problems of interpretation. The poetry of circumcision, which insists on a metaphysical apprehension, can mark out a community as clearly as circumcision did. By associating

21. *Sermons,* 10:114, 104.

the Puritans with the Jews of the Old Testament, and by connecting that with a naive or literal reading style, both Donne and Herrick mark out a community of believers: those who seal a contract with God by circumcising their wit. This circumcised wit, although originating in the life of Christ and the teachings of the early Church—especially those of Paul—can be seen to be a response to a changed conception of the individual, and the individual's contractual relations to society and to God.

Catherine Gimelli Martin

Pygmalion's Progress in the Garden of Love, or The Wit's Work Is Never Donne

In his seminal meditation on "wit work," Freud ponders the problem of distinguishing between a joke that "is an end in itself and serves no particular aim" and one that "does serve such an aim": the difference between an innocent and a tendentious joke. Although this difference initially seems to be great, he finds that as a devious route into the unconscious, a joke cannot ultimately be innocent. As in the dream, since wit's "nonsense often replaces ridicule and criticism in the thoughts lying behind the joke," even when its thought "only serves theoretical intellectual interests" wit is "in fact never non-tendentious." Designed to guard against the criticism of "an inhibiting and restricting power," the joke thus succeeds precisely because we "do not know what is giving us enjoyment and what we are laughing at."[1] This model of wit has obvious implications for the secular lyrics of John Donne, whose wit like that of jokes generally is aggressively designed to circumvent social and sexual inhibitions. Yet at the same time, the very pointedness of this poet's self-conscious display of his design also seems to challenge the Freudian model: unlike the covert tactics of most tendentious *or* "innocent" wit, these lyrics make sure that we know exactly what conventions are being ridiculed and who we are laughing at. Thus, in Elegie 15, "Going to Bed," the exhibitionistic speaker's striptease forces his audience not simply to laugh with him, but also to question why he is walking this hyperbolic tightrope: to astound or belittle his audience, to dare it to follow him, or perhaps even more radically,

---

1. Sigmund Freud, *Jokes and Their Relation to the Unconscious*, trans. James Strachey (New York: Norton, 1963), 90, 94, 107, 132–33.

to demonstrate the absurdity of their common enterprise. Since "Jack" Donne apparently did not pen these games merely for his own amusement, why does he, as Freud might query, openly flaunt the aggressive strategies of the joke work at the risk of exposing the imaginative pleasures of the dream work?

Even a brief examination of the famous bawdry of Elegie 15 will illustrate the puzzling nature of these games and their problematic relation to their audience. After detailing not only each garment he would have his mistress discard but also precisely what it should conceal, the speaker issues an ecstatic imperative:

> Licence my roving hands, and let them go,
> Behind, before, above, between, below.
> O my America! my new-found-land,
> My kingdome, safeliest when with one man man'd,
> My Myne of precious stones; My Emperie,
> How blest am I in this discovering thee!
> To enter in these bonds, is to be free;
> Then where my hand is set, my seal shall be.
>
> (ll. 25–32)[2]

If ever there were a case of poetic "license," it is surely this; nearly every major noun and verb carries a sexual double entendre, beginning with "licence" itself. Imaginatively giving legitimate patent to what can only be illicitly permitted, this license finds release in the "bonds" of a legal body (the female "land"), which ironically frees her possessor (the male "prince") from the "labor" (l. 2) of his lust. Like those of the "midwife" (l. 44) he may (as agent of childbirth) literally become, his hands figuratively rove throughout the "kingdom" of the mistress's body: the speaker dis-covers not merely her "behind" and "before," but also the hidden "Myne" of genital jewels that he now declares "mine." Eventually, this legal terminology casuistically exposes the "law" of the phallus, the cylindrical "seal" that soon shall be placed where his "hand is set" (l. 32)—supplying the "hand-written" charter to his empire. Hence if this lyric is addressed to the coterie audience posited by Arthur Marotti, it could well be taken as a classic example of Freud's analysis of obscene wit:

2. All references to Donne's poetry are from *The Complete Poetry of John Donne*, ed. John T. Shawcross (New York: New York University Press, 1968).

> In the case of obscene jokes, which are derived from smut, [tendentious wit] . . . turns the third person [or coterie] who originally interfered with the sexual situation into an ally, before whom the woman must feel shame, by bribing him with the gift of its yield of pleasure. In the case of aggressive purposes it employs the same method in order to turn the hearer, who was indifferent to begin with, into a co-hater or co-despiser, and creates for the enemy a host of opponents when at first there was only one.[3]

In this context, the wit of Elegie 15 has obviously achieved the speaker's purpose: at once objectifying, shaming, and figuratively raping his "new-found-land," and linking himself to a host of phallic allies who receive his "gift," the shared exploitation of woman.

Yet as suggested above, the very excessiveness of Donne's poetic claims at the same time seem to thwart such an analysis. Beginning with his description of the woman as the "foe" before whom he "Is tir'd with standing" (ll. 3–4), the poet systematically exposes the Petrarchan fictions of feminine idolatry and masculine conquest, revealing them as thinly veiled figures of male aggression, dominance, and undisguised lust. With self-mocking glee, he asks first that his "queen" wear only the "haiery Diadem which on you doth grow" (l. 16), then that this "angel" be sent from the fleshly heaven of "Mahomets Paradice" (l. 21). In the process, he lays bare not only her body but also his own voyeurism: not only the exploitative zeal of men but also their contradictory and highly questionable rationalizations in both law and religion. In discovering this heathen "land" and pretending to patent it, the poet thus discovers the literal and figurative strategies of his gender: using legal "seals" to disguise its sexual privileges, and theories of "imputed grace" to "dignifie" its possession of those forbidden "mystick books, which only wee / Must see reveal'd" (ll. 41–43). In the end, his excessively "liberal" (l. 44) claims are obviously both free and lewd, as his pun suggests; although it still serves his obscene purpose to say so, perhaps a woman should need no "more covering" (clothing or sexual favors) "then a man" (l. 48).[4] In the land of this strangely

---

3. Freud, *Jokes and the Unconscious*, 133; see Arthur Marotti, *John Donne, Coterie Poet* (Madison: University of Wisconsin Press, 1986).

4. The Shawcross edition (58) also points out the first pun, and Thomas Docherty, *John Donne, Undone* (London: Methuen and Co., 1986), 82–83, examines the second in some detail.

"new-found" equality, the teacher must begin by imitating the conduct he would advocate in his pupil: "To teach thee I am naked first" (l. 46).

Unfortunately, although Freud also ponders the equivocal nature of the similarly sophisticated tendentious wit of the poet Heinrich Heine, he ends by labeling rather than resolving the issues this wit raises. Admitting that the three classes of tendentious wit—"exposing or obscene jokes, aggressive (hostile) jokes, [and] cynical (critical, blasphemous) jokes"—also require the addition of another, "the fourth and rarest," he fails fully to define the purpose of "sceptical jokes." Although he grants that their object is "not a person or an institution but the certainty of our knowledge itself, one of our speculative possessions," he approaches these jokes more through the questions they raise than through the roles they imply. Hence he observes that

> the more serious substance of the joke is the problem of what determines the truth. The joke, once again, is pointing to a problem and is making use of the uncertainty of one of our commonest concepts. Is it the truth if we describe things as they are without troubling to consider how our hearer will understand what we say? Or is this only jesuitical truth, and does not genuine truth consist in taking the hearer into account and giving him a faithful picture of our own knowledge?[5]

Although the answer to his final rhetorical question seems as clearly to be "yes" as the answer to the first is "no," Freud never asks the more difficult question implied by both: does the skeptical wit's *shared* divestment of his "speculative possession" of certitude with his audience create a relatively "innocent" or equalized verbal exchange, or is the "truth" of such an exchange finally out of the question altogether?

Thus while extremely suggestive as means of approaching Donne's lyrics, this account does not resolve other nagging questions: even if the speaker defines himself as a skeptical wit coexisting in relative equality with his audience, what happens to the object of his wit, especially when, as so often the case, his literary humor seems to blend all four aspects of tendentious wit: obscene, aggressive, blasphemous, and skeptical? Moreover, since the constantly shifting in- and de-flated tropes of his poetry refuse to resolve into any obvious pattern, they can still be suspected not only of inflating the ego that they so cleverly display but also of reinstating the social structures that they

5. Freud, *Jokes and the Unconscious*, 115.

seem to satirize. Jonathan Goldberg rehearses precisely these suspicions in his view of the *Songs and Sonnets,* which he finds displaying the same hierarchical strategies as those of James I. Using the lyric authority of the sonnet to proclaim "himself a king by Divine Right, ruling in 'the stile of *Gods,*'" in Goldberg's view James establishes the dynastic preoccupation of the period and its artists, who invoke his sense of royal mystery to achieve the same "mystification of the body, the transformation of privacy into public discourse." Thus although he agrees that their imitation of these mysteries has "the potential for subversion" built into it, for Goldberg as for other New Historicists this potential is always already contained. Although Donne's sonnets "begin as if they were rebelling against political values," they end by naturalizing the relations between the sexes and making them "extension[s] of male prerogative and male power."[6] Rather than recognizing the beloved as an independent vehicle of will and desire, the dominant male lover constitutes his power in the very process of praising a female Other who reflects only his own or the "King's reall, or his stamped face" ("The Canonization," l. 7).

The opposite position on the power dynamics at work in Donne's wit is presented by Thomas Docherty, who argues that the hierarchical view of the lyrics rests upon a fundamentally flawed model of communication: "It is as if the Other was no more or less than an empty space, a container of sorts, in which Donne pours his 'influence', his words which are supposed to shape the Other in an imagined repetition of his own image. This extremely crude model of communication, thoroughly discredited in fact though still maintained as valid by much criticism, . . . is fundamentally 'colonialist' . . . The Other, as threat, is domesticated and converted into an aspect of the Self and thus rendered harmless, 'colonized' or appropriated and controlled." According to Docherty, the New Historicist response to Donne's "garden of love" is actually in collusion with the superficial, unironic approach to these "empires" advanced in traditional masculinist readings; like them, "while thinking that it is merely corroborating the ignorance of woman in the texts, [it] in fact is producing that ignorance for the first time, constructing it." Since both positions participate in the mystique of "colonized woman" supposedly circulated in these texts, Docherty proposes a far more dialogical approach to a

6. *James I and the Politics of Literature: Jonson, Shakespeare, Donne, and Their Contemporaries* (Baltimore: Johns Hopkins University Press, 1983), xii–xiii, xv, 27, 66, 97.

poet who not only refuses "to ignore woman" but also pointedly deconstructs the "naturalness" of the female body. In this view, Donne not only creates a new, neither exclusively masculine nor feminine sense of sexual identity, but also imagines a constantly shifting, "eccentric" or de-centered "site" of mutual identity, an early modern microcosm "of a revolutionary land, a society where interchange of social place is the norm."[7]

These diametrically opposed responses to the strategies of Donne's wit work seem inevitably to point toward an excluded middle, an evaluation somewhere between Goldberg's monarchical monologism and Docherty's deconstructive dialogism. The advantages of this middle ground should be obvious: it would account both for the wit's sense of theatrical dis-play, his insistence on forcing "the real world, all the world . . . [to be] replayed in the flesh" as the not-so-hidden motive behind his "state secrets,"[8] and for his sense of re-play, the deconstructive rapidity with which he dons masks only to discard them as ironically open secrets. Yet as both critics variously suggest, these and related polarities have proved remarkably resistant to modification, much less to subversion, throughout the history of Donne criticism. Like the power relations in which wit generally and these lyrics specifically are grounded, these polarities seem to reassert themselves all the more rigorously once they are "undonne." And as we have seen, fully as much as those of the jokester who manipulates language in order to expose its "concealed" object, the female body, Donne's witty poses clearly flaunt the phallocentric verbal devices of which Goldberg accuses them: "the mystification of love, the disguise of sexuality in platonized sexuality, [and] the parade of learning to cover ribaldry." Thus if, as he argues, the anti-Petrarchan, anti-pastoral elements in Donne's gardens of love are domesticated and tamed in the very act of psychic release, then the rebellious elements at work in his verse must also be subverted and canceled, the body finally reinvested in the language of power, "the only language available to Donne to proclaim the mystery, to assert power, to create a sphere of privacy."[9]

7. See *John Donne, Undone*, 52, 62–63.

8. Goldberg, *James I and Literature*, 111–12.

9. Ibid., 107, 111; Docherty examines the same evidence in more detail, and (as one would expect) arrives at quite different conclusions (*John Donne, Undone*, 57, 60, 80–83). The introduction to the Shawcross edition provides a useful survey of the problem(s) of these polarities. For a succinct summary of the function of jokes in "re-establishing old liberties and getting rid of the burden of intellectual upbringing," see Freud, *Jokes and the*

At least superficially, Goldberg's account is supported by Freud's general analysis of the psychology of wit work, where the jokester's initial impulse of pure play is always subverted by the "othering" impulse of the jest. By transferring its random, aggressive energies into more socially sanctioned channels, like the absorption of improvisational theatrics into royal role-playing, or the conversion of private lovemaking into courtly or "coterie" display, the joke delivers psychic gratification only by going public: "Joking as a *play* with one's own words and thoughts is to begin with without a person as an object. But already at the preliminary stage of the *jest*, if it has succeeded in making play and nonsense safe from the protests of reason, it demands another person to whom it can communicate its result. But this second person in the case of jokes does not correspond to the person who is the object, but to the *third* person, the 'other' person in the case of the comic." Much as the kingly lover of "The Sun Rising" needs to display the mysteries of the bedroom by inviting the sun "to witness a royal levée," the joke work requires a witness if its performance is to succeed. Thus both forms of display can be seen as merely masquerades designed to conceal/reveal their unmentionable subtext before an audience, whose awe or laughter releases the pleasure that "is denied to me but is manifest in the other person."[10]

Despite these similarities, Freud's insistence on the continual subversion of humor's altruistic or socially constructive potential is actually less pessimistic than Goldberg's, in large part because his analysis of humor's self-empowering strategies is more dialogic than the Foucauldian knowledge/power equation employed by Goldberg.[11] Particularly in discussing the self-conscious exercise of skeptical wit, he seems to suggest that the "othering" function of jokes partially blends with the free play of the comic, the interactive, free-associative stage through which all wit must pass. Analogous to the silent, ambiguous laughter of aesthetic reception, here first and third persons, or writerly intentions and readerly responses, ambiguously inter-

---

Unconscious, 127–28. Although Freud never precisely says that the scapegoat of this libidinal liberation is always a woman, the presumption is implicit in much of his theory and explicit in his analysis of obscene humor (133), the largest of his categories.

10. Goldberg, *James I and Literature*, 112; Freud, *Jokes and the Unconscious*, 143–44.

11. Freud's is also notably less optimistic than other classic accounts of humor; see *Comedy: "An Essay on Comedy" by George Meredith; "Laughter" by Henri Bergson*, ed. Wylie Sypher (Baltimore: Johns Hopkins University Press, 1980).

change.[12] "At bottom . . . nothing other than the poet's '*Carpe diem,*' which appeals to the uncertainty of life and the unfruitfulness of virtuous renunciation," this simultaneously self-interested and socially critical species of tendentious wit subverts the either/or of praise and blame by scapegoating both self and "Other," recirculating the comic bond ruptured in cruder versions of the joke work, and (as I hope to show) establishing a distinctly anti-imperial private sphere.[13]

Since the tendentious poet can attack his object only by also attacking himself and his own "speculative possession" of knowledge, he succeeds in leveling the pretensions of the powerful only by leveling his own. Like the complex fusion of "poetic subjectivity . . . [and] poetic objectivity" that Joel Fineman finds being invented in Shakespeare's sonnets,[14] the self-canceling ironies of Donne's lyrics restore at least some of the subject/object complementarity that Docherty finds omitted from "colonialist" models of communication. Rather than reappropriating "royal mysteries," this exercise dethrones and displays them as fictions constructed by ignoring our common possession, our awareness of the artificiality of all social positions, high and low. As in Elegie 15, the poet characteristically shows not only that the emperor has no clothes (a possibility that Goldberg considers and rejects) but also that both he and his own claims to power are equally naked. Thus even when he appropriates the form of the obscene jest by appearing to undress a woman in public, he alters its thrust (in a number of senses) by unexpectedly

12. For a fascinating account of this interchange, see Wolfgang Iser, *The Act of Reading: A Theory of Aesthetic Response* (Baltimore: Johns Hopkins University Press, 1978).

13. See Freud, *Jokes and the Unconscious,* 109–11, 142–43. Although these passages are not contiguous, they are linked by explicit internal references. Perhaps owing to this gap, Freud's final analysis of this form of wit is extremely ambiguous. He argues that "the comic" originates as a transaction between two persons, which in satirical humor encompasses three, but when told as a *joke,* is again "really" between two (see 143). Nonetheless, because Donne's wit clearly belongs in Freud's carpe diem category, and because lyrics are not literally jokes, it seems legitimate to include them in the species of skeptical humor where a three-way exchange seems to be maintained.

14. Fineman, *Shakespeare's Perjured Eye: The Invention of Poetic Subjectivity in the Sonnets* (Berkeley: University of California Press, 1986), 10. According to Fineman, instead of a poetics that "produce[s] a praise of 'thee' [that] will regularly turn out to be a praise of 'me,'" the poet "becomes *to himself* an absent third person" by adopting a stance somewhere between praise and the paradox of praise; here "rhetoricity" not only "speaks against itself" but "instantiates . . . the fact that it is false" (9, 27, 31, 35).

reversing the primal scene; as Docherty also observes, the phallus, not the mistress, ultimately becomes the object of the reader's gaze.[15]

Because this "revelation" is itself a fiction, some readers might well suspect that Donne's performances covertly continue to participate in a form of verbal mystification that their speakers only appear to demystify. Since by dramatizing the structure of imperial power relations the poet does not necessarily renounce them, he may still be implicated in the witty shell game of which Goldberg accuses him: not debunking, but celebrating his own superior penetration of the royal mysteries. Far from equalizing the relation between subject and object, this punning "penetration" would then entitle him to become the virtual high priest of their poetic and patriarchal prerogatives. Yet Goldberg's own governing assumption—that the power relations of seventeenth-century England follow the familiar paradigm whereby subversion is ceaselessly circulated and contained—is subject to similar questions of interpretation.[16] If we grant that James's "duplicities paved the way, and Jonson, Donne, and Chapman followed, each seizing the royal road, that doubly crossed path," it is still far from clear how to divide the "doubly crossed" paths of imitative collusion from those of parodic critique. Even if "each author found authority in the royal prerogative of double speech," does each use it in the same way? Or is there sufficient textual evidence to place Donne's lyrics at a

15. Goldberg, *James I and Literature*, 47; Docherty, *John Donne, Undone*, 82–83. Goldberg, *James I and Literature* (262, n. 59) argues that "even the naked body is clothed in the language of power." However, his supporting evidence—Stephen Greenblatt's "More, Role-Playing, and *Utopia*," *Yale Review* 66 (summer 1978): 517–36—universalizes the very mode of self-fashioning that he claims to historicize; applying More's mode to Donne presents a very great stylistic leap indeed.

16. Goldberg's account is persuasive in its outlines. Adopting Clifford Geertz's anthropological analysis of power, he argues, "The real is as imagined as the imaginary," and vice versa (*James I and Literature*, 32–33). However, this general account can be misleadingly applied to the specifics of Renaissance English culture, which is considerably more complex that Geertz's Balinese examples. Arguing that "one mystery could answer another, parodic images could imitate state" (82), Goldberg rarely considers what would constitute a demystifying parody of these mysteries. Instead, as he acknowledges (xiv–xv), he largely adapts the model of Elizabethan manipulations of ideology employed by Stephen Greenblatt in *Renaissance Self-Fashioning: From More to Shakespeare* (Chicago: University of Chicago Press, 1980) and most of his subsequent work. For a critique of the use of the Foucauldian model of power in New Historicism, see Carolyn Porter, "Are We Being Historical Yet?" *South Atlanta Quarterly* 87.4 (fall 1988): 743–86.

more intermediate point on Goldberg's own scale of distinctions: somewhere between Chapman's "absolutism" and Jonson's face-saving exposé of the darker realities of courtly corruption?[17] Although Goldberg himself places Donne closer to Chapman than to Jonson, this alignment becomes extremely dubious if Donne is openly parodying rather than replicating the king's royal "we," and even more so if this parody redistributes rather than reclaims his privileges. That is, if the rites of his lovers critique and implicitly depose the "rights" of patriarchal and aristocratic privilege, his lyrics should be regarded as more socially subversive than either masculinist or New Historicist critical fashion currently decrees.

At this point, supplying some of the gaps in Freud's inquiry into the psychic processes of demystification involved in skeptical wit will provide a valuable theoretical ground for making what might otherwise seem wholly subjective stylistic distinctions. In this troubling "limit case," his examples are actually more instructive than his analysis, particularly in his probing of that other deeply conflicted religious convert, Heine, whose skepticism but not whose faith Freud shares. Like Donne, Heine was nearly as famous for his death as for his life, and his remarkable deathbed witticism is examined by Freud in some detail. When en route to his Eternal Garden and exhorted by his priest to avail himself of God's abundant mercy, the poet retorted, "Bien sûr qu'il me pardonnera: c'est son métier" (Of course God will pardon me: that's his job). According to Freud, this retort represents an "ultimate" revenge in more senses than one: the dying poet adroitly if unexpectedly debunks not only his priest, but God himself. As Freud says, by disparaging the ultimate Other as a mere tradesman, "What was supposed to be the created being revealed itself just before its annihilation as the creator."[18] Nevertheless, this jest seems to possess an additional level overlooked by Freud, one that his own atheistic bias may have ironically caused him to repress. A likely subtext obscured by the brittle surface of the witticism hints at Heine's underlying confession, his admission of skepticism and disbelief undercut by his

---

17. Goldberg, *James I and Literature*, 147. For Chapman's "absolutism," see 155–61; for Jonson's greater hesitation, see 122; and for his ability to turn "the king's self-perception against himself" in order to indulge in social criticism, see 130. Goldberg's remarkably unambiguous readings of Donne seem to me by far the weakest part of his study, and never more so than when he touches on "The Canonization."

18. Freud, *Jokes and the Unconscious*, 114–15.

somewhat wistful desire for faith if not necessarily for pardon. In this sense, his defiance can also be read as a dare, a final challenge to a higher reality that, for better or for worse, he is about to confront. These mixed motives thus impart to Heine's remark in particular and to tendentious wit in general an ambiguous circulation of energies that *cannot* be canceled, that can never fully objectify an Other in and for whom too much of the self is already implicated.

The mixed social and religious circumstances that sharpen the satirical edge of Donne's highly ambivalent Inns of Court and courtly poems possess more than a passing resemblance to those of Heine, as do the poems' strategies. Typically presenting himself as the "creature" of the "Other," a socially or erotically superior lady whom he frankly manipulates and ultimately claims as *his* creature, he either overtly or implicitly portrays himself as her Pygmalion, the creator of the "blissful paradise" of her love, which is essentially also her self: the ironically "original" garden from which he cannot "rightfully" be, but predictably is, evicted, a second Adam suffering for the first's fatal fall. Thus whether he acts as a fictive demiurge or a merely human artist claiming the patent on his perfected Galatea, the stages through which he passes generally imitate the progress of the joke and dream work, with its alternating expansion and condensation, inversion and displacement.[19] Expanding one "little room" until it fills the earth, he condenses both to the point that his figurative universe collapses, the "unruly" Sun who supports it no longer ruling there or anywhere. Like Heine reducing the scope of God's sovereignty to the "narrow room" of his deathbed, in "The Sunne Rising" Donne reduces heaven and earth to the amorous bed he decrees an "everywhere." Yet again as in Heine's jest, the poet's assertion of power is undercut by his own wit, whose strategies succeed only when they are undone *by* Donne. Claudia Brodsky describes the logic at work in these reversals by noting that since the poet's "transformations of 'one little room' into 'an every where' . . . extend and immortalize the lovers by effective default," by "precluding any understanding of its mode," his poem denies "itself in turn as an access to knowledge." As Meg Lota Brown similarly observes, Donne's

---

19. See Freud's summary of the purposes of analogy and substitution (which I take to be variations of Donnean expansion and reversal), and his comparison of the processes of condensation and displacement in the joke work to the same processes in the dream work (*Jokes and the Unconscious,* 87–89).

speaker not only exploits but also flamboyantly dramatizes his abuse of the equitable sanctions of casuistry, sanctions that should adjudicate "the conflicting claims of self and law" but instead abolish them: "Part of the humor of 'The Sunne Rising' is that its elaborate and complex argument is simply a disguise for the speaker's motive of pleasure. His comic maneuvering of casuistical principles enables him to legislate his own gratification, to feign moral and political legitimacy for staying in bed."[20]

Despite Brown's sensitivity to the subversive implications of Donne's blatant sophistry—which not only "invests the lover's motives with a legitimacy that they were never accorded in fact" but also trivializes the pursuits of the king and his emblematic adjunct, the sun—she like Goldberg ultimately overlooks the element of *self*-parody in the speaker's kingly pose. This device, which through his display of imperial presumption ironically manifests his own and the king's actual disempowerment, undermines even as it seems to appropriate "monarchical authority." More clearly than Heine's dismissal of the divine "tradesman," the lover's threat to dismiss the "busy old fool" who voyeuristically intrudes on his lovemaking is obviously spurious; if he makes good on it by eclipsing the sun's "reverend beams" (l. 11) with a wink, he admits that he will be forced to lose the very sight of the self-sufficient "State" on which his "title" rests.[21] Self-consciously sophistic as well as solipsistic, the lover thus "winks" both at his fictive interlocutor and at the solar pretensions of James I.[22] Imitatively deflating the royal appropriation of powers beyond human control, Donne calls attention to the king's egoistic

20. Brodsky, "Donne: The Imaging of the Logical Conceit," in *John Donne and the Seventeenth-Century Metaphysical Poets*, ed. Harold Bloom (New York: Chelsea House, 1986) 54; Brown, "'In that the world's contracted thus': Casuistical Politics in Donne's 'The Sunne Rising,'" in *"The Muses Common-Weale": Poetry and Politics in the Seventeenth Century*, ed. Claude J. Summers and Ted-Larry Pebworth (Columbia: University of Missouri Press, 1988), 24, 31.

21. Brown, "In that the world's contracted thus," 24, 27–29. Since she observes most of these points herself, Brown's conclusion that "Donne's persona appropriates rather than subverts monarchial control" is unconvincing; although not all parody is subversive, not only the text of the poem but the facts of Donne's life (26) suggest that he had good reason to defy authority in ways that do not completely leave its "political structures . . . intact" (28). This is William Zunder's conclusion in *The Poetry of John Donne: Literature and Culture in the Elizabethan and Jacobean Period* (Sussex: Harvester Press, 1982), esp. 39.

22. A number of critics have noted the parodic references to James running throughout the poem; for instance, Marotti, *John Donne, Coterie Poet*, 156–57.

excesses by outdoing them, but also by thereby placing his own "coup" on a less disingenuous basis.

In fact, the excessively phallocentric nature of Donne's complaint against the sun only reinforces the validity of its universal call to rise by tacitly admitting that sexually as well as physically, the lovers *must* obey nature's call. Instead of ruling *out* the "unruly sun," his casuistic strategies thus implicate the strategies of kings, the unruly human rulers who believe (or act as if they believe) in the fantasies of power with which poets merely play. While in one respect (as both Brown and Goldberg agree) Donne's performance merely transfers authority from the actual king to the player king, in another, equally valid sense, his ironic exposure of power plays as mere word plays delegitimizes both. By ultimately robbing not only monarchic but also poetic labors of their truth claims, the speaker's original challenge must be transposed into a new key; when all human authority has been placed in question, the relative positions of sun, lover, lady, and language must be renegotiated.[23]

These strategies, which characterize a wide variety of the *Songs and Sonnets* ranging from well-known examples such as "The Sunne Rising," Elegie 15, "The Canonization," and "The Anniversarie," to lesser-known examples such as "Elegie: Loves Warre," are perhaps most clearly illuminated by Elegie 13, "Nature's Lay Ideot." In this case directly alluding to a third-party audience of sympathetic listeners, the poet bitterly complains that he has undertaken Pygmalion's labors and successfully brought his primary audience, his Galatea, to life, only to be ungratefully driven from her garden of delights. Next, he "reduces" these delights by describing them as man-made fictions, like Heine displacing his loss by implying that it is self-generated, a "death" that is not so much a fall as a rejection of a spurious Eden. Nevertheless, the same rhetorical reversals that seem to assure his success—first belittling the lady and her

---

23. Although we cannot be certain how many of these lyrics were actually sent to the real-life counterparts of the poem's personas, like Heine's "message" to God their primary function seems that of reopening a relationship with a person who may be neither physically nor emotionally "there" for the poet, and whose actual response may thus be fictive, real, or some combination of the two. Certainly it is possible to imagine a wide variety of responses (amusement, anger, scorn, pity, hauteur) to even his most insulting songs, such as Elegie 13 considered below. For convincing evidence of Lady Bedford's actual response to a quite different elegy, see Claude J. Summers, "Donne's 1609 Sequence of Grief and Comfort," *Studies in Philology* 89.2 (spring 1992): 211–31, esp. 227–29.

suitors, then making himself the only real actor in their domestic farce—instead cause it to cancel itself. The very logic of his sophistic, tendentious wit traps him in one of the two "falls" inherent in his position; either he will regain a "blissful paradise" that is actually artificial, or he must relinquish control of the real beauty and spirit that her now humble craftsman (l. 28) concedes he has only tamed or polished. Either way he loses, and while this loss seems compensated by his staging this clever performance for a secondary audience who will admire his wit, because much of its brilliance actually depends upon an open display of its artificiality, his audacity is inherently self-destructive. Thus after disparaging the Eve of Elegie 13 as mere "matter," a rich India that here as in "The Sunne Rising" (l. 17) seems more fit to be molded into a Galatea than into a sister creature, the master pedagogue must demote himself to the role of minor pupil, servant, or groom; his very skill in building his house of cards causes him to expose its flimsiness. When it finally collapses, not only does the "emperor" have no clothes and his palace no walls, but his putative object is reinstated as a potential subject, if only by default.

Precisely like Heine's deathbed humor, then, Donne's wit protests "the social construction of reality" even as it participates in it, and even as it questions the possible existence of an "Other," external reality beyond its own performance.[24] Philosophically, this tactic can be described as using nihilism to defray solipsism in order to provide the grounds of a new dialectic: as with the Cartesian *cogito ergo sum*, once ostensible objects are eliminated, a more relative but also less "dubious" subject/object relation can be established. Of course, as with the *cogito*, since the philosopher/poet retains the ability to mask or unmask, dress or redress, his object, his skeptical stance is neither as disinterested nor as deconstructive as it seems. Although the rules of the game demand that he expose his intentions and call his very identity into question, these self-sacrificial maneuvers remain fictive exercises insuring his control of the craft he is supposedly discrediting.[25] Thus despite the fact that

24. A more specific yet related purpose of this critique is suggested by Marotti in *John Donne, Coterie Poet*, 44–66: that of protesting against and compensating for the subservient male role dictated by Petrarchan love conventions.

25. For a comparable analysis of the effect of the new hermeneutics and aesthetics accompanying the rise of Cartesianism, see Michel Foucault, *The Order of Things: An*

the wit displays his inability to preserve his hierarchical "male" role of creator in relation to subservient "female" matter, he remains an indisputable master *player*. Although the possibility of an-Other voice is never negated, within the limits of this aesthetic circle itself it can never actually be fulfilled. Yet at the same time, because his verbal mastery continues to depend upon a self-parodying shell game, a blatant substitution of illusory rhetorical for physical facts, it also negates his own authority. In the "space" opened by this inevitable if scarcely altruistic negation, a reciprocal appropriation of the wit's double-edged strategies could empower the very Other it had seemed to objectify.

The resulting effect may be regarded as the "hermeneutic circle" of tendentious wit: a self-generating cycle of empowerment, disempowerment, and partially "redeemed" or open-ended reempowerment that governs most of the *Songs and Sonnets*. This structural logic is thus manifest even in poems of compliment when the first scenario is reversed and the poet presents himself as an inverted Pygmalion, an objectified victim of love who figuratively turns himself to stone rather than feel the scorn of God's own Galatea, an "actual" Eve whose miraculous beauty and virtue mock the man until he is nothing more than a man/drake matelessly moaning by the pond of his own tears. Yet because in another form the mandrake is a powerful leveler, a plant with human voice and power over human sexuality, his descent in the chain of being leads to his psychological ascent just as surely as in other lyrics his assertions of power lead to his fall. He declares his tears no ordinary waters, but the miraculous source of a fountain supplying a litmus test of true love, a test that, through his suffering and her virtue, only he and she could pass. Hence in "Twicknam Garden," Pygmalion's progress is again guaranteed by the same circular logic of condensation, displacement, and reversal that characterizes the examples of tendentious wit considered above. By assuming the role of a self-betraying Adam who brings his own serpent into the garden, he gains an ironic martyrdom that at once makes this anti-Edenic "True Paradise" truly his own (l. 9).[26] Just as inevitably, this tactic proves self-canceling.

Archaeology of the Human Sciences (New York: Random House, 1970), esp. 3–16. Foucault's work is susceptible to a number of readings, only one of which is implicated in my objections to the assumptions about power prevalent in New Historicism.

26. Twicknam is "True Paradise" only in the ironic sense that *he* has sinned and fallen

As in Elegie 13, the more he hyperbolically empowers himself the more he trivializes his power, until the only "truth" remaining is that of his own suffering, despair, and defeated desire. Yet in his final "fall," the wit actually accomplishes what had seemed impossible; not only does neither Galatea nor Pygmalion, creature or creator, retain an unqualified upper hand, but the latter's exposure of his unfair advantage opens the possibility of her conceding her own unfair advantage; as Freud reminds us, "a joke is . . . a psychical factor possessed of power."

Yet according to Freud, even in tendentious wit this power is exercised less dialectically than the foregoing analysis would suggest. In order to turn an indifferent hearer into an ally against a common enemy,

> In the first case [the joke work] overcomes the inhibitions of shame and respectability by means of the bonus of pleasure which it offers; in the second it upsets the critical judgement which would otherwise have examined the dispute. In the third and fourth cases, in the service of cynical and skeptical purposes, it shatters respect for institutions and truth in which the hearer has believed, on the one hand by reinforcing the argument, but on the other by practising a new species of attack. Where argument tries to draw the hearer's criticism over on to its side, the joke endeavours to push the criticism out of sight . . . the method which is psychologically the most effective.

Nonetheless, by taking into consideration the elements Freud overlooks in Heine's joke, and by stressing the imaginative complicity between poetic creator and creature that Fineman finds afforded by such "limit cases" as the poetic mock-encomium, we can theorize a form of tendentious wit whose "deductive circularity" not only *refuses* "to push criticism out of sight" but actually seems to invite it.[27]

"Twicknam Garden," with its self-mocking Petrarchan lover and its triply ambiguous "spring" (l. 2), thus provides a paradigmatic instance of this form, one in which self-exposure achieves an advantage that is at once marginally

---

there, while his "Eve" remains faithful; for these and related reasons, it is actually an inverse or anti-Eden, as stated above. See also Sallye Sheppeard, "Eden and Agony in *Twicknam Garden*," *John Donne Journal* 7.1 (1988): 65–72, esp. 67–68.

27. Freud, *Jokes and the Unconscious*, 133; Fineman, *Shakespeare's Perjured Eye*, 35. Although primarily making a case for Shakespeare's sonnets, Fineman sees subsequent performances in this mode (especially Donne's, 123–29) as following similar strategies. For "deductive circularity," see Brodsky, "Donne," 56.

real and really marginal. Here, because *spring* at once refers to the "source" of his Eden, Lady Bedford, to the healing pools or fountains of her garden, and to the season that should end his "winter," the wit dramatizes not only that he cannot be healed by any of these springs but also that he can verbally manipulate them into springs of a quite different kind. Portraying himself first as the victim of a "spider love" that transubstantiates manna to gall and of a female duplicity that causes him, like Adam, to fall at the very threshold of his garden,[28] he denounces his love as a trap that, like a bite of Eve's apple, poisons the garden and blights innocent desire. To reverse this "plot," the poet turns his abject victimization into a mock vehicle of control, with its own appropriately mock auditor and alter ego, the mandrake who helps him convert his poisonous spring into a holy fountain of truth. Yet in contrast to the full recovery Freud finds in the joke work, since the conversion of the poet's tears into liquid touchstones of "true love" is not in any sense a real victory, this recovery remains double-edged. Mocking all lovers except himself and his virtuously wicked fair, the poet ironically neither helps nor vindicates any one, least of all himself:

> Hither with christall vyals, lovers come,
>   And take my teares, which are love's wine,
>   And try your mistresse Teares at home,
> For all are false, that tast not just like mine;
>   Alas, hearts do not in eyes shine,
> Nor can you more judge womans thoughts by teares
>   Than by her shadow, what she weares.
> O perverse sexe, where none is true but shee,
>   Who's therefore true, because her truth kills me.
>
>   (ll. 19–27)

Despite the fountain's putative function of testing the sacramental "wine" of "mistress' tears," no test is really necessary here; not only are all "false, that taste not just like mine," but all women but one are false by nature. Overgoing the conventional Petrarchan complaint concerning the false reflection of hearts in eyes, and thoughts in tears, the speaker infinitely expands it: woman's

---

28. For the theological commonplace that Adam fell during his first day in Eden, see James Grantham Turner, *One Flesh: Paradisal Marriage and Sexual Relations in the Age of Milton* (Oxford: Clarendon Press, 1987).

love now has no more constancy or reality than the appearance of an appearance, her natural or "true" form of reflection, her shadow, being no more indicative of her soul than an arbitrary or conventional form, the clothing that she wears. Yet because it concedes that "*none* is true but she" (italics supplied), the very "controlling fiction" of this hyperbole also cancels the poet's redeeming "gift" to mankind, in the process subverting Petrarchan blame and praise by redistributing it equally between lover and lady. Already having discredited his own probity, the lover begins to attack the lady's, a move that ironically neither justifies his nor tarnishes her motives. Although the wit can still lament that "No where / Lives a woman true, and faire" ("Song," ll. 17–18), here it is only because the "true" woman proves "false" to love by staying true to her marriage vows, which would be a form of praise were it not that she does so only "*because* her truth kills mee.*"* While in one sense this admission vindicates the lover's greater faithfulness, in another it convicts him of greater faithlessness to her husband, her marriage, and in fact to the whole patriarchal system on which his complaints had seemed to rest. Of course, at this level, a more pessimistic Freudian account could also be justified: all human institutions have been exposed to logically unanswerable criticism, not because its terms are logical, but because pure play has been converted to cynical purposes by a bribing of the critical faculties. Nevertheless, this description has some serious limitations, as an examination of an equally skillful but less dialectical protest against the sadistic uses of feminine virtue should show.

Sidney's Sonnet 31 from *Astrophil and Stella,* "With how sad steps," takes up the lover's complaint in much the same terms as do Donne's speakers, but this witty lament wholly lacks the exaggerated self-reflexivity that characterizes the style of the latter. Exposing a quite different object, its ironies continually probe the reason behind the moon's "wan face," concluding with two rhetorical questions:

> Do they above love to be lov'd, and yet
>> Those Lovers scorne whom that *Love* doth possesse?
> Do they call Vertu there ungratefulnesse?
>>>> (ll. 12–14)[29]

---

29. Quoted from *The Poems of Sir Philip Sidney,* ed. William A. Ringler Jr. (Oxford: Clarendon Press, 1962), 180.

Following his complaint that the Petrarchan game of love is heavily weighted on the side of the female, who keeps "score" by attracting lovers and then rejecting them in the name of virtue, Sidney's concluding jibe at a "virtue" that is only vanity seems to parallel Donne's critique of his lady's fidelity, but differs by pointedly hitting rather than deliberately missing its mark. Moreover, Donne's false praise significantly differs from Sidney's both by placing the "truth" of Lady Bedford's "honor" beyond question while Stella's is questioned and by strategically invalidating his own claim to omniscience concerning the nature of all her "perverse sex." In contrast to the consistent logic of Sidney's complaint, both Donne's continual shifts in rhetorical and dramatic stance and his demonstrably false claim to an erotic martyrdom that neither saves nor benefits anyone undermine his related claim that the lady is faithful only "because her truth kills me." Hence his poem finally disproves what Sidney's establishes: the fact that the moon is ironically far less fickle than the female sex. More like Heine's apparent dismissal of God, Donne's persistent questioning of Lady Bedford's motives only exposes his own as an ambivalent admixture of self-knowledge, sour grapes, and a desire for mercy. Magnifying rather than resolving its internal ambiguities,[30] the poem thus exchanges the speaker's claim to verbal superiority for a disguised assertion of moral and spiritual equality, a claim to a humble pride that, if only in loss, equals her proud fidelity. In this sense, social criticism is not so much pushed aside as reactivated.

This assessment is supported by the fact that the poet's self-interested yet undeniable leveling remains essentially the same when his labors are directed at a woman of socially inferior status. In Elegie 13, posing as a pedagogue/creator instead of a creator/victim, the wit also loses his contest with the lady by subverting his assumed authority in a way that questions their common motives. Upbraiding "Nature's lay idiot" for accepting his refining gifts and inheriting "a blissful paradise" (ll. 1, 24) that excludes him, "Dr. Donne" at first claims full credit for her progress in "the mystic language of the eye . . . [and] hand" (l. 4), the lore of deciphering love's maladies, alphabets, and secret codes (l. 11). Yet this Galatea's words and charms remain literally his, his craftsmanship having replaced her foolish "household charms," "broken

---

30. As Marotti observes, the poem's conclusion merely reasserts "the same tension that runs throughout the lyric" (*John Donne, Coterie Poet,* 217).

proverbs, and torn sentences" with true wit (ll. 15–19). Thus although she, too, has "betrayed" him in her choice of husbands, he sues to retain full rights over their relationship:

> Thou art not by so many duties his,
> That from the'worlds Common having sever'd thee,
> Inlaid thee, neither to be seene, nor see,
> As mine: who have with amorous delicacies
> Refin'd thee'into a blis-ful paradise.
> Thy graces and good words my creatures bee;
> I planted knowledge and lifes tree in thee,
> Which, Oh, shall strangers taste? Must I, alas,
> Frame and enamell Plate, and drinke in glasse?
> Chafe waxe for others seales? breake a colts force
> And leave him then, beeing made a ready horse?
>
> (ll. 20–30)

The pun running throughout this final passage—a much bawdier pun than he dares to use in "Twicknam Garden"—here revolves around the word *inlaid*. Although her spouse has "inlaid" the lady in his home and bed, "neither to be seen, nor see," and has figuratively "stamped" her with his sexual "seale," the poet claims to remain the petty god of this pretty world in more senses than one. Because the poet has "inlaid" his Eve/Pandora/Galatea with graces and the very breath of speech, her "good words," and "framed" her to fit a golden world of "plate," he clearly does not merit his exile to a more fragile and transparent age of glass. Yet from the very point at which the godlike poet admits that he has "planted knowledge and lifes tree in thee, / Which, Oh, shall strangers taste?"—a move that directly parallels his admission of a self-provided serpent into Twicknam garden—his argument begins to unravel. By imagining the garden and himself in this way, he undermines even as he exalts his role as the creator-god of a garden already compromised by the fatal apple of desire, once again placing himself in a scene of inevitable temptation and exclusion; not only is his Eve destined to betray her "god," but she also remains behind with the "real" Adam whose place he has attempted to usurp. In this way, the poetic fiction of his spiritual ownership of her or the garden is again undone. By reminding the reader that her many suitors (ll. 13–15) like her own beauty and freedom were always already there, he must concede that her marital "duty" is also beyond his control, a gift to be actualized and "tasted" in a garden that does not merely contain, but belongs to, this Eve.

Like "Twicknam Garden," Elegie 13 concludes with a rapid reversal of its former pretenses and a shift into a newly questioning key. The metaphors framing the Pygmalion-poet as demiurge, tutor, artisan, and finally, after his fall, as a petty clerk chafing "waxe for others seales," abruptly give way to the much more sexually aggressive metaphor of horse-breaker, one that suggests that his nightmare of losing her could vanish should she still prove "a ready horse" or mare. The suddenly stronger, more dissonant rhymes on *alas/glass* and *force/horse* that replace the singsong couplets rhyming with long *es* thus reinforce the suggestion that if he concedes that this "colt" has made an ass of her trainer, she might more graciously enjoy her victory by remitting some of her newfound force. Hence while wit indeed dodges social criticism here, it also attempts to restore equality, if in this case a frankly sexual one. Again retaining only by displaying its self-interest, the jest challenges the Other to revolt, restoring equilibrium and "freeing" desire by repaying the presumptions of her second "proprietor" in the same way that she has repaid those of her first, the wily Dr. Donne.

In conformity with the vastly different social stations of the two ladies, the leveling effect of Elegie 13 is proportionally greater than that of "Twicknam Garden," as is the amount of sexual release and self-empowerment achieved by the wit. Although neither poem approximates the bawdy malice of seduction poems like "The Flea," Elegie 13 comes a good deal closer. Nevertheless, as I have attempted to argue, the release of unconscious or at least highly objectionable criticism—logical, moral, and social—connects Donne's "Inns of Court" poems to his "poems of compliment" by constructing a far more egalitarian form of release than Freud would have predicted.[31] While initially aggressive and in fact openly phallic in their display of verbal power, the speakers of both lyrics are also demonstrably defensive; like Heine and Freud's other Jewish jokesters, the religiously and socially divided Donne claims a hollow victory that converts his tendentious objects of attack (who include himself) into potentially sympathetic allies. In this way, the comic dialectic of the joke work is retained without, as Freud claims, being fully foreclosed after it has been allied with a third-party audience. In fact, since the identity of its

31. The terms are Marotti's; see ibid.

"other" remains less stable or predictable than that of the wit, in one sense humor actually becomes "a psychical factor possessed of power" over the Pygmalion-poet, who must sacrifice his own fictions in order to bestow "life" upon them, and who can at best only hope to gain his projected reward. At once victim and beneficiary of his "social construction of reality," the wit undertakes a wager whose outcome is far from certain; the possibility always remains that "Nature's lay ideot," like God, may finally retain the upper hand.

In this sense, the parodic double bind of the *Songs and Sonnets* should be regarded as a form of self-critique that is only marginally if at all distinct from social critique. By self-consciously enlarging the scope of gendered human interchange in the private sphere, Donne's lyrics enlarge the private sphere itself, a domain that Goldberg would argue is inherently excluded by the royalist logic of public display. Not imperial but rather bourgeois, the lyrics participate in an implicitly subversive critique of the hierarchical limits imposed by the divine right ideology of the Stuart court and its coordinated policies of personal and political mystification. By parodying a style actually well on its way to obsolescence, Donne not only creates a vastly more self-reflective, immediate, and private poetics but also avoids the contemporary fate of James I: to be "subjected, shaped, imposed upon, by the language in which, and with which, he attempted to impose himself on others, to shape their minds to match his." Shaping the minds of his interlocutors in ways that expose, mediate, and finally overturn his own linguistic impositions, Donne's poetic persona is more escape artist than con man, more satirist than clown. Instead of putting on the king's larger-than-life clothes, he turns them inside out: instead of wielding power "by claiming that what it enacts is outside itself and transcendent," Donne's parodic wit exposes its presumed transcendence as actual immanence, effectively erasing its own performance.[32]

Although this inversion of royalist tactics scarcely makes Donne a revolutionary, it does, as Brown remarks, end "by inverting even the customary objective of casuists," although not in ways that, as she claims, "simply confirm . . . the status quo." If only by forging "a new political order in which lovers govern rather than obey society's laws," the poet participates in the long, slow, but rapidly accelerating movement that eventually transformed

---

32. Goldberg, *James I and Literature*, 20, 6 (quoting Michel Foucault, *Knowledge/Power*, ed. Colin Gordon [New York: Pantheon Books, 1980], 93–94).

the ideology of family. The domestic unit whose internal hierarchy reflects and supports the external apparatus of the state becomes a private "garden" whose work is to further its own affective ends in opposition to the state.[33] In this respect, Donne's characteristic insistence that "one little room" can become an everywhere not only subscribes to an incipiently individualistic, anti-aristocratic ethos, but along with his other labors in the garden of love, participates in it. Hence, his Pygmalion's progress is also an amorous pilgrim's progress, a journey through a landscape of courtly love and egoistic temptation whose goal lies beyond—neither in an incarnate nor a "divine mystery,"[34] but in a more egalitarian earthly garden imagined in, but not yet belonging to, this world.

33. Brown, "In that the world's contracted thus," 29. Of course, the state and its ends were changing at the same time. See Docherty, *John Donne, Undone,* 37–47, and Goldberg, *James I and Literature,* 86–87. While Goldberg rigorously documents this transformation, like so many other Foucauldians he fails to account for any pattern of incipient let alone actual transition, at least during the period in question. Somehow the family of the seventeenth century is increasingly authoritarian, while the post-1700 family is egalitarian; see esp. 258, n. 41.

34. See Goldberg, *James I and Literature,* 66. Significantly, Goldberg's remarkably uni-ronic reading of "The Canonization" depends upon a virtual erasure of the poem's two most notorious sexual puns. Surely when the poet claims that "Wee dye and rise the same, and prove / Mysterious by this love" (ll. 26–27), something considerably more earthly than a "divine mystery" is being suggested.

Robert C. Evans

Wit and the Power of Jonson's *Epigrammes*

Wit is not a term that occurs frequently in criticism dealing with Ben Jonson's nondramatic poetry. Certainly the word occurs with nothing like the frequency one finds in criticism devoted to Donne. Yet *wit* is a term that Jonson himself uses repeatedly in his poems, and in a wide variety of senses. Exploring Jonson's many references to wit—in this case in his *Epigrammes*—may help tell us something not only about his complex response to that term but also about his complex understanding of what it meant to be a wit, and a poet, in his era.[1] Jonson seems to have regarded wit as both a source and a display of literary and social *power,* and in doing so he seems to have found sanction in the writings of Quintilian, the Roman rhetorician whose work he regarded as essential to a proper grasp of the poet's craft. Yet Jonson's emphasis on Quintilian has gone largely unexplored, and the implications of Quintilian's discussion of wit—a discussion Jonson knew and recommended—have not received much comment.

Wit, of course, had much wider connotations in the early seventeenth century than it tends to have today, and Jonson seems to have been quite familiar with the term's range of implications. Wit could be variously under-

1. Citations of Jonson's works and relevant secondary material will be from *Ben Jonson,* ed. C. H. Herford and Percy and Evelyn Simpson, 11 vols. (Oxford: Clarendon Press, 1925–1952), referred to parenthetically as "H&S" with volume and page numbers. *Epigrammes* will be referred to as *Ep.* and *The Forrest* as *For.* I wish to thank the Folger Shakespeare Library and the National Endowment for the Humanities for grants that contributed to my research on this article. I am additionally grateful to the Grants-in-Aid program at Auburn University at Montgomery.

stood as the seat of consciousness or thought (the mind); as the faculty of thinking and reasoning (the understanding or intellect); as the faculties of perception (the "five wits"); as the combined intellectual powers; as the quality of saneness; as a synonym for such terms as *genius, talent, cleverness, quickness, sharpness,* or *acumen. Wit* could also imply practical talent, mechanical ability, ingenuity, or skill; suggest something either demanding or displaying wisdom; or connote the qualities of good judgment, discretion, and prudence. In addition, *wit* could be taken to mean a quickness of intellect or liveliness of fancy, a capacity for apt (and especially for amusing) expression, or knowledge and learning generally. Such a list hardly begins to exhaust all the complex connotations the term possessed for Jonson and his contemporaries, but it does suggest why the notion of wit was so important to them and why the word *wit* appears so frequently in Jonson's writings.[2]

Jonson's various uses of *wit,* and his explicit remarks concerning that term, are complicated and not a little ambiguous. His attitude toward wit is marked by an ambivalence rooted in the word's basic double meaning—its association, on one hand, with various qualities of *mind,* and its association, on the other, with various qualities of *expression.* To the extent that wit could be associated with such notions as reason, judgment, understanding, talent, intellect, learning, discretion, or prudence, Jonson seems to have been strongly attracted by the term. However, to the extent that wit could be associated chiefly or merely with such notions as cleverness, quickness, sharpness, liveliness, amusing expression, and simple self-display, he seems to have distrusted it. Certainly he distrusted the kinds of "wits" whose wit consisted mainly of verbal pyrotechnics, of an attention-grabbing but insubstantial play with words.[3] Wit, in the ideal Jonsonian sense, involved both prodigious invention and apt expression. Any separation of these two aspects, and any undue emphasis on wit as mere verbal play or linguistic self-indulgence, usually earned Jonson's scorn. Recognizing this can help us appreciate the kind of wit Jonson both valued and tried to achieve.

2. See the *OED,* s.v. *wit* and the numerous references to *wit* and related words in Steven L. Bates and Sidney D. Orr, *A Concordance to the Poems of Ben Jonson* (Athens: Ohio University Press, 1978).

3. He reported to Drummond "That Done said to him he wrott that Epitaph on Prince Henry . . . to match Sir Ed: Herbert jn obscureness" (H&S 1:136) and also remarked "that Done himself for not being understood would perish" (H&S 1:138).

For Jonson, wit could be understood as both private and public—an individual trait with social implications. It is this social dimension of wit that colors much of his thinking about the term. Many of his attitudes can be quickly glimpsed by surveying the various comments on wit in his prose *Discoveries*. Of course, many of those comments are translations, but nothing the *Discoveries* say about wit conflicts with Jonson's own comments elsewhere. In fact, the translated passages from the *Discoveries* are interesting because they help to suggest, again, how important Quintilian was as a source of Jonson's thinking. In addition, they help to clarify that Jonson understood wit first and foremost as a quality of mind, character, temper, disposition, and innate genius, and only secondarily as a capacity or preference for a particular kind of verbal expression.

The Latin term that Jonson usually translates with the English word *wit* is *ingenium*, a term associated with innate, natural, or in-born qualities of mind; it is a term that stems, ultimately, from a verb meaning "to beget."[4] As I shall suggest, this ultimate link between the power of wit and the power of life, of literally engendering or causing birth, helps explain a great deal about Jonson's complicated response to wit, both as a linguistic term and as a social phenomenon. Wit seems to have been intimately linked in Jonson's mind with notions of individual and social *power*, with all the potential either for creativity or abuse that word suggests.[5] Wit seems to have been a power for which Jonson felt great respect, but one that he also felt should be vigorously monitored and controlled. Self-indulgent wit—wit in the service of individual ambition or pride—was something he despised, whereas wit made to serve some greater good was a quality he both admired and aspired to achieve. The contrast between these two kinds of wit is illustrated at length, for instance, in the contrast between two kinds of wits presented in his early play *Poetaster*—Horace (Jonson's ideal) and Crispinus (modeled on John Marston). The depiction of Crispinus in the play's third and fifth acts provides numerous detailed examples of the kind of poetic wit that Jonson considered bogus.

4. See his translation of Horace's *Ars Poetica* (H&S 8:338–55), esp. ll. 419, 461. In the latter instance, "wit" is explicitly associated with the power of conception. At line 403, however, Jonson uses "wit" to translate the Latin *lepidus* (charming, pleasant, agreeable, elegant).

5. Hobbes had associated wit and humor with the perception of a "sudden glory," a connection explored and justified at length by Charles R. Gruner in *Understanding Laughter: The Workings of Wit and Humor* (Chicago: Nelson Hall, 1978).

However, the comments about wit recorded in Jonson's later *Discoveries* are also highly suggestive. For instance, at one point he praises Sidney and Hooker as "great Masters of wit, and language . . . in whom all vigour of Invention, and strength of judgement met" (H&S 8:591). Here the sense of "wit" as the capacity for intellectual creation is clearly implied, as is the corollary sense that once a thought has been conceived, it needs to be expressed in "language" displaying "judgement." Wit in this double sense—of a power that, by being appropriately mastered, both confers and displays mastery—is essential to most of Jonson's thinking about the term. A true wit is a thinker who has both the power to conceive and the power to express his conceptions, and that expression must be conditioned by a sense of social responsibility. It is this double emphasis that helps explain Jonson's earlier comment, in a passage indebted to Quintilian:

> I doe heare them say often: Some men are not witty; because they are not everywhere witty; then which nothing is more foolish. If an eye or a nose bee an excellent part in the face, therefore be all eye or nose? I thinke the eye-brow, the fore-head, the cheeke, chyn, lip, or any part else, are as necessary, and naturall in the place. But now nothing is good that is natural: Right and naturall language seeme[s] to have least of the wit in it; that which is writh'd and tortur'd, is counted the more exquisite. . . . Nothing is fashionable, till it bee deform'd; and this is to write like a *Gentleman*. (H&S 8:581)

Here as elsewhere, Jonson sees wit as a means of attaining social distinction, of proclaiming, demonstrating, and attaining status or power.[6] The false wit tortures language to seem a "Gentleman," to distinguish himself from those whose language appears plainer or apparently less self-conscious. Yet the self-consciousness of the false wit suggests his social insecurity, his need to perform, to be constantly "on." His wit is labored, contrived, worked up; it seems (to Jonson at least) unnatural, artificial; it lacks the proportion, decorum, discipline, moderation, and self-control he often associates with genuine wit. Of course, part of the paradox of the passage is its implicit admission that "false" wit often succeeds, that it does indeed become "fashionable," a badge of status. Ironically, Jonson must promote a style he considers natural, must

6. On this point see, for instance, George E. Rowe, *Distinguishing Jonson: Imitation, Rivalry, and the Direction of a Dramatic Career* (Lincoln: University of Nebraska Press, 1988).

attack what should not seem to need attacking, must defend what would not seem to need defense. He must, in other words, be just as concerned with achieving or maintaining social distinction as the "false" wits he mocks. Since the wit Jonson regards as "natural" cannot count, naturally or automatically, on popular approval, it needs to be championed, and its allegedly bogus opposite needs to be attacked. Jonson's tone is confident and secure, yet clearly he feels outnumbered: as often happens in his work, at the very moment when he seems most sure of himself, he most clearly acknowledges his own social insecurity, his own need, as a social poet, to prove appealing.[7]

This becomes most clear in the famous comments on Shakespeare. Jonson apparently regarded his great friend and rival as a wit whose wit was insufficiently controlled—that is, as a poet who abundantly possessed *ingenium*, the power of conception, but whose inability or unwillingness to discipline that power simultaneously marred his gifts and won him an acclaim that the more disciplined Jonson clearly resented. When the players commended Shakespeare for never blotting a line, Jonson responded, "Would he had blotted a thousand" (H&S 8:583). However, the crucial passage for our purposes occurs slightly later: "His wit was in his owne power; would the rule of it had been so too" (H&S 8:584). This is as succinct a statement as we are likely to get of Jonson's conception of wit as a double power—the power to conceive and to judge, to create and to discriminate.[8] Shakespeare possessed the first power to an enormous degree, but in Jonson's view he failed to exercise the second power properly. In so failing he failed himself ("many times hee fell into those things, could not escape laughter" [H&S 8:584]), but he also failed in his larger obligations to society. Here again, part of the paradox of Jonson's comments on Shakespeare is that although he regarded some of Shakespeare's failures of wit as literally "ridiculous" (H&S 8:584), he also knew that many failed to share this view. What seemed obvious shortcomings to Jonson did not bother others. Shakespeare's lapses—those errors "hee fell into"—should have diminished his social and literary power, but his many admirers "choose

7. For a general discussion of this topic, see my *Ben Jonson and the Poetics of Patronage* (Lewisburg: Bucknell University Press, 1989).

8. For an overview of discussions of the relations between the two poets, see Russ McDonald, *Shakespeare and Jonson, Jonson and Shakespeare* (Lincoln: University of Nebraska Press, 1988); on wit as a double power, see Gabrielle Bernhard Jackson, *Vision and Judgment in Ben Jonson's Drama* (New Haven: Yale University Press, 1968).

that circumstance to commend their friend by, wherein he most faulted"
(H&S 8:583). Often in Jonson's writings about wit there is exactly this kind of
ambiguity and ambivalence—the sense that what seems natural to him does
not seem so to many others, that what seems commendable to him cannot
count on public acclaim, and that what seems indefensible to him has legions
of defenders. Jonson's thinking about wit everywhere exhibits a consciousness
of wit as *power,* but that consciousness is by no means uncomplicated.

Certainly this is true in his earlier comment, indebted to the rhetorician
Seneca, that "*Expectation* of the *Vulgar* is more drawne, and held with new-
nesse, then goodnesse. . . . Which shewes, that the only decay, or hurt of the
best mens *reputation* with the people, is, their wits have out-liv'd the peoples
palats. They have beene too much, or too long a feast" (H&S 8:576). Here
the phrasing is typically ambivalent. On the one hand, true wit is associated
with something vital and permanent: with something that endures or survives
("out-lives"), indeed with something that nourishes and sustains ("a feast").
Yet while the true wit would seem to feed the public, the public can at any
time reject him; what seems essential can quickly be abandoned. What seems
a source of power can easily cause power's loss. The very wit that Jonson
appears to regard as the basis of all meaningful social distinction ("*Arts* that
respect the mind, were ever reputed nobler, then those that serve the body . . .
the most generous, and exalted wits, and spirits . . . cannot rest, or *acquiesce*"
[H&S 8:568]) is still subject to the vagaries of vulgar, "meaningless" fashion.
This is a tension that runs throughout Jonson's writing about wit, both in the
Discoveries and in his poems.

This tension between needing to use wit to prove appealing without sacri-
ficing one's self-respect finds support in Quintilian, the rhetorician whom
Jonson quotes so approvingly in the *Discoveries.* However, Jonson had already
called attention to Quintilian's importance in his *Conversations* with William
Drummond, transcribed during late 1618 and early 1619. While visiting Scot-
land, Jonson "recommended to [Drummond's] reading Quintilian (who (he
said) [sic] would tell me the faults of my Verses as if he had Lived with me"
(H&S 1:132). More significantly, he told Drummond "that Quintilianes 6. 7. 8.
bookes, were not only to be read but altogither digested" (H&S 1:136). As it
happens, these are precisely the books in the ten-book *Institutio* in which
Quintilian has quite a bit to say about the use of forensic wit.

Many of Quintilian's pronouncements about wit are relevant to Jonson's own poetry, especially the poetry of the *Epigrammes*.[9] Quintilian regarded wit as one very effective means of social appeal (2:411), but he cautioned that wit should never involve the sacrifice of one's social respect or dignity (2:413). This might help explain the typical restraint of Jonson's own wit and the strong sense of personal merit that always seems to underlie it. Unlike Mime in *Ep.* 129, who is willing to make himself look ridiculous for the sake of "some new gesture, that's imputed wit" (l. 14), Jonson seems to have taken to heart Quintilian's advice that many wits ran the risk of appearing to be buffoons.[10] He seems to have been as much concerned as Quintilian with the problem of proper self-presentation; the public wit displayed not only his cleverness but also himself, and it was his character as much as his language or thought that would be judged (2:441).[11] Quintilian had argued that "no jests are so insipid as those which parade the fact that they are intended to be witty" (2:451), and this advice might help explain, again, the subtlety, gravity, brevity, restraint, and understatement that so often characterize the wit of Jonson's *Epigrammes*, especially in contrast with the petulant and obscene wit that many of his readers apparently expected and enjoyed.

9. Citations from Quintilian are to *Institutio Oratoria*, trans. H. E. Butler, Loeb Classical Library, 4 vols. (Cambridge: Harvard University Press, 1920), referred to parenthetically by volume and page. Jonson owned a 1528 edition of this work, now at Emmanuel College, Cambridge; see David McPherson, *Ben Jonson's Library and Marginalia: An Annotated Catalogue*, in *Studies in Philology, Texts and Studies* series, 71.5 (1974): 81. Personal examination confirms the accuracy of McPherson's report on the markings the volume contains. Unfortunately, the markings are not typical of Jonson's style and are probably not his. See also my *Jonson, Lipsius, and the Politics of Renaissance Stoicism* (Wakefield, N.H.: Longwood, 1992). Although Jonson's comments to Drummond indicate clearly which portions of the *Institutio* he found most valuable, the absence of explicit markings by him in his copy makes it impossible to know which passages attracted his attention. Moreover, even if his copy did contain such markings, it would be impossible to say whether Jonson read the rhetorician while or before writing the poems in *Epigrammes*. Thus it seems sensible not to argue for Quintilian's direct influence on the poems, but rather simply to note the similar attitudes of both men concerning the subject and practice of wit. For this reason, I will confine comments on the parallels between Jonson and Quintilian mainly to my notes.

10. Quintilian remarks that "although I want my orator to speak with wit, he must not give the impression of striving after it. Consequently he must not display his wit on every possible occasion, but must sacrifice a jest sooner than sacrifice his dignity" (2:455). See also 2:453, 483.

11. Elsewhere Quintilian notes that "the orator's own contribution to the story should be the most humorous element" (2:459).

Many of the *Epigrammes* suggest this conflict between Jonson's own exalted view of wit and the sort of wit that seems to have been most popular. *Ep.* 2, for instance, wittily attacks those readers who expect epigrams to "hurle inke, and wit, / As mad-men stones" (ll. 5–6). Jonson distances himself from such "mad-men," whose undisciplined, antisocial language betrays both a lack of control and a yearning for the kind of cheap distinction from which Jonson attempts to stand apart.[12] Part of the paradox of the poem, of course, is that it engages in the very sort of wit combat it ostensibly disdains, even as it seeks to elevate the terms and level of such conflict. Another such witty attack on allegedly shallow wit occurs in *Ep.* 29, which mocks "Sir Annual Tilter" for displaying his wit so that "the most may'admire thee" (l. 1)—an admiration from which the poet clearly distinguishes himself. Ironically, however, Tilter's wit wins Jonson's attention as much as the crowd's, and despite his claimed disdain for Tilter, he seems to have felt threatened by the public acclaim Tilter had won—threatened enough, in any case, to write a poem mocking him. Tilter apparently viewed his wit (false in the added sense of being not his own [l. 6]) as a means to social power, and the existence of Jonson's poem ironically confirms that power even while deriding it.

Wit that is false in another way is attacked in *Ep.* 38, "To Person Guiltie." Here Jonson skewers Guiltie for attempting to appropriate one of the poet's own public performances. Typically, Guiltie displays his lack of wit through an alleged lack of self-control ironically born of the very need to impose control. Jonson had advised Guiltie to "conceale [his] ulcers"—not to react with public anger to poems by Jonson attacking him. Guiltie took this advice too much to heart, so that now "You laugh when you are touch'd, and long before / Any man else, you clap your hands, and rore, / And crie good! good!"[13] Jonson, however, thinks that this response "lyes so farre from wit, 'tis impudence," and he threatens to reveal Guiltie's true identity (ll. 3–8). The poem is designed to contrast Jonson's restraint, self-control, and genuine wit with Guiltie's desperately excessive attempts at cleverness.[14] Jonson's apparent self-possession helps define his own brand of wit; yet he still, of course, feels the

12. Quintilian notes that "scurrilous or brutal jests, although they may raise a laugh, are quite unworthy of a gentleman" (2:483).

13. Quintilian cautions that "a humorous look, manner, or gesture" should always "observe the happy mean" (2:451–53).

14. Quintilian notes, "It is a pleasant form of jest to reproach a person with less than would be possible" (2:491).

need to respond, to reseize the initiative, to reappropriate the public attention Guiltie is determined to possess. For Jonson, the almost animalistic excessiveness of Guiltie's display is both bogus and revealing—or rather, it *should* be revealing, if only the poet could count on Guiltie's audience to be sufficiently discerning. Despite the dismissive tone of Jonson's poem, merely dismissing or ignoring Guiltie was something he apparently felt he could not afford to do.

The link between wit and social power appears again in *Ep.* 56, "On Poet-Ape." Even its title suggests the connection, in Jonson's mind, between false wit and the inhuman. Although Poet-Ape "would be thought our chiefe," his "workes are eene the fripperie of wit" (ll. 1–2). They are, in other words, old clothes or stolen finery. Jonson associates lacking true wit with lacking real power, yet he feels the need to attack a shortcoming he claims simply to "pittie" (l. 4). He attempts to make the offense more than merely personal: Poet-Ape "would be thought *our* chiefe"; he "takes vp all, makes each mans wit his owne" (ll. 2; 8). Here the indictment of the supposed stupidity of the false wit's audience—implied in the earlier poems—becomes explicit in the reference to "The sluggish gaping auditor" who "devoures" Poet-Ape's stealings (l. 10). Jonson's attacks on false wits seem to have been written as much for the public from whom those wits derived their power as against the wits themselves. After all, it was the reaction of current audiences that would help determine whether "after-times" would judge a poetaster's wit "to be his, as well as ours" (ll. 11–12).

As that last phrase suggests, Jonson seems everywhere careful of the need to make and keep distinctions, but the phrase also implies that he associated true wit not only with the powers to create and judge but also with the power to endure and survive. Wit was, in many senses, a kind of "life-force" for Jonson, a force associated with a form of distinctly human survival and a force that was, for that reason, also a valuable commodity or *property* (in the literal sense). Jonson seems to have regarded wit, first and foremost, as the power to conceive and express apt thought, and he also seems to have regarded this power as distinctively human because distinctly intellectual and thus ultimately spiritual (that is, God-given). Numerous poems suggest this strong connection between wit and life.[15] *Ep.* 23, for instance, deems John Donne's

15. Interestingly, Quintilian turns immediately from lamenting the death of his sons to discussing the subjects of wit and humor, claiming that he "must find something to make

true, "earely wit" an "example" that "remaines so, yet"; Donne's wit takes "Longer" in the mere "knowing" or appreciation "then most [false] wits doe liue" (l. 3–5). True wit, like Donne's, simultaneously displays, provokes, and withstands study, whereas superficial wittiness quickly dies.

This implicit link between life and wit is suggested again in the acrostic "On Margaret Ratcliffe," whose very form displays some of the wit it extols. The poem cleverly calls attention both to its subject and to its own performance. Margaret's "wit" was "Rare, as wonder, . . . / And like *Nectar* euer flowing" (ll. 9–10)—that is, like the drink of the immortals. However, because Margaret was, finally, human, time "conquer'd hath both life and it" (l. 12). The end of life is here explicitly associated with the death of wit, yet the poem concludes by claiming that "For wit, feature, and true passion" (which might be glossed as "mind, beauty, and virtuous emotion"), "Earth, thou hast not such another" (l. 17). Even in death the young woman's wit lends her an enduring distinction (thanks, in part, to Jonson's poem), and in that sense it was partly her wit that guaranteed the posthumous survival of her identity. Wit may be "conquered" by time, but Jonson's witty acrostic helps ensure that it is never quite extinguished. In fact, one measure of the false wit of the titular character of *Ep.* 81, "To Proule the Plagiary," is that his wit is not self-sustaining; it, and his "belly too," lives by stealing others' inventions. Wit is here associated with intellectual, social, and literal vitality and survival, and this poem is simply one of many that makes it clear that wit—the combined power of thought and expression—had become by Jonson's day a marketable commodity.[16] Recognizing this helps explain one very practical reason Jonson, as a professional poet, disdained wit that was false in being either bogus or purloined.

This notion of wit-as-commodity, as something for sale, is perhaps clearest in *For.* 3, where Jonson mocks the masquing at court by mentioning "the iewells, stuffes, the paines, the wit / There wasted, some not paid for yet!" (ll. 11–12). These lines betray a frustration with the powerful people who value a poet's wit as another means of social display, and yet who fail to value

---

life tolerable, and must needs put faith in the verdict of the wise, who held that literature alone can provide true solace in adversity" (2:381).

16. On Jonson's status in a developing profession, see, for instance, Richard Helgerson, *Self-crowned Laureates: Spenser, Jonson, Milton and the Literary System* (Berkeley: University of California Press, 1983).

it sufficiently to pay for it in a timely fashion. But the lines also suggest the poet's frustration with *himself,* or at least with the circumstances that force him to "waste" his wit on trivial occasions or on ignorant auditors. For Jonson, wit was at once something highly personal, indeed self-defining, and yet also something inevitably caught up in the tangled web of power, performance, and social relations.[17] The lines from *For.* 3 imply what is elsewhere quite clear: that in Jonson's social context, wit could never be entirely self-validating or autonomous, that its value always depended to some degree on social performance and audience response. This was an inescapable but often unpalatable fact of social life, and Jonson's frustration with that fact is everywhere apparent. Ironically, some of his own most effective displays of wit occur when he is condemning wit as self-display.

Examples abound. In *Ep.* 58, for instance, he skewers "Groome Ideot" "For offring, with thy smiles, my wit to grace" (l. 3). The irony of the first verb, of course, is that Ideot's offer, or attempt, is simply that: a lame and labored *effort,* and one that is an offer (or gift) in only the most self-interested sense. Moreover, Ideot's attempt to "grace" Jonson's wit seems (to Jonson at least) graceless in several senses: inept, undignified, ridiculous, and selfish.[18] His contrived smiling—his baring of teeth—implies the ambiguous link that many theorists have posited between humor and aggression, and Jonson's poem becomes an embodiment of the very sort of wit combat that is its subject.[19] Ideot demonstrates a self-interested attention to Jonson's poetry that parodies the disinterested alertness the poet ideally hoped for. The poem

17. On the ambiguities of Jonson's social position, see David Riggs, *Ben Jonson: A Life* (Cambridge: Harvard University Press, 1989), and my discussion of his career in *Seventeenth-Century British Nondramatic Poets: First Series,* ed. M. Thomas Hester, vol. 121 of *Dictionary of Literary Biography* (Detroit: Gale, 1992), 186–212. On these general issues, see my *Ben Jonson and the Poetics of Patronage* and *Jonson and the Contexts of His Time* (Lewisburg: Bucknell University Press, 1994).

18. In an important passage, Quintilian discriminates among the various kinds of wit, including *urbanitas* (which "suggests a certain tincture of learning" and is "the opposite of rusticity") and *salsus* ("the salt of wit" or "a simple seasoning of language"). *Venustus,* another form of wit, "means that which is said with grace and charm" (2:447).

19. Quintilian notes that "laughter is never far removed from derision" (2:443); on this point, see Gruner, *Understanding Laughter,* 24. Interestingly, many of the word combinations listed at the end of the *OED*'s definition of "wit" include phrases suggesting aggression: "wit-battle," "wit-combat," "wit-contest," "wit-pride," "wit-sally," "wit-shaft," "wit-assailing," "wit-oppressing," "wit-abused," "wit-beaten," "wit-stung," and "wit-cracker."

trivializes Ideot, yet its very existence suggests that Jonson could not ignore him, and in fact this tension between dismissive contempt and obsessive response characterizes many of Jonson's comments about the allegedly false wit of his antagonists. In *Ep.* 71, for instance, he seeks to skewer "Covrt-Parrat," noting that "To plucke downe mine, POLL sets vp new wits still, / Still, 'tis his lucke to praise me 'gainst his will" (ll. 1–2).[20] The name Jonson ascribes to his target suggests Parrot's lack of the independent wit or creativity that would make him fully human. At the same time, the phrase "sets vp" implies that the rival wits whom Poll elevates also themselves lack any real autonomy. Their power is purely social, purely a function of Poll's status and promotional efforts, yet Jonson obviously feels threatened enough by these efforts that he must respond. He claims that Poll is forced to acknowledge Jonson, and yet the poem also displays Jonson's forced acknowledgment of Poll—his inability or unwillingness to ignore a figure for whom he obviously feels contempt.[21]

The mere fact that Parrot is a *Court*-Parrot elevates his importance as a threat. The same is true of the figure lambasted in the following poem, "To Covrt-ling" (*Ep.* 72). It is Courtling's position—socially and even physically—that seems threatening: he sits "At MADAMES table, where thou mak'st all wit / Goe high or low, as thou wilt value it" (ll. 3–4). Jonson attempts to display his own wit, his own independent authority, by mocking Courtling's power, which derives from the latter's affiliation with "madam." However, his very need to mock Courtling suggests his own lack of full autonomy. A similar tension exists in *Ep.* 115, "On the Townes Honest Man," in which the target, probably Inigo Jones, is mocked for using a "fit / Of miming" to get "th'opinion of a wit" (ll. 27–28). The public "opinion" or reputation Jones thereby wins is debased—or so Jonson insists. To be an acknowledged wit, Jones must display himself; his reputation must be contested for, and is therefore (Jonson implies) unstable and insecure. The very word *fit* suggests the odd quality of Jones's performance—at once labored and frenetic. In fact, *fit* suggests a lack of precisely that sort of mental autonomy its rhyme word should connote. It

20. It seems relevant to note, about this and other equally short poems, Quintilian's comment that "brevity in wit gives greater point and speed" (2:463).

21. Quintilian notes that urbane wit is "specially suitable to resistance or attack" (2:497).

suggests again a kind of animalistic, irrational debasement of a trait—wit—that Jonson usually considers distinctly and definingly human.

This same play on rhyme words occurs in another poem—*Ep.* 64, written to celebrate Robert Cecil's accession as Lord Treasurer. Jonson protests that he, unlike other celebrants, is not "glad for fashion. Nor to shew a fit / Of flatterie to thy titles. Nor of wit" (ll. 7–8). Once again "fit" suggests exaggerated public display, loss of self-control, loss of personal dignity. Although flattery might seem the opposite of wit (the first associated with craven submission, the second with autonomous power), Jonson's lines collapse any distinction between the two terms. The sort of wit he wittily lampoons here is itself a kind of flattery, an admission of subservience of a kind from which Jonson attempts to distance himself. The broken, measured quality of his own syntax in these lines suggests a dispassionate, laconic tone; his own apparently disinterested style of expression seems the very opposite of an undisciplined "fit."[22] His satire here is witty in the triple sense of being clever, thoughtful, and in apt contrast with the precise vice he attacks. Similarly apt and witty satire on false wit is evident again in *Ep.* 112, "To a Weake Gamster in Poetry." Here the notion of wit combat, which seems to underlie so many of Jonson's satirical poems, is explicit, and the witty appropriateness of Jonson's pointed epigrammatic attack on a poetaster who considers the epigram genre his "proper game" is clear. The poem's final lines allude to a card game, primero, and Jonson manages to make the allusion explicit in the very last word: "There's no vexation, that can make thee prime" (l. 22). There is, that is to say, no laborious effort (an idea that itself contradicts the very spirit of "wit") that can make Gamester the winner in his competition with Jonson or, indeed, the first in any kind of importance. The fact that Jonson sustains the gaming metaphor at such length, combined with the fact that he makes his poem's very last word one that literally means "first," exemplifies a subtlety of wit for which he is given credit too infrequently.[23]

Such subtlety is lacking in most of the targets Jonson wittily attacks,

22. Quintilian observes that *"urbanity* involves the total absence of all that is incongruous, coarse, unpolished, and exotic whether in thought, language, voice, or gesture, and resides not so much in isolated sayings as in the whole complexion of our language" (2:499).

23. Quintilian comments on witty ambiguity and insinuation and notes that "the essence of all wit lies in the distortion of the true and natural meaning of words" (2:487).

including the title figure of *Ep.* 100, "On Playwright," who, "by chance, hearing some toyes I'had writ, / Cry'd to my face, they were th'elixir of wit" (ll. 2–3). Playwright then proceeded to steal five of Jonson's jests—both his exaggerated flattery and his brazen theft implying his lack of independent power, his own lack of wit. By contrast, Jonson's restrained, understated response suggests that Playwright is more a pest than a serious threat.[24] However, it is the noun here associated with wit—*elixir*—that makes the poem most interesting. This is one of several poems by Jonson that associates wit with strong or powerful drink,[25] but the connotations of *elixir* are particularly illuminating. Elixirs were used in alchemy in the misguided attempt to change base metals into gold (a sense perfectly appropriate to Playwright's plagiarism). However, they were also drugs supposedly capable of indefinitely prolonging life; they were considered sovereign remedies for disease; and they were regarded as the quintessence or souls of things. Playwright's fulsome praise, although dishonest, is not inappropriate to Jonson's own very positive conception of wit. The word *elixir* succinctly sums up many various ways in which the right kind of wit, in Jonson's mind, seems to have been associated with conception, transformation, life, and intellectual immortality.

All these connotations lie at the heart of the various poems in which Jonson not only demonstrates but also celebrates wit—a wit he usually attributes to others but that also reflects his own. Typical is *Ep.* 121, "To Beniamin Rvdyerd," which pays respectful tribute to Rudyerd's "learned *Muse*" and "better studies" (ll. 2–3), qualities the poet modestly hopes to emulate. The poem consists of a series of neatly finished couplets, and its structure, comprising two sentences, also divides perfectly in half. Here Jonson displays the highly polished, genteel, yet genuine "manners" he extols in the final line, where he claims to strive that "his manners should precede his wit" (l. 8). It isn't until we read that final word, of course, that we realize that he has wittily contrived just such a precedence in this concluding line. *Ep.* 121 is a small but perfect display of its author's double command of wit—wit as intelligence and wit as apt expression.

24. Quintilian notes that "wit always appears to greater advantage in reply than in attack" (2:445).

25. For example, in *Ep.* 84 Jonson describes how, in reaction to the promised gift of a buck, "most like a *Poet,* / I fancied to my selfe, what wine, what wit / I would haue spent: how euery *Muse* should know it" (ll. 5–7).

The same qualities are on display in another poem addressed to Rudyerd, *Ep.* 123, which begins by claiming that "Writing thy selfe, or iudging others writ, / I know not which th'hast most, candor, or wit" (ll. 1–2). Here again, the poem's balanced construction suggests a mind in perfect control of its words, and such balance also pays mute tribute to the balanced person it extols. Rudyerd harmonizes honesty and expression, plainspokenness and real judgment. By praising Rudyerd as a judge even while judging him, Jonson demonstrates the very qualities he celebrates.[26] Once again, the wit of this poem is evident in its rational thought and apt expression, yet the apparent plainness of its statement momentarily conceals the further wit of subtlety: one notices, for instance, that the first line can be read in at least two ways, both mutually reinforcing. It can mean, "When you yourself write, or when you judge what others have written"; but it can also mean, "When you express your essence or self in writing, or when you judge other selves expressed that way." Rudyerd, then, is implicitly depicted as a judge both of written expression and of something more essential, more basic. He is, in other words, a wit capable of judging both the internal and external aspects of wit in others. And, by implication, so is Jonson himself.

The close bond between wit and manners—between the personal and the social—praised in the poems to Rudyerd appears also in *Ep.* 113, "To Sir Thomas Overbury." The poem begins by claiming that merely to speak of Overbury is praise—that is, praise of Overbury, but also praise of the poet associated with his name. Jonson thus wittily turns what might be seen as self-aggrandizement into a tribute to his subject. The poem's double emphasis on the personal and the social, the private and the public, first appears in line 3, which commends Overbury for having so "liu'st" that he "mak'st life vnderstood."[27] His personal behavior, in other words, has definite public implications, and the same notion is suggested again in line 6, where Overbury is praised for helping to have "sau'd" both the "wit" and the "manners" of the court. Overbury's balanced qualities have helped drive out much of the court's "ignorance" and "pride," helping to replace them with "letters" and "human-

26. Quintilian describes one kind of wit, *facetus*, as exhibiting "grace and polished elegance" (2:449).
27. Quintilian notes that the *ethos* of "an orator is commended to our approval by goodness more that aught else" (2:423).

itie," and thereby helping both the "men" and the "place" to "repent" (ll. 7–10). Jonson's pairings of such key words give the poem, rhetorically, the kind of balance it extols, but the pairings also emphasize the close connection between personal attributes and public expression or conduct that is essential to Jonson's conception of wit.

This same emphasis on public and private is wittily emphasized in the penultimate couplet, which both begins and ends with "repent," but in which the first use refers to Overbury's private intentions, while the second implies his public influence. (Of course, one function of Jonson's own poem is to help promote the process of public or courtly repenting that it credits to Overbury.) Jonson's ability to shift so quickly from one connotation of "repent" to another demonstrates his witty mastery of language, and this is a mastery he exhibits again in the final couplet, where "ambition" is associated not with self-promotion but with public service, and where the idea of "follow[ing]" Overbury's lead is associated with being true to one's own best self.[28] One needn't fear to "loose . . . degree" by emulating Overbury—at least, not the sort of degree or respect that matters (respect for oneself and respect by ethically worthy persons [ll. 11–12]). The poem is witty in exploiting such equivocations, but its deeper wit is also evident from the fact that it is constructed as a chain of *reasoning*, of consequences logically derived from clearly stated premises ("So . . . So . . . I thinke . . . For since" [ll. 1–7]). By the end of the poem we see how much more than merely to "speake" of Overbury Jonson accomplishes. The example Over-bury sets through his life is one that Jonson propagates through his poem. If Overbury is depicted almost as a savior (whose "comming" was "crau'd" in order that the court might be "sau'd" [ll. 5–6]), Jonson functions, in this poem, as a kind of apostle or disciple. Certainly the cooperative relationship here between the poet and his subject contrasts greatly with the competitive relationship sketched in the immediately preceding "To a Weake Gamster in Poetry." By juxtaposing these two epigrams, Jonson illustrates both the abuse and the proper use of wit. Both Overbury and Jonson exemplify a kind of "wit" at which a figure like Gamester can only "plucke" (l. 18).

Much the same seems true in *Ep.* 116, "To Sir William Iephson." Once again, the qualities of wit that Jonson ascribes to his subject implicitly reflect

---

28. For comments by Quintilian on the link between wit and the mastery of language, see 2:451.

his own, and once again wit is implicitly associated with a kind of social power. However, this poem is particularly interesting because it suggests not simply how the power of wit could benefit a single person in individual competition, but how it could also ultimately benefit a whole class of persons whose power was rooted less in birth than in worth, less in inherited wealth or status than in intellectual merit. This is a note that Jonson emphasizes at once:

> IEPHSON, thou man of men, to whose lou'd name
>   All gentrie, yet, owe part of their best flame!
> So did thy vertue'enforme, thy wit sustaine
>   That age, when thou stood'st vp the master-braine:
> Thou wert the first, mad'st merit know her strength,
>   And those that lack'd it, to suspect at length,
> 'Twas not entayl'd on title. That some word
>   Might be found out as good, and not *my Lord.*
>
> (ll. 1–8)

Jephson is a "man of men," an exemplary human being, but he is also a sterling representative of his social class, the "gentrie."[29] The precedent he set depended not merely on his goodness (or "vertue") but also on his "wit," which made him the "master-braine." The "merit" whose "strength" he embodied was not, then, simply ethical; it was also, and significantly, intellectual. Here "wit" is clearly identified with this basic intellectual power, and Jephson is taken to exemplify the fact "That bloud not mindes, but mindes did bloud adorne, / And to liue great, was better, then great borne" (ll. 11–12). "These," Jonson continues, were Jephson's "knowing arts," and whoever fails to acknowledge Jephson's example "must commit / A desperate soloecisme in truth and wit" (ll. 15–16). To deny Jephson's merit, in other words, is to reveal oneself both as unwise and as ignorantly misspoken. Jephson has helped create a precedent of social mobility and ascent ("thou stood'st vp") from which Jonson and other intellectuals might benefit, but the kind of self-assertion celebrated here is also, ultimately, one that benefits society at large by ensuring that the best minds prevail. Jephson helps not only his own class but his whole nation by helping to ensure that talent and wisdom are accorded their proper influence. Jephson embodied these values, and Jonson

29. Don E. Wayne notes the importance of this poem in *Penshurst: The Semiotics of Place and the Poetics of History* (Madison: University of Wisconsin Press, 1984), 153–55.

helps promote their survival by extolling them in this poem. Jephson displayed his wit through his life, but Jonson displays his own wit additionally through the very words and structure of his poem, whether the chiasmatic phrasing of line 11 or the series of clauses, beginning in line 7, that suggest a chain of sequential reasoning leading to the epigram's logically "inevitable" conclusion. Even the use of "soloeicism" in the final line suggests the poet's own concern with precision of thought and expression, and the very phrase "truth and wit" seems to suggest, once again, the double emphasis on wise thought and intelligent expression that seems to characterize all of Jonson's thinking about "wit."

Wit is clearly one of Jonson's preoccupations in the *Epigrammes*. That term or its variants occur in no less than 24 of the collection's 133 poems, and sometimes the word appears more than once. The epigram genre, of course, lent itself well to the expression of some kinds of wit, and, as the poem "To My Booke" makes clear, Jonson was aware of his audience's expectations in this regard. That poem seeks to dissociate his writing from the kind of petulance often linked in the public mind with wit (including the wit he himself arguably displayed in such corrosively satirical lampoons as *Poetaster*). By the same token, *Ep.* 49 seeks to dissociate the wit of epigrams from mere obscenity or bawdy humor (l. 4).[30] Instead Jonson seeks, as in his epigram "To Sir Edward Herbert" (*Ep.* 106), to associate wit with more substantial qualities such as "learning" and "iudgement" (ll. 5–6). Yet this very effort inevitably gave Jonson's thinking about wit a kind of social dimension it might otherwise have lacked, because Jonson had to champion a particular ideal of wit in the face of the differing expectations, and sometime even the resistance, of many members of his audience. Paradoxically, then, even when he conceives of wit in ways that might seem to intellectualize it and distance it from conventional notions of wit combat, that very effort becomes an assertion in a particular social arena. It becomes, that is, part of the contention from which it might seem to assert its difference. For this and for all the other reasons sketched above, Jonson's notions of "wit" in his *Epigrammes* are very much involved in questions of personal, mental, linguistic, and social power.

30. Quintilian notes, "Sarcasm that applies to a number of persons is injudicious. . . . A good man will see that everything he says is consistent with his dignity and the respectability of his character" (2:457). Too, he considered "ribald jests" to be "unbecoming" and suggested that "obscenity . . . should not merely be banished from [the orator's] language, but should not even be suggested" (2:453).

M. C. Allen

George Herbert's Pastoral Wit

O that I might some other hearts convert.
"Praise (III)"

George Herbert's wit is an "unruly engine," difficult to define and more difficult still to reconcile with his devotional aims.[1] In *The Temple*, Herbert seems both to celebrate and to spurn wit—to deride it as shameless and to deploy it shamelessly.[2] For example, despite the reservations about wit expressed in "Perirrhanterium" (ll. 235–46) and "The Sacrifice" (ll. 141–42), both poems are ingenious, paradoxical, and conceited. Although "Proud wits" are faced with God's judgment in "Justice (II)," Herbert employs the witty conceit of judicial scales becoming buckets to convey the penitents heavenward. And while the voice bids enchanting and embroidered language farewell in "The Forerunners" (ll. 9–11), his concluding salutation expresses reservation ("*If* you go . . ."). Turning to the prose, however, we can see that Herbert's attitude toward wit is discriminating rather than ambivalent. Her-

1. "Perirrhanterium," l. 241. All quotations of Herbert are from *The Works of George Herbert,* ed. F. E. Hutchinson (Oxford: Clarendon, 1941). For further discussions of Herbert's wit, see Anthony Low, "Metaphysical and Devotional Poets," in *George Herbert and the Seventeenth-Century Religious Poets,* ed. Mario di Cesare (New York: Norton, 1978), 223, 232; R. Darby Williams, "Two Baroque Game Poems on Grace," *Criticism* 12 (1970): 180–81; and Judith Dundas, "Levity and Grace: The Poetry of Sacred Wit," *Yearbook of English Studies* 2 (1972): 93, 102.

2. In light of my later discussion of literary history, I should note that Ben Jonson also dismisses wit in a highly witty fashion. See Robert C. Evans's essay in this volume.

bert's remarks in *The Country Parson* (1652) indicate his suspicion of "wits" (courtly practitioners of wit).[3] But Herbert's sprightly, and indeed witty, commendation of "witty speech" in his letter to his brother Henry suggests that wit per se (the capacity for ingenuity and invention) is good.[4] Most important, Herbert's proverb that "Every one is witty for his owne purpose" implies that witticisms (the products of wit) should be judged according to their purpose rather than according to their dexterity. What, then, is the purpose of wit in *The Temple*?

I believe that Herbert's purpose is pastoral. The wit of *The Temple* displays a particular kind of ingenuity, sometimes verbal sometimes not, which suggests the priest rather than the scholar or courtier or cavalier. We are aware, if we think about it, of the priestly persona in the poems: of someone with a profound sense of ceremony who catechizes, admonishes, preaches, and performs the liturgy. His peculiar attitudes inform *The Temple*, and his kindly but persistent efforts to "rhyme [us] to good" provide some sense of continuity ("Perirrhanterium," l. 4). Because the priest's ingenuity demands a congregation and employs public modes, Herbert's poetry may not seem as powerfully "metaphysical" as Donne's nor as personally "devotional" as Traherne's.[5] Nonetheless, Herbert's poetry *is* witty, and *The Country Parson* provides the best commentary upon his wit.

Although we tend to dissociate the urbane and witty poet from the humble country parson, Herbert's vocation was always both religious and artistic. Herbert probably wrote and revised his English poems throughout his adult life, as his religious vocation developed. The sonnets from Izaak Walton's *Life of Herbert*, the accompanying letter to Magdalene Herbert (1609), and the early poems of the Williams manuscript suggest that Herbert began his poetry at Cambridge, long before he became an Anglican priest in 1630. But as early as 1617, Herbert speaks, in a letter to his stepfather, Sir John Danvers, of "setting foot in Divinity to lay the platform of [his] future life." Herbert's

---

3. See *The Country Parson*, chap. 26, p. 264, ll. 9–14, and chap. 32, p. 275, ll. 5–10. Subsequent references to this work will follow this edition and be indicated parenthetically by chapter, page, and line.

4. See *Works of Herbert*, ed. Hutchinson, 366. In "Witty by Design," below, Roger Rollin describes this conception of wit as "capacity."

5. On the devotional qualities of Herbert's wit, see Helen Wilcox's essay in this volume and Low, "Metaphysical and Devotional Poets," 221–32.

assiduous theological study, his subsequent letters to Danvers and Magdalene Herbert, and his permission for immediate ordination to the diaconate (1624) all suggest a growing pastoral perspective.

Herbert's pastoral wit is characteristically public, for the persona is always calculating the public effect of his personal devotion. As we learn from *The Country Parson*, neither personal morality nor personal piety is purely private:

> The Countrey Parson is exceeding exact in his Life . . . Yet he labours most in those things which are apt to scandalize his Parish. (chap. 3, p. 227, ll. 1, 10–11)

> The country parson, when he is to read divine services, composeth him-selfe to all possible reverence; lifting up his heart and hands, and eyes, and using all other gestures which may expresse a hearty and unfeyned devotion. . . . that being first affected himself, hee may affect also his people. (chap. 6, p. 231, ll. 1–4, 12–13)

So it is that one does not merely read a Herbert poem, but finds one's self ingeniously drawn into it. Sometimes, one is aware of the pastoral overture. In "Obedience," for example, the persona invites the reader to participate, "to thrust his heart / Into these lines" (ll. 42–43). Again, in "The Invitation," he repeatedly invites everyone to God's holy feast.

More often, however, one begins by admiring what seems to be a personal statement, only to be drawn into a communal act, a process similar to what Roger Rollin describes as poetic "entrapment." For instance, "Praise (II)" presents a series of apparently personal propositions, yet becomes a beautifully spare hymn of praise and thanksgiving. "Home" might be misconstrued as a private poem—a direct, individual address to God—but it works like a psalm, ingeniously forcing the reader to take up the voice's repeated cry ("O show thy self to me / Or take me up to thee!"). The reader is "taught" the refrain because it is written only twice, and then must be recalled. More ingeniously still, "The Discharge" encourages participation through double entendre: its "busie enquiring heart" is not only the voice's heart but also the reader's (as in "dear heart"). *Thys* and *thous* and general statements predominate toward the end of the poem, drawing in the reader and creating public meaning.

There are, of course, many anguished notes in *The Temple*, but the voice's personal struggles have been overemphasized. The pastor characteristically comforts the afflicted:

> The Countrey Parson, when any of his cure is sick, or afflicted with losse
> of a friend, or estate, or any ways distressed, fails not to afford his best
> comforts, and rather goes to them, then sends for the afflicted, though
> they can, and otherwise ought to come to him. (chap. 15, p. 249, ll. 13–17)

The parson's wit consists largely of his ingenuity in overcoming doubt with assurance and in using his private suffering for the good of others. For instance, "Marie Magdalene" is less notable for its Donnean paradoxes than for its portrayal of spiritual comfort and its subtle insinuation that "we" ("dear soul[s]") might be cleansed like Mary. In "A Parodie," Herbert portrays a life without spiritual joy, but the poem ends hopefully in a prayer for God's presence and forgiveness. As one might expect, the pastor's comforting wit is at its dramatic and ingenious height as he encounters death. The opening of "Death" recalls Donne's "Death be not proud": "Death, thou was once an uncouth hideous thing, / Nothing but bones." Here is a ragged "strong line" to be proud of. Herbert's conceit is, if anything, more grotesque and "intellectual" than Donne's, but Herbert's ingenuity is pastoral. Rather than Donne's catalog of abstractions and final broadside of spondees, Herbert provides us with a comforting story and melodious conclusion. The pastor can befriend even Death and make him sing, can help once-frightful Death to be "full of grace." The last stanza provides a note of quiet consolation to the assembled congregation ("we" the readership).

As Helen Wilcox and Roger Rollin suggest elsewhere in this volume, Herbert's wit ultimately favors communication over obscurity.[6] This pastoral necessity is articulated most clearly in Herbert's discussion of preaching in *The Country Parson:* "The Parsons Method in handling of a text consists of two parts: first, a plain and evident declaration of the meaning of the text; and secondly, some choyce Observations drawn out of the whole text" (chap. 6, p. 235, ll. 1–4). Despite the protestations of the Jordan poems, Herbert's poetic method is often more complex than his preaching method; however, his pastoral purpose, and therefore his need to communicate clearly, is felt throughout *The Temple.* To see how much Herbert valued poetic clarity, we

6. Rollin rightly notes the "accessible" quality of Herbert's architectonics. Wilcox nicely describes the usefulness of Herbert's wit for conveying religious experience and prompting devotion, as well as Herbert's ability to draw upon and sanctify diverse literary traditions. This concern for the useful and this willingness to incorporate diverse traditions are typically Anglican attitudes.

have only to follow his revisions of "Charms & Knots" or to examine the poems in the Williams manuscript that he did not include in the Bodleian manuscript. If Herbert's meaning does not appear to be clear, it is usually because his poems are taken out of context or because we are too intent on "crumbling a text into small parts."[7]

At times, Herbert's poems may seem difficult to follow, but the problem is usually more apparent than real, and relief is usually forthcoming. In "Clasping of Hands," for instance, what seems complicated is merely a paradoxical commonplace (that one is really one's self when in God), and Herbert's turns of logic are not intended as a maze to wander in distracted, for his end couplets provide resolution. The wonderful conceit of crying up to heaven in "Praise (III)" is typically apt and clear. Even when Herbert's conceits are more complicated, as in "The Foil," we are characteristically left with an epigrammatic moral instead of in confusion.

Another general characteristic of Herbert's pastoral wit is the imposition of formal order upon ragged personal emotions. This formal modulation of individual experience is one of the main attributes of the Anglican liturgy. Hence the emphasis upon "composing one's self to prayer" in chapter 6 of *The Country Parson*. Just as the priest's part in the liturgy is both visual and aural, the poet imposes order both visually and aurally.[8] For example, the turbulence of "Affliction (I)" is progressively dissipated as a cross emblem grows in "Repentance," "Faith," and "Prayer." The same visual device is used also, appropriately, in "Assurance." In "Affliction (IV)," however, the voice's angst is offset by the workmanlike use of dimeter couplets that convey a pervasive sense of order, of self-conscious staging and control. Similarly, the five identical quatrains of "Submission" moderate the poem's urgency and emotion. "The Search" meditates upon God's absence but is so evenly constructed as to

7. See *The Country Parson*, chap. 7, p. 233, l. 23, and p. 235, l. 6. In context, Herbert's warning against wittiness is a comment upon the inappropriateness for rural congregations of Lancelot Andrewes's sermon technique of sophisticated linguistic analysis ("crumbling a text"). Herbert does not reject wit altogether.

8. Sharon Seelig, in *The Shadow of Eternity: Belief and Structure in Herbert, Vaughan, and Traherne* (Lexington: University Press of Kentucky, 1981), 17, considers the passage I allude to from "The Parson praying" (*CP*, chap. 6, p. 231) with respect to the posturing of Herbert's poetic voice. For further discussions of the imposition of form visually and aurally, see P. G. Stanwood's description of Herbert's "structural wit" in this volume.

forestall despondency. Even the emotional outburst of joy in the opening of "A True Hymne" is moderated by the extreme regularity of its iambics and its approach to isochronism: "My joy, my life, my crown!" The implicit moderation of violent personal experience is particularly evident in "The 23d Psalme," in which the only upset in the flawless metric order established in stanza 1 comes briefly in the valley of death in stanza 4—a nice touch of pastoral decorum.

Characteristically, Herbert's pastoral wit is more relational than doctrinal. Although the country parson is theologically acute and always ready to defend his faith, and indeed his church (chap. 24), he is less interested in doctrine than in his relation to others; less interested in winning arguments than in winning souls. Something of this typically pastoral attitude is implied in Herbert's curious assertion that "the Countrey Parson's Library is a holy Life" (chap. 33, p. 278, l. 11). It is not surprising, then, that although many of Herbert's poems assume doctrinal positions, they are more concerned with relationships than with doctrine. The obvious example is "Divinitie," in which theological abstractions ("curious questions and divisions") are abandoned in favor of the more relational golden rule ("do as ye would be done unto").[9] "Judgement" does not argue for or expound justification by faith; rather, it portrays the relationship with God enjoyed by a sinner who is confident of the scriptural promises of forgiveness. And "The Banquet" describes the intensely relational experience of receiving the elements, without attempting to adjudicate between the conflicting theories of transubstantiation and memorialism.

Although *The Temple* is, to some extent, "a compendium of literary novelties," Herbert is not simply amusing himself, nor is he experimenting for the sake of experimentation.[10] The country parson strives to adopt a "winning" attitude to all (chap. 8, p. 236, l. 16); however, he is particularly concerned to

9. On Herbert's attitude to doctrine, see also my "The Priest in *The Temple*" (Ph.D. diss., University of British Columbia, 1993); Christopher Hodgkins, *Authority, Church, and Society in George Herbert: Return to the Middle Way* (Columbia: University of Missouri Press, 1993); Claude J. Summers, "The Bride of the Apocalypse and the Quest for True Religion: Donne, Herbert, and Spenser," in *"Bright Shootes of Everlastingnesse": The Seventeenth-Century Religious Lyric,* ed. Claude J. Summers and Ted-Larry Pebworth (Columbia: University of Missouri Press, 1987); and John N. Wall, *Transformations of the Word: Spenser, Herbert, Vaughan* (Athens: University of Georgia Press, 1989).

10. M. M. Mahood, "'Something Understood': The Nature of George Herbert's Wit," in *Metaphysical Poetry,* ed. Malcolm Bradbury and David Palmer (New York: St. Martin's Press, 1970), 124.

win over "young and unwary spirits" (chap. 28, p. 252, l. 6). Herbert's pastoral wit is seen in his ingenious devices to win "sweet youth," particularly in his "baits of pleasure"—an important mode of pastoral wit in *The Temple* ("Perir-rhanterium," ll. 1–6). Once the youth is attracted to church, he is slyly instructed. The witty and paradoxical "Charms & Knots" turns out to contain useful axioms. "Jesu" is a word game, but a serious moral underlies the joy of playing: "That to my broken heart he was *I ease you*, / And to my whole is JESU." "Love-joy" also appears to be a toy, but turns out to be a dialogue to discover meaning. The diminishing acrostic-like line endings of "Paradise" are not ends in themselves so much as witty reminders of the cross. Even the cheerful parlor game of echoes is ingeniously designed to uncover "delights on high" in "Heaven" (l. 1).

Another prominent mode of pastoral wit in *The Temple* is best described as "ceremonial." As D. J. Enright observes, one senses in "The Altar" and "The Windows" that "orderly, deliberate, and business-like nature which built churches."[11] Indeed, as chapter 13 of *The Country Parson* suggests (and Walton attests), Herbert took great pains to arrange the furniture and fixtures of his churches. Part of his pastoral wit involves the spatial arrangement of his poems in *The Temple*, what Rollin calls the "wit of juxtaposition." Sometimes this ceremonial mode of thinking involves a note of wry pastoral humor, as when "Sinne (II)" occurs between "Mattens" and "Even-song." Sometimes the ceremonial mode reflects a more profound pastoral observation, for instance that affliction may follow a profession of faith but lead to deeper consolation ("The Pearl," "Affliction," "Man"). But, like the members of a congregation, the poems in *The Temple* rely upon one another for meaning.

Herbert's pastoral wit also involves the mode of priestly offices: preaching, catechizing, admonishing, praying.[12] We might begin with the most obvious

11. "George Herbert and the Devotional Poets," in *The New Pelican Guide to English Literature: From Donne to Marvell*, 2d ed., ed. Boris Ford (London: Penguin, 1982), 195.

12. See A. Alvarez, *The School of Donne* (New York: Pantheon, 1961), 86; J. B. Leishman, *The Monarch of Wit: An Analytical and Comparative Study of the Poetry of John Donne*, 4th ed. (London: Hutchinson, 1959), 226; Mahood, "Something Understood," 125; William Shullenberger, "*Ars Praedicandi* in George Herbert's Poetry," in *"Bright Shootes of Everlastingnesse,"* ed. Summers and Pebworth, 97; Terry Sherwood, *Herbert's Prayerful Art Power* (Toronto: University of Toronto Press, 1989), 4; Stanley Fish, *The Living Temple: George Herbert and Catechizing* (Berkeley: University of California Press, 1978).

example, Herbert's poetic sermons, for "the Countrey Parson preacheth constantly" in *The Temple* (chap. 7, p. 233, l. 20). Following the edicts of *The Country Parson* (chap. 7, p. 232, l. 27), Herbert chooses "moving and ravishing texts" for such poems as "Coloss. 3.3: Our life is hid" and "Ephes. 4.30: Grieve not the Holy Spirit."[13] Just as the country parson procures attention by expostulating with the audience (chap. 7, p. 233, ll. 18–22), so the pastor's poetic voice expostulates, "Weep foolish heart, / And weeping live" ("Ephes.," ll. 8–9). Just as the overcoming of temptation is a "sermon ready penn'd" for the country parson (chap. 33, p. 278, ll. 24), so poems such as "The Pearl" and "The Glance" ingeniously describe such victories. Just as the country parson must use his "utmost art" to "particularize his speech" for various listeners, so a poem such as "Affliction (V)" seeks to convince by spectacle, by shifts in mood, and by argument. Just as the country parson often tells stories from the pulpit (chap. 7, p. 233, ll. 11–15), so "Peace" insinuates instruction through a cunningly wrought narrative. The feeling one has reading "Joseph's Coat" is particularly like the experience of listening to a sermon: mild confusion, as one tries to figure out what the preacher's remarks have to do with the text, a slowly dawning understanding, and a final sense of conviction from the preacher's clear and emphatic conclusion.

"The Countrey Parson values Catechizing highly" and has developed this skill to an art (chap. 21, pp. 255–57), an art that informs many of the poems in *The Temple*. In "Businesse," for example, the voice interrogates the "foolish soul" (a parishioner) who is spiritually idle despite his "busyness." The couplets are questions; the regular three-line stanzas provide the answers. "Time" is an amusing vignette suggesting the country parson's frustration in catechizing thickheaded yokels. Though he is led relentlessly to the correct answer, time still misses the point (ll. 29–30). "Heaven" is an ingenious example of the catechetical mode, for it works on the audience at one remove, as advocated in *The Country Parson* (chap. 21, p. 255, ll. 25–35). Questions are posed, but the responses are not altogether predictable. Like a member of the congregation witnessing the catechism, the reader looks on, intrigued by the questions, edified as well as entertained by the responses.

One of the recurrent themes in *The Country Parson* is the parson's duty to rebuke and encourage his parishioners without fear or favor. At times, admo-

---

13. See Stanwood's discussion of "Coloss. 3.3" in this volume.

nitions from *The Country Parson* seem to inform *The Temple* directly. For example, the parson's denigration of spices and dietary excess (chaps. 17, 23, 26) adds poignancy to the "greedie heart" lusting after spices, and to the "thinne and spare" Christian, in "The Size." In "Bitter-sweet," the priestly voice overtly proclaims his pastoral duty of admonition and encouragement:

> Since thou dost love, yet strike;
> Cast down, yet help afford;
> Sure I will do the like.
>
> (ll. 2–4)

In "The Familie," however, the voice subtly discharges the same pastoral duty. Here, Herbert presents what appears to be a personification of individual spiritual struggle, which eventually implicates the refractory and dilatory members of the congregation (ll. 5–6) who are suitably admonished in the closing prayer:

> This is thy house, with these it doth abound:
> And where these are found,
> Perhaps thou com'st sometimes, and for a day;
> But not to make a constant stay.
>
> (ll. 21–24)

Rebuke and encouragement also figure prominently in "Love unknown," "The Method," and "Love (III)."[14]

Public prayer is another of the country parson's chief employments, his main salve for his own cares and for his parishioners' suffering. Accordingly, many of Herbert's poems resolve themselves in prayer, and not just personal prayer. The many irritants of "Complaining" are resolved in the last stanza, a prayer tacitly inviting the reader's participation. In "The Glimpse," the voice adds a prayer (stanza 6) to a testimonial (stanzas 4–5). The final couplet of "Clasping of Hands" is a joyful petition. In "A Parodie," stanza 4 is a prayer for God's presence and against the sin of unbelief, and the final stanza recalls "The Authour's Prayer before Sermon" in *The Country Parson:*

---

14. The style of these poems sometimes suggests catechism as well, for the reader "overhears"—and therefore tacitly participates in—the process of examination.

O what a deadly cold
Doth me infold!
I half beleeve,
That Sinne sayes true: but while I grieve,
Thou com'st and dost relieve.
(ll. 26–30)

How shall we dare to appear before thy face, who are contrary to thee, in all we call thee? for we are darknesse, and weaknesse, and filthinesse, and shame. . . . But thou Lord art patience, and pity, and sweetnesse, and love; therefore we sons of men are not consumed. (p. 288, ll. 8–11, 20–21)

The Eucharist is obviously central to *The Temple;* what is not so obvious is that the Eucharist is often described from the point of view of the celebrant. Herbert's pastoral wit is most obviously seen in the articulation and resolution of his priestly concerns in "The Priesthood" and "Aaron."[15] But Herbert's pastoral wit also draws the reader into an experience of the Eucharist in more subtle and ingenious ways. For instance, the refrain "come ye hither all" in "The Invitation" invokes the Eucharist by repeating the first sentence before communion in the Anglican liturgy: "come unto me all ye that travail and be heavy laden." "The Banquet," which follows "The Invitation," answers the voice's persistent worries about self-indulgence in worldly delights (l. 33) and writing mere ditties (ll. 50–51) by submerging these concerns in the heavenly delights of the sacrament. "The Poesie," the sanctified ditty that follows "The Banquet," demonstrates the efficacy of the sacrament by its sense of joyous repose.

Although I have provided a number of small examples of Herbert's pastoral wit, many other poems might be mentioned in this context, and some deserve our special attention. In particular, "The Call," "The Offering," "Affliction (V)," and "The Invitation" demonstrate respectively the communicative, prayerful, homiletic, and liturgical qualities of Herbert's wit.

"The Call" nicely illustrates Herbert's pastoral emphasis on communication and consolation. Like "Prayer (I)," "Paradise," and "Coloss. 3.3," this

---

15. See Richard Todd, *The Opacity of Signs: Acts of Interpretation in George Herbert's "The Temple"* (Columbia: University of Missouri Press, 1986), 99, as well as Diana Benet's detailed discussion of "The Priesthood" and "Aaron" in *Secretary of Praise: The Poetic Vocation of George Herbert* (Columbia: University of Missouri Press, 1984). I quote below the "comfortable words" of the Anglican liturgy from *The Book of Common Prayer (1559),* ed. John E. Booty (Washington: Folger Shakespeare Library, 1976), 260.

short poem has a strength beyond its witty paradoxes, for its ingenuity is a means of communication rather than an end in itself.

> Come, my Way, my Truth, my Life:
> Such a Way, as gives us breath:
> Such a Truth, as ends all strife:
> Such a Life, as killeth death.
>
> Come, my Light, my Feast, my Strength:
> Such a Light, as shows a feast:
> Such a Feast, as mends in length:
> Such a Strength, as makes his guest.
>
> Come, my Joy, my Love, my Heart;
> Such a Joy, as none can move:
> Such a Love, as none can part:
> Such a Heart, as joyes in love.

The strength of "The Call" derives largely from Herbert's proclamation of Scripture, most obviously in its opening line but also in the first lines of the second and third stanzas, all of which echo Jesus' claims about himself: "I am the way, the truth, and the life" (John 14:5); "I am the light of the world" (John 8:12). Herbert emphasizes his joyful invitation verbally by the repetition of terms, visually by the capitalization, and vocally by the extra beat that begins each line and creates a mystical seventh syllable.

The priest instructs the reader "how to behave [him]self in church" most obviously in "The Church-porch." But the reader is also instructed how to pray in "The Offering":

> Come, bring thy gift. If blessings were as slow
> As mens returns, what would become of fools?
> What hast thou there? a heart? but is it pure?
> Search well and see; for hearts have many holes.
> . . . .
> But all I fear is lest thy heart displease,
> As neither good, nor one: so oft divisions
> Thy lusts have made, and not thy lusts alone;
> Thy passions also have their set partitions.
> These parcell out thy heart: recover these,
> And thou mayst offer many gifts in one.

> There is a balsome, or indeed a bloud,
> Dropping from heav'n, which doth both cleanse and close
> All sorts of wounds; of such strange force it is.
> Seek out this All-heal, and seek no repose,
> Untill thou finde and use it to thy good:
> Then bring thy gift, and let thy hymne be this.
>
> (ll. 1–4, 13–24)

Herbert follows these instructions with a hymn written in the dimeters familiar from "Praise (II)." Behind the hymn lie the Anglican prayer after communion ("Accept this our sacrifice of praise and thanksgiving") and the exhortation before communion ("oblation and satisfaction").[16] Similarly, "The Method" concludes with a strong admonition to prayer and a proclamation of grace (ll. 29–32).

Perhaps "Affliction (V)" best demonstrates the use of multiple appeals to the auditor advocated in "The Parson praying" (*The Country Parson*, chap. 6). Although the "Affliction" poems are commonly read simply as statements of personal struggle, the voice in "Affliction (V)" quickly moves from the personal ("I") to the corporate ("we," "us," "ours"), from despair ("tempests") to consolation ("Angels" and "relief"):

> My God, I read this day,
> That planted paradise was not so firm
> As was and is thy floating Ark; whose stay
> And anchor thou art onely, to confirm
>   And strengthen it in ev'ry age,
>   When waves do rise, and tempests rage.
>
> At first we liv'd in pleasure;
> Thine own delights thou didst to us impart:
> When we grew wanton, thou didst use displeasure
> To make us thine: yet that we might not part
>   As we at first did board with thee,
>   Now thou wouldst taste our miserie.
>
> There is but joy and grief;
> If either will convert us, we are thine:
> Some Angels us'd the first; if our relief

16. See ibid., 263–64.

> Take up the second, then thy double line
> > And sev'rall baits in either kinde
> > Furnish thy table to thy minde.
>
> Affliction then is ours;
> We are the trees, whom shaking fastens more,
> While blustring windes destroy the wanton bowres,
> And ruffle all their curious knots and store.
> > My God, so temper joy and wo,
> > That thy bright beams may tame thy bow.

The striking simplicity and intimacy of the opening of this poem recall the opening of "Man" ("My God, I heard this day"). This is the intimacy not only of the devout but also of the priest whose duties require constant discourse with God. Herbert develops an analogy between Eden (pleasure) and the Ark (tribulation), leading to the syllogism of stanza 3: "There is but joy and grief; / If either will convert us, we are thine." But as closely argued as it is, this poem also relies upon its visual suggestions of the cross and its resolution in prayer. Here, as in "Coloss. 3.3," Herbert follows his advice to the parson in prayer to use visual as well as auditory effects. The reason is obvious, once one adopts the parson's perspective, for some members of the congregation will respond most to spectacle, others to shifts in mood, still others to argument.

The priest's administration of the sacraments provides continuity to "The Church," reflecting the centrality of the Eucharist in Anglican worship. Most notably, "The Priesthood" and "Aaron" reflect the priest's hesitation over "what behaviour to assume for so holy things . . . being not only to receive God but to break and administer him" (*The Country Parson*, chap. 22, p. 257, ll. 26–30).

> But th' holy men of God such vessels are,
> As serve him up, who all the world commands:
> When God vouchsafeth to become our fare,
> Their hands convey him, who conveys their hands.
> O what pure things, most pure must those things be,
> > Who bring my God to me!
> > ("The Priesthood," ll. 25–30)

The order of the poems in "The Church" sometimes conveys the celebrant's perspective. "The Church" begins with "The Altar," a poem that recalls "the sacrifice of praise and thanksgiving" of the prayer following Holy Communion in the Book of Common Prayer.[17] "The H. Communion" is linked to "The British Church" by its concern with "fine aray." "Love (I)" and "Love (II)," which describe the purification of desire, look back to "The Altar" and forward to "Love (III)." And the implied setting of "The Dawning" is the mystical banquet of "Love (III)" and "The Altar" at which a sad heart becomes thankful and eyes are restored.

Sometimes the reader is particularly aware that he is being led to worship by the priest. For example, the priest brings the reader and worshiper under the divine gaze in "The Glance," and then leads him to worship in "The 23d Psalme." The priest does not merely receive the Eucharist, he also celebrates it for us. For instance, Herbert fashions hieroglyphs of altars in "Marie Magdalene," not only conveying the idea of sacrifice but also bringing us visually to the altar. Then, in "The Invitation," the poet-priest not only invites us to approach the altar ("Come ye hither All") but also prays that God will inform the "dainties" at the "feast":

> Lord I have invited all,
> > And I shall
> Still invite, still call to thee:
> For it sees but just and right
> > In my sight,
> Where is All, there All should be.
> > (ll. 31–36)

Surely this is an exhortation or prayer, rather than a personal reflection.[18]

I am well aware that by emphasizing the public aspects of Herbert's poetry, its characteristic clarity, and the importance of Herbert's Anglican priest-

---

17. Ibid., 264.

18. Herbert's "Come ye hither All" recalls the priest's exhortation before confession in the service of Holy Communion ("You that do truly and earnestly repent . . . Draw near, and take this holy Sacrament to your comfort"), as well as the "comfortable words" repeated by the priest ("Come unto me all that travail and be heavy laden, and I will refresh you"). Herbert's invitation to God to join (and become) the feast suggests the priest's invocation immediately before communion ("Hear us, O merciful Father, we beseech thee; and grant that we receiving these thy creatures of bread and wine . . . may be partakers of [Christ's] most blessed Body and Blood") (ibid., 259–60, 263).

hood, I am going against the flow of current critical opinion. I do not, of course, wish to make Herbert's poetry simpler than it is. Herbert's poetic voice does sometimes seem to grope toward the truth; as readers, we may sometimes be "led into temptation that we may be delivered from evil."[19] However, I do not think that Herbert's poetry is quite as intricate, private, reformed, and equivocal as it is often thought to be. Perhaps we have overemphasized the view of *The Temple* as "a picture of [Herbert's] many spiritual struggles." After all, Walton also records Herbert's pastoral hope that *The Temple* might "turn to the advantage of any dejected poor soul" who read it. And poems such as "Perirrhanterium," "Providence," and "Praise (II)" could hardly be simpler, clearer, or more public.

The stylistic reevaluation I suggest may also involve a reconsideration of Herbert's place in literary history. We tend to assume that Herbert's wit is typically Jacobean because of its ingenuity.[20] But if Elizabethan wit involves the rhetorical conception of poetry and the penning of courtly trifles, Herbert's wit is sometimes more Elizabethan than Jacobean. With few exceptions, critics still assume that Herbert falls in the Donnean tradition of strong lines, strong emotions, and witty conceits; however, the controlled, polished, and monumental aspects of his poetry suggest an equal affinity with the Tribe of Ben.[21] The spareness and classicism of his poetry might even be thought to anticipate eighteenth-century poetics. Perhaps, like Gerard Manley Hopkins, whom Herbert so obviously inspired, George Herbert transcends the conventional literary-historical categories.

But one thing is certain: Herbert is not merely a pale disciple of Donne. Herbert's pastoral wit is no less ingenious than Donne's scholastic wit. In-

---

19. Todd, *Opacity of Signs*, 167, 170; Seelig, *Shadow of Eternity*, 11.

20. See Robert L. Sharp, *From Donne to Dryden: The Revolt against Metaphysical Poetry* (Chapel Hill: University of North Carolina Press, 1940), 36–37, and George Williamson, *The Proper Wit of Poetry* (Chicago: University of Chicago Press, 1961), 12–13, 45.

21. Joseph H. Summers proposes an alternate view of literary history in *The Heirs of Donne and Jonson* (New York: Oxford University Press, 1970), as does Low in "Metaphysical and Devotional Poets," 221–32. Michael Schoenfeldt, in *Prayer and Power: George Herbert and Renaissance Courtship* (Chicago: University of Chicago Press, 1991), 1–18, has also challenged the conventional classification of Herbert's poetry and has drawn *The Temple* into the realm of public discourse. On Jonson and Herbert, see *Classic and Cavalier: Essays on Jonson and the Sons of Ben*, ed. Claude J. Summers and Ted-Larry Pebworth (Pittsburgh: University of Pittsburgh Press, 1982), 13–14, 47, 157.

deed, honeybees and orange trees have one distinct advantage over twisted eye beams and stiff twin compasses—ready comprehensibility.[22] So, if we consider Donne to be the "Monarch of Wit," we should imagine Herbert not as the bloodless prince, but as the Bishop of Wit, or—as he would undoubtedly prefer—the humble country parson.

---

22. See "Employment (I)," ll. 17–18, and "Employment (II)," ll. 21–22: these images or conceits are not only understandable because they are familiar, they are actually interpreted for the reader.

Roger B. Rollin

Witty by Design

Robert Herrick's Hesperides

by *Apollo*! . . . I worship wit.
　　　—Robert Herrick[1]

Whatever seventeenth-century wit is, it is not a quality modern criticism tends to associate with Robert Herrick. Yet as far as the poet himself was concerned, wit he did have. For example, in the terse epigram "His Losse" (H-830), he wryly notes: "All has been plundered from me, but my wit; / Fortune her selfe can lay no claim to it."

This couplet on wit is itself witty. The verb "plundered" may be an allusion to Herrick's expulsion from his vicarage in 1647 by the Puritan regime's "Committee of Plundered Ministers," a form of persecution that in line 2 is regarded, somewhat unexpectedly, with ironic equanimity.[2] Moreover, there is wit in the epigram's self-referentiality: its second line amusingly demonstrates what its first claims, that Herrick does indeed still have his wit about him—that is, his "capacity for apt expression" (*OED* 7), or "That quality of [his] writing which consists in the apt association of thought and expression, calculated to surprise and delight by its unexpectedness" (*OED* 8). What the

---

1. "To Master Denham, on his Prospective Poem," *The Complete Poetry of Robert Herrick*, ed. J. Max Patrick (New York: New York University Press, 1963), H-673. All citations from Herrick are to this volume and will be given parenthetically, using its numbering for the poems.

2. I am indebted to Claude J. Summers for this suggestion and for his recommendation that I include in my discussion a brief consideration of Herrick's epigrams.

OED does not note, however, is that wit can be "structural" as well as intellectual and rhetorical. Structural wit—what I shall term the "wit of design"—is in plain view in the "architectonics" of George Herbert's The Temple. But, as I shall argue later in this essay, it is also present, if in more subtle form, in Herrick's highly conscious arrangement of the more than fourteen hundred poems that make up the first edition of his Hesperides (1648).

Herrick is not at all subtle about proclaiming the *rhetorical* wittiness of his poems. For example, in one of his several addresses "To his Verses" (H-626) he plaintively-comically asks:

> What will ye (my poor Orphans) do
> When I must leave the World (and you)
> Who'l give ye then a sheltring shed,
> Or credit ye, when I am dead?
> Who'l let ye by their fire sit?
> Although ye have a stock of wit,
> Already coin'd to pay for it.
>
> (ll. 1–7)

The answer to this question turns out to be a patron, like "Noble *Westmorland*; / Or gallant *Newark*," who might become "fost'ring fathers" to these soon-to-be "orphaned" poetic "Babes." Thus, what appears to be a conventional apostrophe to the poet's own book, replete with its "stock of wit," unexpectedly—the unexpected is what we expect of wit—turns out to be a begging poem.

It might be expected that Herrick's famous—or infamous—epigrams would offer plentiful examples of his wit. The majority of them, however, are relatively serious or at least gnomic utterances. A few are romantic, a few autobiographical. Even most of the satiric epigrams, such as "Upon Cuffe . . ." (H-109), are more humorous than witty:

> *Cuffe* comes to Church much; but he keeps his bed
> Those Sundayes onely, when as Briefs are read.
> This makes *Cuffe* dull; and troubles him the most,
> Because he cannot sleep i'th'Church, free-cost.

Even those (relatively few) exercises in what Michael C. Schoenfeldt feelingly terms "The Art of Disgust," Herrick's poems of "coarse vulgarity,"[3] display more scatological humor than wit:

> *Skoles* stinks so deadly, that his Breeches loath
> His dampish Buttocks furthermore to cloath:
> Cloy'd they are up with Arse; but hope, one blast
> Will whirle about, and blow them thence at last.
>
> ("Upon Skoles. Epigram," H-650)

Only a few epigrams, such as "Nothing new" (H-352), exhibit anything like the kind of irony, ingenuity, and surprise generally associated with true wit: "Nothing is New; we walk where others went. / Ther's no vice now, but has his president." The reason may not be far to seek: in a sense, the wit of most epigrams, including Herrick's, resides more in their form than in their content, that is, in their ability to maximize expression within a minimal structure. Wit prolonged is wit dissipated. Brevity itself is the soul of the wit of the epigram.

Earl Miner remarks that it has "become common to think of wit in terms of conceits,"[4] and here too Herrick's *Hesperides* is not wanting. For example, another of his apostrophes, "His Winding-sheet" (H-515), might be expected to be merely one more lugubrious seventeenth-century meditation upon death, but it begins in rather sprightly and conceited fashion: "Come thou, who art the Wine, and wit, / Of all I've writ." These lines constitute a highly compressed example of the self-referentiality that is a hallmark of Herrick's poetry (and a neglected dimension of seventeenth-century wit).[5] Anyone who has been carefully reading straight through *Hesperides* might recall that, long before "His Winding-sheet" appears, in his paired comic tours de force "His fare-well to Sack" (H-128) and "The Welcome to Sack" (H-197), Herrick claims that the main source of his wit (his creativity) is not death but *wine*, "Of which, sweet Swans must drink, before they sing / Their true-pac'd-

---

3. "The Art of Disgust: Civility and the Social Body in *Hesperides*," *George Herbert Journal* 14 (1990–1991): 127.

4. *The Metaphysical Mode from Donne to Cowley* (Princeton: Princeton University Press, 1969), 118.

5. See my *Robert Herrick*, rev. ed. (Twayne: New York: 1992), 8, 130, 161, 164, 181–82, 189–91, 193.

Numbers, and their Holy-Layes" ("His fare-well," ll. 34–35; see also "The Welcome," l. 89). Herrick's ingenuity in attributing his poetic force to his winding-sheet at this later point in his collection resides in his implicit and ironic acknowledgment of all those poems in which he has portrayed himself as near death or imagines himself to be already dead—poems so numerous that the reader can hardly have missed them either.

The same kind of hyperbole with which Herrick addresses canary wine in the sack poems is now applied to his winding-sheet, which becomes:

> The Grace, the Glorie, and the best
> Piece of the rest.
> Thou art of what I did intend
> The All, and End.
> And what was made, was made to meet
> Thee, thee my sheet.
> (ll. 3–8)

Some of the wit of these lines resides in their self-referential double meaning. Although death has figured importantly in many of the poems up to this point in the collection, so many others have celebrated life and love that it becomes hard to take Herrick's predictions of his own imminent demise very seriously.

The controlling conceit of "His Winding-sheet" is that of death (symbolized by his shroud) as his lover:

> Come then, and be to my chast side
> Both Bed, and Bride.
> We two (as Reliques left) will have
> One Rest, one Grave.
> (ll. 9–12)

Thirty-six more lines wittily elaborate upon this triple trope: though Herrick's winding-sheet is his spouse and then (adding yet another layer to the conceit) his marriage bed, "Lust," "Desires," even "Affections" (all words prominent in the sack poems) have been put behind them. Behind them as well, he sarcastically notes, are such worldly annoyances as the legal system and the court (ll. 19–34). The poem's deepening irony finally gives way to the peculiarly de-Christianized religiousness that is a salient characteristic of Herrick's secular collection—the promise of the poet's transfiguration with the advent of "that great Platonick yeere" (l. 47)—a distant echo, five hundred poems into *Hesperides*, of "The Argument of his Book" (H-1): "I sing (and ever shall) / Of Heaven, and hope to have it after all" (ll. 13–14). Whereas wit typically trades in a sense of disjunction, the wit of self-referentiality can enhance continuity.

"His Winding-sheet" is not, of course, the only poem in *Hesperides* to exhibit the kind of extensively explored and exploited metaphors that modern criticism associates with seventeenth-century wit and that A. J. Smith labels "conceited wit." For example, a Julia poem, "The Eye" (H-133), is an elaborate conceit in the metaphysical manner; "Corinna's going a Maying" (H-178) exhibits the dialectical structure, the dramatic mise-en-scène, and the ingenious metaphors we have come to think of as witty in the Donnean mode; and surely some of the appeal of the oft-anthologized "Upon Julia's Clothes" (H-779) lies in its ingeniously "submerged" conceit that compares fishing and flirtation.[6]

The distinctiveness of Herrick's wit, however, does not in the main reside in the rhetorical ingenuity of some of his poems: after all, there is not a seventeenth-century poet still being read today (including Milton) whose work is wholly lacking in this quality. Rather, as mentioned above, the uniqueness of Herrick's wit manifests itself most importantly in the ingeniousness of his ordering of the poems of *Hesperides*, a volume he saw through the presses. This highly conscious but often highly subtle arrangement endows Herrick's book with a "wit of design" that goes beyond that of any other poetry collection of the time.

Indeed, Herrick's wit of design is a unique example of another salient quality of seventeenth-century poetic wit in general—its frequently "adversarial" nature. Witty writers are, after all, nothing if not aggressive: they challenge readers to recognize, to decipher, and to savor plays on words, irony, multiple meanings, allusion, ambiguity, reversal, surprise, and self-referentiality. Rhetorical challenges like these transform such common authorial personae as guide, friend, mentor, suppliant, confidant—all of which Herrick, for example, effects—into intellectual adversaries. However, once the challenge has been successfully met by the capable reader and the poet's wit adequately

6. Smith, *Metaphysical Wit* (Cambridge: Cambridge University Press, 1991), 20–23; Rollin, *Herrick*, 79, 85; Louis H. Leiter, "Herrick's 'Upon Julia's Clothes," *Modern Language Notes* 73 (1958): 331; for other examples, see Rollin, *Herrick*, 220.

appreciated, poet and reader become confederates, bonded together by the presumed superiority of their intellects, their learning, and their taste. Thus, the reader who is able to discern something of *Hesperides's* witty design can experience a form of intellectual pleasure akin to that of Robert Herrick himself. One of the rewards of poetic wit for the reader is momentary complicity, even identification, with the poet.

The origin of the idea of organizing a poetic miscellany in some way other than by chronology (as in Milton's *Poems*, 1645) or by genre (as in Jonson's *Epigrammes*, 1616) is the subject for a separate investigation. Here it can only be speculated that, for English poets, Sidney's *Astrophel and Stella* (1591), with its loose narrative structure, may have provided an impetus that reached its culmination in a very different kind of arrangement—the architectonics of *The Temple* (1633).

Both the rhetorical wit and what P. G. Stanwood and Lee M. Johnson and Helen Wilcox call the "structural wit" of Herbert's *individual* poems, of course, pose frequent challenges to his readers. But the poet's *arrangement* of his collection constitutes a more accessible kind of wit of design—and, in all likelihood, deliberately so. Herbert's poetry is after all an extension of his ministry, as M. C. Allen observes, and therefore "all good structure" may not be "in a winding stair" ("Jordan" [I], l. 3).[7] Thus, if the title of his book and its introductory poem, "The Church-porch," do not make Herbert's design apparent, most readers will become aware of his architectonics in the transition from "Superluminare" to the division labeled "The Church" and its first poem, the hieroglyphic "The Altar." The wit of Herbert's design, however, resides not only in his juxtaposing and "clustering" of some poems but also in his verbal linking of others: thus, the final refrain of "The Sacrifice"—Christ's "Never was grief like mine"—is confirmed in the first line of the poem that immediately follows ("The Thanksgiving"), where the Savior is addressed as the "King of grief." Similarly, the last two lines of "The Thanksgiving" ("Then for thy passion—I will do for that— / Alas, my God, I know not what") evoke the response that opens the next poem ("The Reprisall"): "I have consider'd it, and finde / There is no dealing with thy mighty passion."

---

7. See the essays by Stanwood and Johnson, Wilcox, and Allen in this volume. All quotations from Herbert are from *The Works of George Herbert*, ed. F. E. Hutchinson (Oxford: Clarendon Press, 1941).

This kind of wit of design, like the self-referential wit mentioned above, can in a poetic miscellany be a strong if subtle force for continuity.

The continuity of *The Temple* is enhanced as well by what might be called "title replication," a phenomenon also characteristic of *Hesperides*. Thus, poems spatially separated in the collection become implicit series by virtue of their identical titles (for example, Herbert's "Affliction" and "Jordan" poems and Herrick's self-apostrophes). Given *Hesperides*'s more than fourteen hundred "verses," Herrick's title replication may be due as much to the limits of his invention as to deliberate wittiness, but the consequences for readers—a sense of unity and coherence through repetition—can be similar.

Because the particulars of design in *Hesperides* are still far from being fully mapped, even though three hundred years have passed since its publication, it is patent that the wit of Herrick's arrangement is less accessible than Herbert's. Whereas the controlling design of *The Temple* is "architectural" and thus of necessity somewhat formal, that of *Hesperides* is "horticultural." Herrick's book is, as J. Max Patrick has said, "a garden of poetry" as well as green and flowery Devonshire itself.[8] The poet's own conceits characterize his volume as a "Sacred Grove" (H-265, l. 3) and a "rich Plantation" (H-392, l. 4). A formal garden it is not, although some of its features betray the gardener's handiwork more than others—for example, the deliberately pastoral "entrance" to *Hesperides* through "The Argument of his Book" (H-1) and that collection's statuary "exit," "The pillar of Fame" (H-1129). Between those two poems, however, stand 1,127 others, the golden "blossoms" of this Hesperidean garden, whose very profuseness and diversity threaten to transform it into a wilderness. Small wonder then that Herrick, a poet ever conscious of his readers,[9] saw the need for—and the artistic value of—giving some kind of design to the arrangement of his miscellany.

Read—as most students today read him—in anthology selections or—as some critics read him—highly selectively, the wit of Herrick's design is hardly apparent at all. For his is not a book meant for browsing: it is quite clear that the poet himself thought of *Hesperides* as a "long [continuous] work" ("To the generous Reader" [H-95], l. 6), to be read from beginning to end, in sequence, as one might follow a garden path. Experienced thus, the wit of his design has

8. *Complete Poetry*, ed. Patrick, 5.
9. Rollin, *Herrick*, 4, 8, 11.

more chance to work its effects—some obvious, some highly subtle—upon the reader. Such effects begin with the book's first eight poems, which have to do with the collection itself, or more precisely, with what today we would call reader response to that collection. Thus, the opening work, "The Argument of his Book" (H-1), appears to be a versified table of contents, but more important, from a phenomenological point of view, it is a conscious effort to create a "Hesperidean world," a world that is pastoral, ceremonial, sexual, natural, transient, partly supernatural, and ultimately *sub specie aeternitatis*. Moreover, as noted above, the poem also offers readers a profile of the poet who will be their guide through that garden world, a profile that will be both filled in and problematized as readers proceed through the collection. As a table of contents, though, "The Argument" is only relatively accurate: for example, it gives readers no hint of the more realistic Hesperidean realm reflected in the collection's political, epideictic, and epigrammatical verses. The poem thus effects the kind of "entrapment" of the reader that is characteristic of seventeenth-century wit: we expect one thing and (sooner or later) get something else.

Entrapment of this sort figures in the rest of Herrick's introductory sequence as well. In the seven poems immediately following "The Argument," readers, instead of being flattered or cajoled into responding favorably to the poet's labors, are indirectly warned against being surly "Critick[s]" ("To his Muse [H-2], l. 22); or hypocrites who protest risqué verse in public and find delectation in it in private ("Another" [H-4]); or gross philistines who use poems for toilet paper ("Another" [H-5]). Moreover, readers who, weaned on a pickle, like nothing Herrick has written, find themselves cursed in advance for their perversity ("To the soure Reader" [H-6]) and condemned for lack of judgment ("To his Booke" [H-7]). Finally, his readers are instructed by Herrick as to "When he would have his verses read" (H-8) and by implication admonished not to be "rigid *Cato*[s]" when they do so. While these varied admonitions are not without their humorous elements, their importance resides in their cumulative wit—in their surprising, even daring, attempt to manipulate readers, to shape them into the kind of ideal reader (infinitely sensitive, understanding, and tolerant) who will best appreciate the kind of poetry written by the idealized poet profiled in Herrick's "Argument."

Seventeenth-century wit always puts readers on the defensive, primarily by challenging their capacities for understanding and appreciation. The wit of the opening sequence of *Hesperides*, however, takes a different tack: the poet's preemptive assaults on unfit audiences disarm criticism by forcing us to perceive those assaults as being directed toward readers less open-minded and less cultured than ourselves. It is a bold move on Herrick's part, with the potential for alienating his audience. But boldness—intellectual and rhetorical boldness at least—is one of the chief marks of a seventeenth-century wit.

The reader who appreciates Herrick's wit of design may notice that, as Ann Baynes Coiro has shown, his secular collection concludes as it began, with a series of eight poems on poetry, this time of a valedictory nature, with farewells to his book, to the writing of poetry, and finally, in "On Himselfe" (H-1128), to life itself. Between the latter epigram and that famous example of typographical wit, the hieroglyphic "pillar of Fame" (H-1129), it is implied that Robert Herrick "dies," for, as John L. Kimmey has pointed out, his versified monument, fame's pillar, is erected not by himself but by an anonymous "we."[10] Thus, the fiction of the poet's decline and imminent death that is played out through the course of *Hesperides* becomes, at that book's end, a climactic "factoid," a fictional fact that gives the collection dramatic closure.

Such witty design also characterizes Herrick's sacred collection: for example, *His Noble Numbers* begins, surprisingly, with an apologia for writing the poems the reader has just finished reading, "those Lines, pen'd by my wanton Wit" ("His Confession," [N-1], l. 3), the very same lines that initially were bold "to sing of cleanly-*Wantonnesse*," lines that became for the poet "Fames pillar." To make assurance doubly sure, the next poem, "His Prayer for Absolution" (N-2), likewise apologizes "For Those my unbaptized Rhimes, / Writ in my wild unhallowed Times" (ll. 1–2), lines and rhymes that Robert Herrick did, of course, publish. Departing from this self-flagellating mode, the third poem in the series employs another convention, that of the catalog of impossibilities, to dramatize the intellectual folly of trying to find God (N-3). That principle established, Herrick immediately and unexpectedly abandons it with a group of seven poems that confidently enumerate the deity's characteristics—even while insisting that God is "not to be comprehended" (N-8).

The main effect of this cluster of introductory verses is confusion. Cer-

---

10. Coiro, *Robert Herrick's "Hesperides" and the Epigram Book Tradition* (Baltimore: Johns Hopkins University Press, 1988), 214, 215; Kimmey, "Order and Form in Herrick's *Hesperides*," *Journal of English and Germanic Philology* 70 (1971): 263.

tainly the abject and seemingly muddled pietist that they figure forth seems quite unlike the Robert Herrick the reader has come to know in the course of reading through his secular poetry. As it turns out, however, this problematic introduction to the persona of *His Noble Numbers* is in fact quite appropriate for a collection that is grounded in a Christian's unequal struggle with a God who seems as angry as he is loving, a collection that progresses in fits and starts from a mood approximating religious melancholy to one of calm acceptance of a Heavenly Father and of feeling accepted by him. This is another case in which the wit of Herrick's design is in a sense cumulative, becoming apparent only after sequential reading.

Wit of design also marks the arrangement of the final "pious Pieces" of *His Noble Numbers*, a series of five epigrams about or prayers to God that parallel the collection's introductory sequence. Encountering the last of these, "To God" (N-262), readers are to be forgiven if they expect it to conclude the volume, for here the poet seems about to receive the absolution he has sought so earnestly from its onset: "The work is done," the first line announces with finality,

> now let my *Lawrell* be
> Given by none, but by Thy selfe, to me:
> That done, with Honour Thou dost me create
> Thy *Poet,* and thy *Prophet Lawreat.*

But there is to be one last surprise—a series of nine vivid and highly dramatic meditations upon the Crucifixion and the Resurrection—"Herrick's Passion play," as they have been called.[11] The best known of these is the first, "Good Friday: Rex Tragicus, or Christ going to His Crosse" (N-263). This tour de force—a theatrical employment of a theatrical motif—is one of those relatively few works of Herrick's whose wit is rhetorical *and* structural, featuring the exploration and exploitation of the conceit of the Son of God as tragic actor. Succeeding poems in this series constitute a kind of dramatic narrative in which the poet (and his reader) seem to be physically present at the Passion, even to the extent of hearing the "Saviours words" as he addresses onlookers (N-266). The sequence (and *His Noble Numbers* itself)

---

11. Robert L. Deming, *Ceremony and Art: Robert Herrick's Poetry* (The Hague and Paris: Mouton, 1974), 76.

concludes with Herrick's "coming to the Sepulcher" (N-271), encountering a "white Angell" there, and vowing, like a heroic Christian militant, to "live in Hell, if that my *Christ* stayes there."

It would be simplistic to suggest that the marked difference between Herrick's tone and attitude here and in the opening of "His Pious Pieces" indicates an evolution from abject sinner to God's "*Poet, and . . . Prophet Lawreate*": *His Noble Numbers* is more complex than that. Nonetheless, some such evolution does take place and becomes a unifying aspect of the wit of the sacred collection's design. In this respect *His Noble Numbers* (too readily dismissed by too many critics) generally resembles Herrick's secular collection, even down to the fact that both close with couplet-length epigrams— the well-known (and witty) "To his Book's end this last line he'd have plac't, / *Jocond his Muse was; but his Life was chast*" (H-1130) of *Hesperides* and the less familiar sacred epigram of *His Noble Numbers*, "Of all the good things whatsoe're we do, / God is the ΑΡΧΗ, and the ΤΕΛΟΣ too" (N-272). Such symmetry prompts the speculation that some kind of symmetry may indeed be fundamental to the wit of design—in fact, may be fundamental to seventeenth-century wit generally—for nothing would more likely subvert wit than a "yoking together" of nonsymmetrical expressions, images, or ideas.

Less formal than the wit with which Herrick "frames" his books and his volume as a whole is his ordering of individual poems within the main body of his collection—ordering them in such ways, in fact, that they seem to "comment" upon one another. Such "commentary," usually operating through comparison or contrast, tends to be more implicit than explicit but can generate cumulative effects as *Hesperides* unfolds. A few love lyrics will serve to illustrate the point.

For many readers Herrick's reputation has been chiefly (if erroneously) that of an amatory poet, and that reputation derives in large part from such favorites as "To the Virgins, to make much of Time" (H-208) and "Corinna's going a Maying" (H-178). Neither poem is without wit, but it is likely that their popularity and power reside in much more than their wit. The irony of transiency—"this same flower that smiles today / To morrow will be dying" (ll. 3–4)—of "To the Virgins" is a commonplace, but its expression is at once magisterial and graceful, serious and light. "Corinna" is more ambitious and more witty—witty in its conception (as an original, dramatic, and specifically English conflation of the aubade and the pastoral invitation to love), in its

ingenious conceits linking humanity and nature, and in its emergent dialecti-
cal structure. But the most originally witty aspect of Herrick's love poems
resides less in their manner of expression than in the ways they are sometimes
arranged within *Hesperides*. For example, one effect of that arrangement is
that, as a reader proceeds through the collection, there gradually emerges an
often mocking self-portrait of the poet, at once a Petrarchist and a misogynist,
a romantic and a rake, a boyish lover and a *senex amans*—truly a practitioner
of "cleanly-Wantonnesse."

The first poem after the introductory series of *Hesperides* is a love lyric, one
that celebrates the "Recovery" (H-9) of a mistress named "Julia." Next,
however, is a plea "To Silvia to wed" (H-10)—which would seem to settle
early on the matter of the poet's romantic intentions. But "To Silvia" is
immediately followed by yet another love lyric to the aforementioned Julia
(H-11), and within but a few pages will also be found amatory verses to
"Perilla" (H-14), "Perenna" (H-16), and "Anthea" (H-22). Finally, in *Hesperides*
more than a dozen other mistresses will be addressed, described, or named as
characters in the scores of love lyrics that are distributed throughout the
volume. Such promiscuity has troubled those who suspect that behind the
well-crafted lyrics a naughty reality lurks, whereas others, seeing male fanta-
sies run rampant, are merely amused. But the wit, again, resides in Herrick's
self-referentiality: the portrait of the poet that gradually emerges is not infre-
quently unflattering, for Herrick can depict himself as a cynical roué ("No
Loathsomeness in love," H-21), as a distraught victim of love-melancholy
("The Wounded Heart," H-20), as a fleshly voyeur ("The Vision," H-142), as a
pretentious priest of love ("The Perfume," H-251), or as a dreary confirmed
bachelor ("No Spouse but a Sister," H-31). These lovers' roles (and many
more) continually play off against each other, as do Herrick's varied amatory
subjects (women's clothes, women's anatomy, male fantasies) and themes
(sexual aesthetics, lovers' rituals), subjects and themes that continually com-
pare or contrast and thus qualify one other. (Comparison, as William G.
Crane has observed, is "without doubt, the chief element of wit.")[12]

The order of *Hesperides* is full of those unexpected pleasures that arise out
of the wit of Herrick's design. For example, "To Cherry Blossomes" (H-189),
which begins a "bouquet" of five flower poems, takes the brutal fact that all

---

12. *Wit and Rhetoric in the Renaissance* (Gloucester, Mass.: Peter Smith, 1964), 141.

living things have their ends and renders it natural, even beautiful: "But (sweet things) ye must be gone; / Fruit, ye know, is comming on" (ll. 3–4). By contrast, beginnings are the subject of the next poem in the grouping, the almost Crashavian fantasia "How Lilies came white" (H-190), while the verse that follows, "To Pansies" (H-191), notes the solace to be found in flowers. In the fourth poem in the cluster, "On Gelli-flowers begotten" (H-192), a flower-sweet mistress is romanced. Finally, completing this poetic bouquet is "The Lilly in a Crystal" (H-193). The title object of this oft-anthologized poem symbolizes the triumph of artistic stasis over natural flux, but in Herrick's hands the lily then becomes the text of a lesson in sexual aesthetics—women's clothes "Raise greater fires in men" than their nakedness. In effect, this cluster of five poems constitutes a kind of literary game in which flowers are put to five different poetic uses.

The element of game, indeed, might be said to be yet another characteristic of a good deal of seventeenth-century wit,[13] John Donne being the most notable case in point. For example, like Herrick, Donne can play the game of representing contradictory views on love and women (his *Songs and Sonnets*) and religion (his *Holy Sonnets*), leaving his readers to wonder when the real John Donne will stand up. And while Herrick never tries (like Donne) "to match Sir Ed[ward] Herbert in obscureness" within his poems,[14] the obscurity of his volume's witty design has proved for readers to be a challenging game indeed.

(At this point, a caveat: some of the time, Herrick's arrangement of his poems appears to be simply for the sake of variety rather than for some more witty end. To cite but one of many examples, a pair of bitter epigrams on poets' "Detracter[s]" [H-173, 174] is sandwiched between two witty Julia poems: "A Ring presented to Julia" [H-172] is, like Donne's "The Funeral," with its wreath conceit, analogically developed, while "Julia's Petticoat" [H-175] is a playful exercise in hyperbolic personification; yet there is no discernible wit involved in the *juxtaposition* of these four poems.)

Another way in which the wit of Herrick's design sometimes manifests

13. Earl Miner, *The Cavalier Mode from Jonson to Cotton* (Princeton: Princeton University Press, 1971), 124.
14. Ben Jonson, "Conversations with William Drummond of Hawthornden," in *Ben Jonson*, ed. Ian Donaldson (Oxford: Oxford University Press, 1985), 597.

itself is in "strings" of poems on select addressees—a notion explored by Ann Baynes Coiro in connection with the poet's Julia verses.[15] The effects of such arrangements, however, must be more subliminal than conscious: not many readers will in the course of reading through *Hesperides* be able to recall hundreds of short poems and piece together their relationships. There are limitations to the echo effect, even echoes that repeatedly call the name of "Julia." On the other hand, "clusters" of poems located in close proximity to one another can influence readers' responses to individual works. For example, a loose grouping of poems on poetry and poets just beyond the midpoint of *Hesperides* acts rather like a series of versified snapshots that together add up to a composite self-portrait of the poet—this time, however, a flattering one. Thus, the epigram purportedly addressed "To his Booke" (H-603) is actually a remonstrance to unsympathetic readers and a self-advertisement: "all here is good, / If but well read; or ill read, understood" (ll. 3–4). This pronouncement is immediately followed by the self-validating "His Prayer to Ben Johnson" (H-604), a witty exercise in the "religion of poetry" in which Herrick proclaims himself to be a "son of Ben." On the next page of the 1648 edition an address "To his Muse" (H-611) further establishes Herrick's credentials as a poet, one whom the Prince of Wales himself might love. Charles's royal parents and their precarious political situation are lamented in the last poem of this cluster, "The bad season makes the Poet sad" (H-612). Thus, within the space of three pages Herrick wittily crystallizes his literary and political identity and demonstrates that for serious poets like himself the poetic and the political are inextricably linked.[16]

Another such cluster consists of seven poems whose combined effect is to reinforce a sense of Herrick as something of a philosopher poet. These include a meditation upon the body's fate ("Proof to no purpose," H-720); epigrammatic observations upon "Fame" (H-721) and upon the necessity of constant practice ("By use comes easinesse," H-722); an imitation of a Roman prayer for modest creature comforts ("To the Genius of his house, H-723);

15. "Herrick's 'Julia' Poems," *John Donne Journal* 6.1 (1987): 67–89.

16. See Claude J. Summers, "Herrick's Political Counterplots," *Studies in English Literature* 25 (winter 1985): 165–82, and "Herrick, Vaughan, and the Poetry of Anglican Survivalism," in *New Perspectives on the Seventeenth-Century English Religious Lyric*, ed. John R. Roberts (Columbia: University of Missouri Press, 1994), 46–74.

followed by a verse catalog of such comforts as a country gentleman can enjoy, including, as a humorous if not witty touch, the only poet's dog to be mentioned by name in English poetry up to this time ("His Grange, or private wealth," H-724); next, "Good precepts, or counsell" (H-725), issued by an optimistic stoic, is followed—to conclude this series—by a cynical (or realistic) epigram announcing that "Money makes the mirth" (H-726). This kind of a verse cluster further broadens and deepens the reader's image of the *Hesperides* persona by, for example, counterbalancing the impression conveyed in the amatory lyrics of a Herrick who plays so many roles in the game of amour that he sometimes appears to be merely a fool for love.

In addition to its other functions, then, Herrick's wit of design contributes to the development of a "unifying personality" that lends coherence as well as human interest to a large and various poetic collection. Moreover, John L. Kimmey has suggested that this Herrickean personality is the protagonist of a kind of loose narrative about a poet's life, partly imaginative, partly autobiographical, that lends further unity to *Hesperides*'s almost infinite variety.[17] This "story" tells, among other things, of the quest for literary fame, of inconclusive affairs of the heart, of the search for personal contentment amid social and political upheaval, of attempting to deal with aging and death, and (in his devotional poems) of the vicissitudes of religious faith. Kimmey proposes that this sweeping though subtle design is accompanied by a gradual shift in the tone of Herrick's collection, from less to more serious, culminating in the sobriety and piety of *His Noble Numbers*. It is a pattern of greater scope even than the architectonics of *The Temple*, a pattern whose contradictions, ironies, self-referentiality, and dialectic, it can be argued, constitute a very special kind of seventeenth-century wit.

"A goodness of natural wit" was, for Ben Jonson, the first requisite of a "poet or maker"—along with *Exercitatio, Imitatio, Lectio* ("exactness of study and multiplicity of reading"), and "art." Wit (*Ingenium*) enables the poet, Jonson explains, "to pour out the treasure of his mind." Quoting Aristotle ("nullum magnum ingenium sine mixtura dementiae fuit"), he associates wit

---

17. "Robert Herrick's Persona," *Studies in Philology* 67 (1970): 221–36. On "unifying personality," see T. S. Eliot, *On Poetry and Poets* (New York: Farrar, Straus, and Cudahy, 1957), 43–44.

with "poetical rapture."[18] Would "Father Ben" have credited his "son" Herrick with *ingenium*? On the strength of some individual poems, the answer is, most probably, yes. And had Jonson lived to read *Hesperides*, who more than he, who himself wrestled with the problem of organizing one's *opera*, would have been more likely to appreciate the wit of that collection's design?

18. Jonson, "Timber, or Discoveries," in *Jonson*, ed. Donaldson, 584–86. Robert C. Evans's sense that wit for Jonson primarily meant a "capacity for intellectual creation" more than a "particular kind of verbal expression" (see his essay in this volume) lends support to my supposition.

Sharon Cadman Seelig

My Curious Hand or Eye

The Wit of Richard Lovelace

Richard Lovelace, as David Judkins reminds us, "is often considered the great lover of the Cavaliers. He does not display the libertinism of Carew or the cynicism of Suckling; instead, he is remembered for a romantic attitude toward ladies, love, and honor."[1] Because Lovelace's reputation is so well established—as the most graceful and idealistic articulator of the cavalier ideal, the poet who expresses the relationship between love and honor (most notably in "To Lucasta, Going to the Warres") and the paradox of physical imprisonment and spiritual liberty (most memorably in "To Althea, From Prison")—and perhaps because he seems to go so well with port and leather chairs and cigars—Lovelace has received little recent critical attention, certainly none that would challenge the conventional notion of gallant cavalier and witty lover. But the nature of cavalier as distinguished from metaphysical wit and the nature of the audience for that wit have been insufficiently examined. In this essay, I shall suggest that wit and our understanding of it are more deeply involved with issues of gender and audience than most descriptions of cavalier poetry have acknowledged.

In addressing what seems to me an imbalance in the critical view of Lovelace, I want at the outset to take note of the rather remarkable range of his verse, which extends from highly polished lyrics to the uneven production of the gentleman amateur, and which includes not only the better-known love lyrics in imitation of Donne, celebrations of the Petrarchan mistress, and

---

1. Judkins's statement prefaces the Lovelace section of his bibliography of the Cavalier poets in *English Literary Renaissance* 8 (1977): 249.

libertine verse but also satires, poems of praise, philosophical consolations, and translations. I do not hope here to account for the whole of this corpus, but rather to focus on the nature of Lovelace's wit, to show that it is not only a matter of quick turns of phrase, reinterpretation of situations, or intellectual domination, but of sexual mastery as well; and to suggest that, far from being superficial or merely verbal, Lovelace's wit seems to have its sources deep within his experience, both personal and political.

Manfred Weidhorn, in the most recent full-length study of Lovelace,[2] does note that Lovelace wrote a good deal of libertine as well as Petrarchan verse, but he fails to notice what I want to argue here—that in much of Lovelace's poetry, including his best-known verse, a dominant male figure controls, visually, verbally, or rhetorically, a female subject; and that what has been seen as wit, even as idealism, has much to do with control—both sexual and intellectual—expressed in sensuous and complex images. A careful reading of both lesser-known and well-known lyrics indicates that Lovelace is not simply the idealistic, gallant cavalier of the Dulwich portrait but the creator as well of poems in which a masculine figure envisions and controls a female subject, with hand or eye, metaphor or logic. Without discounting Lovelace's deliberate use of rhetorical strategy and far-fetched conceit, one must also acknowledge that these poems are more powerfully erotic than has heretofore been suggested, and that the wit that they so evidently display is achieved through sexual as well as intellectual dominance. Lovelace is not only more disturbing than we may have supposed (and in some ways more disturbing than the poets with whom he is usually associated) but also more versatile: in the sensuous, even shocking, images of Lovelace's poetry there are intriguing similarities, not only with the metaphysicals, whom he sometimes inadequately emulates, but also with that which is usually termed baroque and associated with Crashaw, a poet whom Lovelace knew from his days at the Charterhouse School. If Lovelace performed best in the subgenres for which he is usually remembered, he also wrote well in a surprising variety of forms, including poems that force us to confront sensuous images not as graceful compliment but as part of a complex rhetorical and psychological strategy.

The qualities I've been describing may be seen in "La Bella Bona Roba," which opens with a startling vision of woman as a purely physical object, not

---

2. *Richard Lovelace* (New York: Twayne, 1970).

merely in a sexual sense but as a configuration of contrasting colors and interesting textures:

> I cannot tell who loves the Skeleton
> Of a poor Marmoset, nought but boan, boan,
> Give me a nakednesse with her cloath's on.
>
> Such whose white-sattin upper coat of skin,
> Cut upon Velvet rich Incarnadin,
> Ha's yet a Body (and of Flesh) within.[3]

Both the opening reference to "a poor Marmoset" and the poem's very title designate a prostitute—in the one case by analogy with an inferior creature, a small monkey, in the other, by an identification of a woman with inanimate material substance ("bona roba" refers to things, goods, but also garments).[4] The woman is possessed (or rejected) according to how she is seen—and in this poem she is the object of a radical glance, a voyeuristic probing that not only cuts through clothing but also pierces flesh to the bone, revealing the strongly erotic contrast between red and white, velvet and satin, skin and blood. The poem expresses the speaker's preference for a woman, as it were, with a little meat on her bones, through a number of analogous metaphors of masculine control, intrusion, or incorporation: he is the huntsman, the husbandman, the voyeur; she is the doe to be shot with the speaker's shafts, the rib to be reincorporated into his flesh, the body stripped bare.

There is precedent in both sacred and secular verse for the representation of flesh as clothing: Suckling, in a striking image, speaks of "that fresh upper skin, / The gazers Joy, and sin," which covers the death's-head. Herrick, more conventionally, writes, "Give me my Mistresse, as she is, / Drest in her nak't simplicities," but he then goes on to distinguish between the two coverings: "For as my Heart, ene so mine Eye / Is wone with flesh, not *Drapery*."[5] But

---

3. The text quoted throughout is *The Poems of Richard Lovelace*, ed. C. H. Wilkinson (Oxford: Clarendon Press, 1930).

4. *Bona roba* was a common term for prostitute (*OED* and Wilkinson), but the identification of woman with her clothing, with something merely material, is also significant, analogous to the modern slang designation of a woman as a "skirt."

5. Suckling, "Farewel to Love"; Herrick, "Clothes do but cheat and cousen us"; the quotations are from *The Works of Sir John Suckling*, ed. Thomas Clayton (Oxford: Claren-

Lovelace's use of such imagery is peculiarly striking, indeed, probing: to see his poem simply as conventional is to ignore its discomfiting aspects, for much of what has been admired in the poem, although often attributed to other causes, derives from the frisson it occasions.[6] There is certainly wit here, in the sense that the poet sees and makes us see something—in fact someone— in a new way. But that "new perspective," concentrated in the opening stanzas of the poem, involves treating a woman, and her living body, as if she were a particularly striking still life.

Images and issues of control are found also in "Ellinda's Glove," in which the speaker, unable to address Ellinda herself directly, pays his respects to her glove:

> Thou snowy Farme with thy five Tenements!
>   Tell thy white Mistris here was one
>   That call'd to pay his dayly Rents:
> But she a gathering Flowr's and Hearts is gone,
> And thou left voyd to rude Possession.[7]

Several critical accounts of "Ellinda's Glove" suggest something special in the poem while missing its essence. Weidhorn calls it "a touchstone of taste," but his report of the critical history emphasizes decorous wit without danger or depth; he finds it a "lovely little poem" with a "playful tone."[8] In this poem of ostensible compliment the would-be lover places himself in a subordinate position (as "one / That call'd to pay his dayly Rents"). But in the rather strained conceits that follow another picture emerges: the glove, the pure and snowy white representative of its mistress/owner, supposedly dominant over the speaker, is so described and handled that the situation is reversed. An empty vessel normally filled by the woman's hand, the glove is in Ellinda's absence "left

don Press, 1971); and *The Poetical Works of Robert Herrick*, ed. L. C. Martin (Oxford: Clarendon Press, 1956).

6. Donald Davie points to the conventionality of both title and the skin-clothes imagery (*Scrutiny* 16 [1949]: 234–41); Marius Bewley (*Masks and Mirrors* [New York: Athenaeum, 1970], 55–58) finds the opening image "strange and personal" but reads this part of the poem as a memento mori, thus minimizing the sexual content of the poem.

7. Touchstone's parodic verse may serve as gloss for this passage: "If a hart do lack a hind, / Let him seek out Rosalind. / If the cat will after kind, / So be sure will Rosalind, / Wint'red garments must be lin'd, / So must slender Rosalind" (*As You Like It*, 3.2.101–6).

8. *Lovelace*, 88.

voyd to rude Possession": the speaker imagines a spatial intrusion that is repelled but that, in the very envisioning (and the clear sexual implications thereof), becomes thinkable and even likely:

> But grieve not pretty *Ermin* Cabinet,
>> Thy Alablaster Lady will come home;
>> If not, what Tenant can there fit
> The slender turnings of thy narrow Roome,
> But must ejected be by his owne dombe?

The poem concludes with a stanza in which, in the very act of expressing apparent subservience, the speaker lays claim to the glove in a way that also appropriates and includes its owner:

> Then give me leave to leave my Rent with thee;
>> Five kisses, one unto a place:
>> For though the *Lute's* too high for me;
> Yet Servants knowing Minikin nor Base,
> Are still allow'd to fiddle with the Case.

Of this remarkable ending Weidhorn says merely, "The kisses he leaves are proper to both his roles here, as lover and as tenant paying his rent. . . . Instead of randomness and extravagance, we see a nimble mind readily find-ing apt analogies in conveying what it feels like to be, on the one hand, disappointed by the absence of a lady one comes to visit and, on the other hand, cheered by the presence of an object associated with her." But the implications of "fiddle," which means not only to play aimlessly, to toy, but also to take liberties with a woman, are anything but decorous.[9] To be sure, the tone of much of the poem is delicate, almost strained in its compliment, but in the last lines, the lady—absent, apparently unapproachable, and revered— is in fact quite adequately represented by a physical object that may be touched, manipulated, and played upon.

9. Ibid., 88–89. On "fiddle," *OED* cites Chapman and Shirley, 1632. More recently, Gerald Hammond, *Fleeting Things: English Poets and Poems, 1616–1660* (Cambridge and London: Harvard University Press, 1990), goes to the opposite extreme, reducing Love-lace's sly innuendo to crass literalism: "Behind the coded kisses upon the sockets of the glove lies the message that he knows what his function is. She will not allow him to penetrate her, but may let him masturbate her, playing with the case rather than plucking the lute" (305).

A similar pattern obtains in "Her Muffe," in which, again in the last stanza, the speaker, who has depicted the article of clothing with great care and attention, makes clear that it is a representative of the woman—but in this case a less than satisfactory one, as he indicates his wish to move from the symbol to the thing itself. Within the rhetorical structure of "Her Muffe," the first three stanzas, and in a sense the fourth as well, propose a series of possible interpretations of Lucasta's wearing of the muff, all rejected in favor of a final, conclusive reading. As in "Ellinda's Glove," these successive possibilities have a commonality of meaning, rather insistently raising images of sensual passion even while denying their validity. The poem opens with a vivid contrast between Lucasta's "polish'd hands" and the "shagg'd furs" in which they are covered:

> 'Twas not for some calm blessing to receive,
> Thou didst thy polish'd hands in shagg'd furs weave;
>   It were no blessing thus obtain'd,
>   Thou rather would'st a curse have gain'd,
> Then let thy warm driven snow be ever stain'd.

This stanza seems to refer obliquely to the story of Jacob, who to receive from his father the blessing belonging to his brother Esau covered his smooth skin with the hair—the "shagg'd furs"—of a goat (see Gen. 27). Lovelace puts forth a series of potentially negative interpretations of Lucasta's actions, only to reject them, yet leaving disturbing suggestions behind, in the curious tension between the "calmness" of the blessing, which actually involved an act of deception, and the erotic and transgressive quality of the "shagg'd furs"— in the notion of Lucasta's being both pure as "driven snow" and "warm."

There follow further images of enclosure, of sexual intensity, and of heat that run counter to the apparently innocuous declarative statements of the apostrophe:

> Nor could your ten white Nuns so sin,
> That you should thus pennance them in
> Each in her course hair smock of Discipline.

Lovelace has it both ways: the speaker repeatedly asserts Lucasta's innocence, while the images of the poem suggest restlessness and ruthless violence. Not content with wearing an animal image on a crest, as a male hero would, this woman thrusts her hands into its body:

> Thou would'st thy hand should deeper pierce,
> And, in its softness rough, appear more fierce.

Yet, the speaker insists, Lucasta is guiltless; the animals thus violated are willing sacrifices, for

> destiny Decreed
> That Beasts to thee a sacrifice should bleed,
> And strip themselves to make you gay.

The final stanza, whose rhetorical function is to supply the true reading of Lucasta, both confirms and denies this sexually charged discourse: the first lines appear to move beyond the inadequate images used thus far (those that are only for inferior "Lay-Lovers," a clear allusion to the Donnean priesthood), but the final lines of the poem are of course even more explicitly and definitively sexual than what has gone before.

> This for Lay-Lovers, that must stand at dore,
> Salute the threshold, and admire no more:
> But I, in my Invention tough,
> Rate not this outward bliss enough,
> But still contemplate must the hidden Muffe.

In a turn of wit designed to gratify his male audience, in a gesture that the lady can hardly miss but dare not understand, the speaker claims for himself the dominance that had appeared to belong to Lucasta throughout much of the poem.

In each of these poems, then, with a wink and a witty turn, the speaker's apparent adulation of a woman or expression of inferiority to her leads to a reassertion of masculine control, to a new definition of the situation. These poetic situations seem to bear out Freud's notions of wit as requiring a third party, an audience, as well as his assertion of a connection between wit and sexual domination.[10] But why should one be surprised to find this pattern in Lovelace? Shared masculine attitudes are surely a given in libertine verse; and

10. *Jokes and Their Relation to the Unconscious*, trans. James Strachey (New York: Norton, 1963), chap. 3.

even in the most frequently taught lyrics in the canon, as students are quick to point out, sexual equality is hardly to be expected. We're accustomed to poems in which the lady, though apparently adored, never gets to speak (most obviously in Donne); poems in which male logic—or more often flagrant sophistry—asserts itself over female objection or action (as in "The Flea"); poems in which the lady is broken up into separable parts, humorously, as in Marvell's "To His Coy Mistress," or in the cannibals' admiration of Serena in the *Faerie Queene,* and more conventionally in the blazons of many another poet.[11] We're certainly used to poems in which the female body is the object of the male gaze and hand—most notably in Donne's elegies or Carew's "A Rapture"; we're used to the comic cynicism of Suckling's "Give me the woman here!" or Rochester's explicit identification of orifices.

But whereas the qualities I've mentioned in other poets are well known, in thinking of Lovelace one is more likely to think of the dominant lady than of the dominant lover—as in "Gratiana dauncing and singing," in which the graceful movement of a dancer creates a universe; or as in "Lucasta's World," in which in typical Petrarchan fashion the lady's sighs are "Cold as the breath of winds that blow / To silver shot descending snow," whose "frowne to Rubies frose / The blood boyl'd in our veines." Moreover it seems important that in Lovelace's case the issue of dominance is not simply rhetorical and obviously outrageous as in "The Flea," or flip and cynical as in the insouciant Suckling, or professionally scandalous as in the case of Rochester. It is in fact a significant, though little noticed, feature of Lovelace's poetry.

It might be objected that a logical implication of my argument is the view that all speech is controlling, that no matter what a man says he may be said to be enforcing his will on a woman. That is not what I wish to imply, although the case for speech as a means of control is eloquently made by Edgar in *King Lear:* "the worst is not, / So long as we can say, 'This is the worst'"; and by John Donne in "The Triple Foole": "Grief brought to numbers

---

11. *The Faerie Queene,* 6.8.37–45, and *Amoretti,* 76, 77, for example. See also Nancy J. Vickers, "Diana Described: Scattered Woman and Scattered Rhyme," *Critical Inquiry* 8 (1981): 265–79; Paula Johnson, "Carew's 'A Rapture': The Dynamics of Fantasy," *Studies in English Literature* 16 (1976): 145–55; as well as the important work of Laura Mulvey, "Visual Pleasure and Narrative Cinema," in her *Visual and Other Pleasures* (Bloomington: Indiana University Press, 1989), 14–26, and John Berger, *Ways of Seeing* (New York: Viking, 1973), 45–64.

cannot be so fierce, / For, he tames it, that fetters it in verse." One might suggest, in fact, that compliment itself presupposes that the person paying the compliment is in a position of power, able to bestow something on another. But I mean to argue that, in the poems considered, Lovelace uses speech quite deliberately and explicitly to control. And certainly the witty turns I've been describing go beyond compliment as tribute.

Nor are such patterns of dominance as I've been observing merely idiosyncratic features of lesser poems; they figure also, more subtly, in a number of Lovelace's best-known lyrics: in "To Amarantha, That she would dishevell her haire," the lady is invited to freedom from restrictions that have both physical and moral dimensions:

> Amarantha sweet and faire,
> Ah brade no more that shining haire!
> As my curious hand or eye,
> Hovering round thee let it flye.

The implications here are complex: Amarantha is being invited to abandon the rigidity represented by the braiding of her hair, which will now fly as free and unconfined as the wind.[12] But the extent of her liberty is in fact limited and prescribed by the speaker's vision and definition of her, by the way in which he sees and hence controls her, by his "curious hand or eye." He becomes both connoisseur and curator of her body. The second stanza of "To Amarantha" suggests even greater liberty—but then, paradoxically, both greater control and violation by a masculine figure.

> Let it flye as unconfin'd
> As it's calme Ravisher, the winde;
>   Who hath left his darling th' East,
> To wanton o're that spicie Neast.

Here the woman is a passive object of a male presence that is oxymoronically depicted both as highly active, sexually intrusive and as lovingly caressing, emotionally composed: she is ravished; he [the wind] is calm.

---

12. C. V. Wedgwood has connected this poem with the new fashion in women's hairstyles—away from the tight control associated, for example, with the coiffures of Queen Elizabeth's court to the looser, freer styles associated with France and Italy (noted by Weidhorn, *Lovelace*, 129, who also makes the connection with Propertius).

I do not want to engage here in a kind of crude misreading, a substitution of vehicle for tenor. This poem is not about violent possession or rape but about sensuousness. The wind, not the speaker, is a ravisher, and a "calm" one at that. If the poem begins with masculine control, its middle stanzas emphasize the power of the lady who can "shake [her] head and scatter day," and its later stanzas explicitly depict mutual sexual enjoyment. But the poem also depicts a male figure in intimate and controlling contact with a female body. Lovelace's images balance sexual force and playfulness, but the poem's initial appreciative metaphors are explicitly intrusive and dominating.

Sometimes, as we've seen, Lovelace uses a reversal of the power dynamic as a witty strategy of control; in other poems, as in "To Amarantha," Lovelace's treatment of the female figure seems the result as much of a general or habitual perception as of a witty ploy; occasionally, especially in his less-polished poems, one wonders how fully Lovelace controls the implications of his verse. But there is no doubt about the degree of rhetorical control in "To Lucasta, Going to the Warres," one of Lovelace's most accomplished poems, and one that reveals both habitual ways of seeing and rhetorical strategy. In this poem, the speaker defines not only himself, the relationship between his two vocations of love and war, but also the lady, creating for her a new creed that goes against her previous inclinations. The poem begins in response to what is evidently a complaint on the part of a female interlocutor; its strategy is to defeat her complaint and to redefine the relationship between love and war, man and woman—to explain that, in leaving this woman for the battle-field, he does her no injustice, that she in fact approves his choice. In wittily economical fashion, the first stanza states the lady's objection (in the process of implicit denial by the speaker): "Tell me not (Sweet) I am unkinde"; the second stanza acknowledges what may be said for her point of view: "True; a new Mistresse now I chase"; and the third stanza refutes her argument to his satisfaction and, as he assures her, to hers as well: "Yet this Inconstancy is such, / As you too shall adore." But this gracefully symmetrical arrangement also constitutes a series of controlling gestures toward Lucasta, who is literally bracketed as "(Sweet)" in stanza 1 and "(Deare)" in stanza 3, and so made to frame and accommodate the rival mistress of stanza 2.

Lucasta, as her name implies, is identified with chastity, with "the Nunnerie / Of thy chaste breast, and quiet minde," a locus that has both religious and sexual implications and from whose confines the speaker flies. The "new

Mistresse" that he now "chase[s]," namely military honor, is seen by the lady as a competing force but is defined by him as being altogether in harmony with his love for her. What is seen in the first stanza as being possibly perverse, unkind, perhaps unnatural, is in the final stanza defined as truest religion, truest faith, truest love and honor: "Yet this Inconstancy is such, / As you too shall adore."

One is always tempted to remember this poem, I think, as one in which the poet, as if this were Chrétien's *Erec and Enide,* defines the conditions under which he would be worthy of a lady's love, in the sense that his honor in war makes him more appealing in love.[13] In fact, the poem defines, brilliantly, the terms under which *he* will love the lady, so that both action and definition remain in his hands: "I could not love thee (Deare) so much, / Lov'd I not Honour more."

"To Lucasta, Going to the Warres" is clearly one of Lovelace's finest and most graceful poems, one in which he articulates the relationship between the cavalier's two chief occupations—love and war. It wittily forges a link between the faith of love and the faith of religion, first placing love and war in opposition and then forcefully uniting them in the final stanza. But the kind of praise this poem has received has generally failed to acknowledge that it achieves its effects by a sleight of hand: the poem uses a series of oppositions and tensions that appear absolute (love/war; honor/dishonor; fidelity/infidelity) but that are in fact subtly shifted (love/honor; war/dishonor), so that infidelity to Lucasta becomes fidelity, and love to the new mistress becomes highest truth and faithfulness. Thus Lovelace's act of definition is also an act of imposition, and the wit that invites admiration from one part of its audience— the reader, construed as male—also imposes itself on another—the lady to whom it is addressed. This is a poem in which love of woman is clearly subordinate to love of arms, indeed, in which the woman becomes lovable only insofar as she allows and accepts, even embraces, this set of priorities.

If "To Lucasta, Going to the Warres" is an exercise in witty control, a much more flagrant instance of sexual and rhetorical domination as the basis for wit is "The faire Begger." Despite its play with logical categories, the poem lacks

---

13. Weidhorn's description, *Lovelace,* 88, comes close to doing just that. Compare also Mark Van Doren's praise of the poem in his *Introduction to Poetry* (New York: Hill and Wang, 1966), 21–26.

the dazzling display of sophistic reasoning that one admires in "The Flea" or the wit and humor of Donne's Elegy 19. But precisely because its strategy is less brilliant and its execution less polished than the very best of Lovelace, the critical admiration it has received suggests that the definition of wit has been something other than purely intellectual.[14]

The poem has its antecedents in the European baroque; earlier examples of the motif of a beautiful woman clad in rags achieve one kind of wit by juxtaposing and contrasting the woman's beauty and her ragged clothing.[15] But in Lovelace's hands the real issue is not sensuous contrast but power; the woman's situation becomes the basis for a sophistic persuasion to love or, more precisely, to have sex.

> Comanding Asker, if it be
>   Pity that you faine would have,
> Then I turne Begger unto thee,
>   And aske the thing that thou dost crave;
> I will suffice thy hungry need
> So thou wilt but my Fancy feed.

The wit of this poem consists in turning the tables on the woman, redefining the categories of the situation, refiguring her as the dominant party and the speaker as her suppliant. But in fact power remains in the speaker's hands: it is he who possesses food and wealth, sexual and verbal dominance. The function of his attribution of power to the woman is to make her yield that supposed power to him: since, the argument goes, she possesses something that he desires, her fate is not so much in his hands as in her own.[16]

The speaker argues that although the woman looks poor—"In all ill yeares, wa'st ever knowne / On so much beauty such a dearth?"—she is richer than all that would adorn her, whether clothing or jewels. But her wealth is consistently defined in terms of male enjoyment: "Yet happy he that can but tast / This whiter skin who thirsty is"; she will manifest her beneficence and

14. Weidhorn, *Lovelace*, 110, finds it one of Lovelace's best lyrics.
15. M. J. O'Regan, "The Fair Beggar—Decline of a Baroque Theme," *Modern Language Review* 55 (1960): 186–99. O'Regan rejects the label *baroque* for this poem, finding it sensual and concrete rather than *precieux*, a decline from the earlier baroque renderings of this theme.
16. The argument, without the wit, figures in *Measure for Measure*.

love (or is it charity?) by giving "almes," by supplying his sexual need. The poem has been seen as a clever variation on a conventional topic, but it becomes something more in its intertwining of motifs of compliment with baser physical ones—he will feed on her, he will clothe her. In fact, both its wit and its disturbing quality derive from what is a rather uncertain movement between the Platonic and the sexual; it mingles claims of high-mindedness with intimidation, as in the speaker's assertion that his failure to supply the woman's need for food would be a lesser offense than her failure to feed what he variously calls "my Fancy" and "my minde." This poem juxtaposes the ostensible demonstration that she is in control of her own destiny with the supposed proof that his needs are greater and his desires higher than hers, and concludes with a threat of starvation and of universal opprobrium that at once undermines and drives home its argument:

> But Cruel, if thou dost deny
>   This necessary almes to me;
> What soft-soul'd man but with his Eye
>   And hand will hence be shut to thee?
> Since all must judge you more unkinde;
> I starve your Body, you my minde.

The reference to the shutting not only of the speaker's hand of supposed generosity but also of his eye shows the power of the male gaze on the female subject: a woman will be powerful or abused, sought after or neglected, according to how she is seen. Perhaps the true wit of the poem consists in attributing power to the woman while simultaneously demonstrating that the speaker—with his definitions, images, language, and logic—remains dominant.

How are we to read such a poem? And how shall we place it within Lovelace's work, within his period or ours? Clearly the poem goes beyond its baroque antecedents to create a quite different kind of wit. And clearly those critics who have praised that wit assume a shared understanding among readers. Quite aside from its obvious political incorrectness in today's terms, it is evident that the poem invites us to admire mental ingenuity but assumes that no woman reader will imagine a real situation, certainly not one that places her at a serious disadvantage. Although the speaker formally addresses a woman, he in fact plays to a particular kind of male audience, one that will find clever the assertion that the feeding of his "Fancy" (with implications of imagination and sexual desire) is a higher priority than the feeding of her "hungry need," one that relishes his promise of mutual satisfaction and his offer to furnish her wardrobe with his own body:

> Thou shalt be cloath'd above all prise,
>   If thou wilt promise me imbrac't;
> Wee'l ransack neither Chest or Shelfe,
>   I'll cover thee with mine owne selfe.

M. J. O'Regan sees in "The faire Begger" a decline from the baroque concentration on sensuous surface; but it seems to me that Lovelace retains a good deal of emphasis on that surface, spinning out a series of extravagant conceits without regard to emotional content, and so evoking an unexpectedly deep response, leading at least some of his modern readers to imagine a painful situation where he intends only sexual gamesmanship and the display of intellectual prowess.

The fully erotic, even perverse, implications of such images of dominance are seen in "A Guiltlesse Lady imprisoned; after penanced," in which Lovelace depicts a beautiful woman exposed to public humiliation for a sexual offense. The poem emphasizes the contrast between the punishment planned for this woman (barefoot, and dressed, as was common, in a white sheet)[17] and the adulation that she in fact receives:

> And as thy bare feet blesse the Way
>   The people doe not mock, but pray,
> And call thee as amas'd they run
>   Instead of prostitute, a Nun.

In a motif similar to that of "The faire Begger," Lovelace articulates the paradox that the woman, supposedly imprisoned by the jailer, in fact dominates him; but he also depicts in sensual terms the encounter between her wrists and their confining shackles in a way that suggests mutual enjoyment of her pain:

> The Gyves to Rase so smooth a skin,
> Are so unto themselves within,

---

17. Lawrence Stone, *The Family, Sex, and Marriage in England, 1500–1800* (New York: Harper and Row, 1979), 324, describes the punishment.

> But blest to kisse so fayre an Arme
> Haste to be happy with that harme.

> And play about thy wanton wrist
>   As if in them thou so wert drest;
> But if too rough, too hard they presse,
>   Oh they but Closely, closely kisse.

The explicit argument of this poem is that the lady, though imprisoned and shamed, is not only beautiful but also desirable; but the clear implication, which emerges in the opening stanza, is that she is the more enthralling because enthralled. She exists for the speaker in a tantalizing state between guilt and innocence, pain and pleasure; his use of the verb *enjoy* conveys not only her beauty but also his strongly sexual anticipation; despite the assertion of her sexual innocence, her wrist is described as "wanton," with the implication that she welcomes, even prompts, the speaker's sexual fantasies, drawing him on to delight in her subjugation:

> Heark Faire one how what e're here is
>   Doth laugh and sing at thy distresse;
> Not out of hate to thy reliefe,
>   But Joy t'enjoy thee, though in griefe.

That it is not simply the image but also Lovelace's treatment of it that is significant may be seen in Herrick's far lighter treatment of the motif of female imprisonment in "Upon a black Twist, rounding the Arme of the Countesse of Carlile":

> I saw about her spotlesse wrist,
> Of blackest silk, a curious twist;
> Which, circumvolving gently, there
> Enthrall'd her Arme, as Prisoner.

Unlike Lovelace, Herrick concludes not with male enjoyment of female captivity, but with a wish for his own imprisonment, as a means of getting closer to the lady:

> but if there be
> Such Freedome in Captivity;
> I beg of Love, that ever I
> May in like Chains of Darknesse lie.

Although I have been pointing out ways in which a modern reader may find it difficult to applaud Lovelace's cleverness, my discomfort is less with his poetic strategies than with more recent critics' assumptions about the universe of his readers. It seems to me that Lovelace aimed (if I may presume to judge) not at a tasteless sadomasochistic display, but at the witty demonstration of his abilities as a poet, using what seemed to him an interesting and paradoxical subject. Like many another Caroline poet, he uses extravagant conceits to show his verbal mastery and rhetorical skill. But what may have been Lovelace's lack of serious emotional involvement in his subject leads to a quite different effect on a modern reader. The powerful and disturbing quality of many of these poems is created by Lovelace's emphasis on the sensuous surface—the "white-sattin upper coat of skin" of "La Bella Bona Roba," the tasting of "This whiter skin who thirsty is" of "The faire Begger," and the erotic contrast between Lucasta's hands and the "shagg'd furs" of her muff, which implies also imprisonment and containment of sexual desire.

Although we have often compartmentalized the varieties of seventeenth-century wit into metaphysical, cavalier, and baroque, a number of Lovelace's poems in fact show striking similarities not only to Donne, whom he obviously imitated, but also to Crashaw and the baroque more generally. For like Crashaw, Lovelace sometimes focuses on the sensuous surface in a way that is inherently unstable, as his images hover in an area between sensuality and devotion; this is the case in poems like "Gratiana dauncing and singing," in which "The floore lay pav'd with broken hearts," and "A Guiltlesse Lady imprisoned." The kind of attention to the senses used by Crashaw to direct passion toward devotion—as in the "sweet and subtile pain" of a Saint Teresa—has a wholly secular purpose in "A loose Saraband," in which Cupid subjects the speaker's heart to a series of emblematic erotic torments:

> Then as a Top he sets it up,
>   And pitifully whips it;
> Sometimes he cloathes it gay and fine,
>   Then straight againe he strips it.

The experiences of the captive lover's heart partake both of medieval love allegory and of representations of the sufferings of Christ; in this case the pain can be eased only by Lucasta, who, after washing the wound with her tears,

> Then prest the *Narde* in ev'ry veine
>   Which from her kisses trilled;
> And with the balme heald all it's paine
>   That from her hand distilled.

The power of the woman here and the intensity of the speaker's experience are conveyed not merely by narrative but by strongly sensuous language ("trilled," "Narde," "balme," "paine") that links this poem with the overwhelming sensuousness of "Music's Duel."

Although not a poet of the stature of Donne or Crashaw, Lovelace was versatile enough to practice a variety of forms of wit, both the flip and the revealing, the controlled and the controlling; on occasion he imitated the metaphysical and indulged in the baroque. In this essay I've chosen to focus on a group of poems that depict imprisonment as sexually charged, that represent a female subject held by a controlling male gaze or defining conception, fixed by a glance or a metaphor. But these poems, though significant, are only part of a larger and extremely varied corpus, one in which Lovelace's fascination with power and imprisonment is manifested more generally, and which depicts a world in which the speaker is not always in control. In "To Althea, From Prison," for example, which is conventionally dated by Lovelace's confinement in the Gatehouse in 1642, it is the speaker himself who is imprisoned; while he distinguishes between the physical state of imprisonment and the state of moral freedom, he also finds himself sensuously entangled:

> When Love with unconfined wings
>   Hovers within my Gates;
> And my divine *Althea* brings
>   To whisper at the Grates:
> When I lye tangled in her haire,
>   And fetterd to her eye;
> The *Gods* that wanton in the Aire,
>   Know no such Liberty.

Lovelace, who depicts the erotic attraction of the "Guiltlesse Lady imprisoned," also represents with sympathy the confinement of the king—"the chain'd Prince," "the Royal Captive"—in terms that suggest pathos, dignity, and integrity, but also a certain erotic power. In "The Lady A. L.: My Asylum *in a great extremity*," Lovelace, using ironic language, makes the king's experience a metaphor for the speaker's own dread:

> With that delight the Royal Captiv's brought
> Before the Throne, to breath his farewell thought,
> To tel his last tale, and so end with it;
> Which gladly he esteemes a Benefit;
> . . . .
> With such a Joy came I to heare my Dombe,
> And haste the preparation of my Tombe.

But whereas the king is executed, the speaker is rescued by the powerful woman to whom the poem is addressed, becoming, in the final lines of the poem, her willing slave:

> In this, wilt an unthankful Office do:
> Or wilt I fling all at her feet I have?
> My Life, my Love, my very Soule a Slave?
> Tye my free Spirit onely unto her,
> And yeeld up my Affection Prisoner?

Lovelace's fascination with confinement, seen in male-female relations and in captive-captor relations, extends even to the plight of trapped insects and other confined small creatures, depicted in a series of emblematic poems— "A Fly caught in a Cobweb," "A Fly about a Glasse of Burnt Claret," "The Snayl," "The Falcon."

The dynamic of power and sexuality, as I've been arguing, is an important and too little noticed element in Lovelace's verse, but it is also part of a larger concern with the limitations of liberty widespread in his work. Without suggesting a single or simple biographical explanation, one might note that Lovelace had good reason to find such images powerfully expressive: he wrote "To Althea, From Prison" while himself confined; his very ardor in support of the king's cause, the boldness with which he presented the strongly pro-royalist Kentish petition to the House of Commons, led to his imprisonment in 1642; unmoved by his argument that "beeinge confined here in this Springe-tide of Action, . . . [your petitioner] is to his farther Greefe disabled from discharginge parte of that duetie, which he owes unto his Kinge and Countrie,"[18] the Commons, even after his release, did not permit him to join the king's forces. During much of the civil war, Lovelace was in Holland, doing what he could there for the Royalist cause; in 1648–1649 he was imprisoned for ten months, consequent to his taking part in an uprising in Kent. For all the confident expression of "To Lucasta, Going to the Warres," Lovelace in fact experienced relatively little control in his own life, losing even the family inheritance and dying in obscurity, if not in poverty. His ambiguously positive representation of imprisonment relates to Lois Potter's more general descrip- tion of the royalist "who represents himself as a helpless figure, a defeated cavalier, often a prisoner, who achieves a sense of freedom by voluntarily submitting himself to other kinds of passive experience."[19] Writing from prison, he refigures imprisonment as sexually charged; he exercises, as Donne would put it, "his masculine persuasive force" in verse.

The wit of Lovelace's poems, then, is not simply a matter of intellectual prowess, not simply an assertion of the transforming power of a controlling mind, but also a matter of domination, with sexual and psychological as well as intellectual dimensions. If Lovelace's wit has more to do with domination and less with gallantry than we have supposed, it also is less superficial, less merely imitative and casual, than his reputation might suggest. While Love- lace shares a good many subjects and motifs with other cavalier poets, the note he strikes is to be distinguished from Herrick's exuberant relish of detail, Carew's cool elegance and deliberate self-indulgence, or Suckling's impudent insouciance, and the subtle attention to control that we've seen in his poetry differs from the more open, more robust, or more obviously cynical views of Suckling, Herrick, Carew, or Rochester. Though distinct in its manifestations and often in its subject matter from the wit of Donne and Herbert, Lovelace's wit, like theirs, is not mere witticism but something more intimately con- nected with the poet's deeper concerns, with his ways of knowing and seeing the world. In trying to understand the wit of Richard Lovelace we are perhaps finally, if perplexingly, closer not only to the biblical use of the word *know*, with its sexual implications, but also to the Anglo-Saxon root of wit, *witan*,

18. Lovelace's petition to the House of Commons, quoted in Wilkinson, *Poems*, xxxviii.
19. *Secret Rites and Secret Writings: Royalist Literature, 1641–1660* (Cambridge: Cam- bridge University Press, 1989), 147. Potter also notes "the eroticism which figures so strangely in the literary treatment of Charles I . . . and the nervousness about femaleness which is the other side of the royalist taste for romance" (211).

"to know" in its wider sense. To acknowledge the more serious as well as the more sobering dimensions of Lovelace's poetry is to begin to consider what is at stake in cavalier wit, even in the work of its supposedly most idealistic practitioner, and to begin to construct a view of Lovelace more adequate to the complexity of his poetry.

Lorraine Roberts

The "Truewit" of Crashaw's Poetry

Few poets demonstrate so well the changing definitions of *wit* from the seventeenth century to the present as does Richard Crashaw. The fundamental degeneration of meaning that the word underwent—from wit as wisdom or understanding to wit as ingenuity, mere "fancy," or even speciousness—while not reflected in Crashaw's poetry itself, has certainly been evident in the critical commentary on it through the centuries. In his own day Crashaw was thought of as a wit, a term often used to denote a poet in his role as maker and craftsman and not meant in a pejorative sense.[1] But later, in the second half of the seventeenth century, Crashaw's poetry, like that of all the other metaphysical poets, suffered a decline, being thought not wisdom, but mere ingenuity; and this opinion remained strong until the 1920s, when Grierson and Eliot restored metaphysical poetry to the canon. The attention that they and later critics gave to isolating and defining the wit of the metaphysical conceit, indeed in equating wit with conceit, has resulted—in Crashaw's case in particular—in the unfortunate neglect of the wit involved in the structure and concept that underlie each of his poems. Much attention has been given to surface features such as imagery and the use of rhetorical devices, but little or none to the way Crashaw structures his poems around a central idea. Indeed, the received opinion has been that structure is not Crashaw's strength

---

1. See, for example, Henry B[elasyse], "An English Traveler's First Curiousity: or The Knowledge of his owne Countrey (April 1657)," in Historical Manuscripts Commission, *Report of Manuscripts in Various Collections* (London: Printed for Her Majesty's Stationery Office by Mackie and Co., 1903), 2:193–204, who lists Crashaw along with Jonson, Shakespeare, Donne, and others as examples of the "good witts in England" (p. 194).

as a poet, that it is, in fact, sacrificed to a pyrotechnics of ingenious imagery, rhetoric, and metrics.

Crashaw's use of the term *wit* in his own poetry (eight times in his English poems) seems to indicate that to him the word meant something much more substantive than ingenuity or fancy. In all instances he seems to have intended the fifth definition of the word as listed in the 1989 second edition of the *OED*, that is, a "[g]ood or great mental capacity; intellectual ability; genius, talent, cleverness; mental quickness or sharpness, acumen"; or the sixth, "Wisdom, good judgement, discretion, prudence." One of the most arresting and paradoxical uses of the word occurs in the Nativity Hymn, in which Crashaw praises the shepherds to whom Christ first revealed himself as "home-spun things: / Whose Wealth's their flock; whose witt, to be / Well read in their simplicity" (ll. 94–96).[2] Probably the most famous line in all Crashaw's poetry—one that he used twice—is the likewise paradoxical one from stanza 15 of "The Weeper," in which the speaker proclaims dramatically and thematically, "O wit of love! that thus could place / Fountain and Garden in one Face" (ll. 5–6). The climax of "To the Name Above Every Name" repeats this famous paradox: "It was the witt of love o'reflowd the Bounds / Of WRATH, and made thee way through All Those WOUNDS" (ll. 223–24). Undoubtedly Crashaw would have agreed with Emanuele Tesauro that human wit is a "vestige of the Deity in the human mind" and that the role of the poet is to "discover" this wit in Scripture and in Nature. Or he might have agreed with Michelangelo that

> [not] even the best of artists has any conception
> that a single marble block does not contain
> within its excess, and *that* is only attained
> by the hand that obeys the intellect.[3]

Crashaw's "A Hymn to the Name and Honor of the Admirable Sainte Teresa" explicitly calls attention to this symbiotic relationship of divine and human wit in its praise of Teresa's writings:

2. All quotations from Crashaw's poetry are from *The Complete Poetry of Richard Crashaw*, ed. George Walton Williams (Garden City, N.Y.: Anchor Books Doubleday, 1970).
3. Tesauro, *Il Cannochiale Aristotelico*, 1654, quoted in S. L. Bethell, "The Nature of Metaphysical Wit," in *Discussions of John Donne*, ed. Frank Kermode (Boston: Heath, 1962), 140–41; no. 151 in James M. Saslow, *The Poetry of Michelangelo: An Annotated Translation* (New Haven: Yale University Press, 1991), 302.

Those rare WORKES where thou shalt leave writt
Love's noble history, with witt
Taught thee by none but him.

(ll. 155–57)[4]

Crashaw's meaning of the term *wit*, deduced by the reader from his poetry, is not the meaning that has generally been ascribed to his wit since the second half of the seventeenth century. It is not his genius, but his ingenuity that has been noted, especially in relation to his use of conceits. Historically, the term *wit* narrowed in meaning, especially in relation to the metaphysical poets; it became, generally speaking, equated with the term *conceit,* and not with the more encompassing faculty of mental powers of understanding and wisdom.[5] Through time one sees this narrowing in the criticism on the metaphysical poets, Crashaw included. In his own century, the few who commented on Crashaw's poetry were appreciative of it, even singling out his capacity for wit, presumably his understanding and wisdom; later, beginning with Pope's assessment of 1710 in which he disapproved of Crashaw's "forc'd and inextricable conceits," Crashaw's verse declined in estimation, partly because of its wit, or more precisely its conceits. Dr. Johnson in the eighteenth century did not speak specifically of Crashaw in his evaluation of metaphysical conceits (although he quoted him 103 times in his *Dictionary*),[6]

---

4. Crashaw's other uses of the word *wit* are in *Sospetto d'Herode,* st. 35, l. 1, in which Satan exhorts his troops to use whatever means they can to overcome God "if usuall wit, and strength will doe no good"; in the English epigram "Neither durst any man from that Day aske him any more Questions," in which the persona contrasts Christ's wisdom with the "Blacke wit" (l. 2) of those who tried to ensnare Him; in "The Hymn" of the Third Hour of the "Office of the Holy Crosse," in which, after reflecting on the crowd's choice of Barabbas over Christ, the persona says, "But there is witt in wrath, and they will try / A HAIL more cruell then their crucify" (ll. 5–6); and in the Epiphany Hymn, in which two of the three speakers dismiss the false gods, calling them "(1.) Proud sons of death! that durst compell / Heav'n it self to find them hell; / (2.) And by strange witt of madnes wrest / From this world's EAST the other's WEST" (ll. 109–12).

5. In a review of Hazlitt's edition of Lovelace (*North American Review* 99 [1864]: 336), James Russell Lowell, speaking briefly of Crashaw and other metaphysical poets, said "conceit means wit; they could carve the merest cherrystone of thought in the quaintest and delicatest fashion."

6. Pope, letter to Henry Cromwell, December 17, 1710, in *Letters of Mr. Pope, and Several Eminent Persons. In the Years 1705, &c. to 1717* (London: J. Roberts, 1735), 147; For Johnson's *Dictionary* (New York: AMS Press, 1967), see entries 81 and 756 in John R. Roberts,

but by the mid-nineteenth century those who wrote on Crashaw tended to focus on his conceits and to isolate them from the structural and conceptual wit that is their foundation.

Crashavian conceits of wounds, tears, nests, breasts, sucking, and bleeding in reference to religious subjects are shocking to readers if they are divorced from the symbolic Christian tradition that invests them with meaning. Yet even some readers who are aware of the symbolic system cast an unsympathetic eye toward Crashaw's mingling of the sacred and profane and tend to feel that the poet's judgment has given way to ingenuity or even bad taste. It is difficult for some readers to believe that Crashaw, whose education at Cambridge was classical and scriptural, is one of the most intellectual of poets, whose exercise of wit functions on the level of wisdom as well as that of cleverness. Crashaw's methods of revision and his art of fusing a variety of traditions at one time—emblematic, liturgical, classical, meditative—demonstrate that his wit was exercised not just on surface features such as images and rhetorical devices but on structural features such as concept and form as well in order to highlight the major subject and theme of almost all his sacred poetry—the Incarnation and its meaning in human history. As noted, too often discussions of wit in seventeenth-century poetry have focused on surface manifestation—the conceit and image—and have ignored the underlying structure that is a product of wit as well. Indeed, the word *conceit* does not apply only to image, but has its roots in the concept *idea;* thus it is appropriate to emphasize that the wit of a poem may reside not just in its surface images but in its structure as well, in its subtle unveiling of a theme.

It is instructive to look briefly at this problem of surface versus structural wit as it related to an artist in other media to whom Crashaw is often linked—Gianlorenzo Bernini. Like Crashaw, Bernini has often been criticized for having "a creative fantasy run amok." But as Rudolf Wittkower reminds us, Bernini subscribed to the humanistic theory of art, which, allying the sister arts of poetry and painting/sculpture, believed a work of art must be controlled by a literary theme, or *concetto.* In this theory the *concetto,* while perhaps ingenious and even awe-inspiring, was never simply decoration. One might be impressed by the surface techniques of the drapery folds of Bernini's

Richard Crashaw: An Annotated Bibliography of Criticism, 1632–1980 (Columbia: University of Missouri Press, 1985).

The Ecstasy of St. Teresa (1645–1652, Rome, Santa Maria della Vittoria, Cornaro Chapel), a surface technique that moves the emotions, but the sculptural group and its surroundings are fundamentally controlled by an intellectual idea. The same is true of Crashaw's poetry and can be demonstrated by aligning Crashaw's "The Flaming Heart" with Bernini's Saint Teresa; indeed, Howard Hibbard thought that the conclusion of "The Flaming Heart" "describes the state Bernini desired to create in the mind of the beholder better than any other English poem" and that "it may be useful to approach [Bernini's] Ecstasy of St. Teresa through Crashaw."[7] The conclusion he is referring to is the one praised by critics from Coleridge to the present, but which has nevertheless been seen as an "ill-welded fragment" to the poem proper (partly because it was added later).[8] Yet there is an idea or concetto that informs this fragment and its relationship to the poem as a whole, as there is to Bernini's famous group. In other words, structural wit underlies Crashaw's poem.

Just as Bernini's sculpture of saint and seraphim needs to be seen in the grand idea of its entire space, Crashaw's twenty-four concluding lines need to be seen in the context of the redrawn "painting poem." Alone, Bernini's duo of seraphim and saint capture one dramatic moment of ecstasy, but placed above the communion altar—whose floor symbolizes the grave, whose dome symbolizes resurrection, and whose "theater" of spectators wondering about the mystery represents all earthly viewers of the union of God and human person—the overall concetto unfolds the meaning of a Christian life from cradle to grave to resurrection. These intertwined baroque perspectives are present in "The Flaming Heart" as well, because Teresa, as represented in her Vida and her ecstasy, along with the poet as witness, must be put in their context or niche as well.

Crashaw's poem begins, of course, as "advice to the painter," a type of address deriving from Anacreon; the advice offered is that the painter needs to transpose angel and saint because of his anemic presentation of the latter,

7. Wittkower, Art and Architecture in Italy, 1600–1750, 3d rev. ed. (Baltimore: Penguin, 1973), 170, 157–60; Hibbard, Bernini (Baltimore: Penguin, 1965), 241.

8. Coleridge, "Lecture XI, 8 March 1819," in The Philosophical Lectures of Samuel Taylor Coleridge, ed. Kathleen Coburn (London: Pilot Press, 1949), 312–38; for the present, see Joseph H. Summers, The Heirs of Donne and Jonson (New York: Oxford University Press, 1970), 114; Mario Praz, The Flaming Heart (Garden City, N.Y.: Anchor Books, 1958), 261–62.

who in reality should be presented as more seraphic than the angel because of her special flaming dart—her *Vida,* which has inflamed the hearts of all who have read it. While the controlling idea of this poem would appear to be hagiography and little more, ultimately it is a praise of the love of God, as all Crashaw's poems are. His concluding twenty-four-line litany is not just a praise of Teresa, but a supplication that Teresa teach him how to love God to such an extent that he will be dead to self and sin and exist only in a state of ecstasy such as that recorded by Teresa. The role of Teresa in this poem is the twofold role intended for saints—that is, that they be not only models worthy of imitation but also intercessors between the sinner and God. Thus the concluding litany of "The Flaming Heart" is not an "ill-welded fragment," but a means to unite not only saint, poet, and reader, but all three with God. It paradoxically transforms the poem from hagiography to meditation and liturgy; it completes structure and theme.

But one poem cannot be the burden of the argument that the true wit of Crashaw's poetry consists of more than its surface images. One has only to look at the very appealing "Hymn in the Holy Nativity" to find further evidence of Crashaw's structural and thematic wit. There are approximately twenty-eight references to eyes or to the act of seeing in the 108 lines of the poem, certainly appropriate when the hymn of praise by the shepherds results from God's manifestation to them in the form of the Infant Jesus, who is called "the fairer ey" in the 1648 revision of the poem (l. 7). Through a series of paradoxes and antitheses, the world of the "fairer ey," while superior, will not supplant that of the natural sun and "mortall Sight" (l. 12), but will *join* it by Christ's "all-embracing birth" (l. 83). Other revisions from the 1646 to the 1648 version further testify to Crashaw's interest in making his theme evident through structure. Such was the conclusion of Kerby Neill after a careful examination of the two versions, and what should be emphasized is his conclusion that the revised version has an improved "conceptual unity" and a change of focus—from Virgin to Christ.[9] I have claimed that Christ is almost always the focus of Crashaw's sacred poetry; that is true even of those poems that seem to be concerned primarily with saints such as Teresa and even Mary Magdalen, as I hope to demonstrate. But while Christ is the focus, he is not the end of the action of these poems, for they almost always call for the liturgical or devotional

---

9. "Structure and Symbol in Crashaw's 'Hymn in the Nativity,'" *PMLA* 63 (1948): 101–13.

response of self-offering to God. This is true of the end of the Nativity poem, where the shepherds, privileged by sight of the Lamb, say

> To THEE, meek Majesty! soft KING
> Of simple GRACES and sweet LOVES.
> Each of us his lamb will bring
> Each his pair of sylver Doves;
> Till burnt at last in fire of Thy fair eyes,
> Our selves become our own best SACRIFICE.
>
> (ll. 103–8)

It is also true of "The Flaming Heart":

> By all of HIM we have in THEE;
> Leave nothing of my SELF in me.
> Let me so read thy life, that I
> Unto all life of mine may dy.
>
> (ll. 105–8)

And it is likewise true of "The Weeper." The mingling of different times and different places of poem and reader, of the created world of art and the external world of reality, is liturgical as well as baroque.

But it is easy to appreciate the structural wit of the Nativity Hymn. What about the most infamous of ingenious poems, however, Crashaw's "The Weeper"? Can a defense of it be made on the grounds that a structural wit underlies it as well?

Crashaw's use of wounds, tears, and bleeding hearts, which are the elements of the opening distich of "The Weeper," has, in the past decade, been psychoanalyzed, even potentially deconstructed into meaningless signifiers; but these reductionisms of Crashaw's conceits are really no more harsh than the ridicule that the poem has been subjected to from the eighteenth century onward. There have been, on the other hand, a few valiant efforts to defend the poem, and on more grounds than its use of images. For example, there have been conscientious attempts to elicit dramatic movement and structure in the poem, to counter Praz's contention that neither movement nor structure exists in what he calls this "rosary of epigrams or madrigals."[10] Nevertheless, these attempts have not been wholly successful, for to most contempo-

---

10. Praz, *Flaming Heart*, 218–19; see Stephen Manning, "The Meaning of 'The Weeper,'" *ELH* 22 (1955): 34–47, and Paul A. Parrish, "Crashaw's Two Weepers," *Concerning Poetry* 10.2 (1977): 47–59.

rary readers the poem may have some excellent lines, but the overall effect is like Bernini's "creative fantasy run amok," an effect that obscures coherent meaning. Such is the judgment of one recent critic, who contends that "the poem is about tears *and nothing else*. . . . Mary Magdalene as the repentant sinner has completely disappeared from this poem. There is no exploration of her emotions, of her relationship with Jesus, of the nature of repentance: All this has yielded to a series of brilliant conceits about weeping."[11]

While it is true that the person of Mary Magdalen is not present in the poem except as addressee (in stanzas 28 and 29 the tears are distilled and addressed directly, and then they answer in stanzas 30 and 31), and while it is also true that there is no exploration of her emotions or her biography as sinner, the poem is not just "about tears, *and nothing else.*" Indeed, implied in the poem are the nature of repentance and, even more important, the sinner's relationship with Christ. There is, in other words, a *concetto* that underlies the "series of brilliant conceits about weeping."

The *concetto* of "The Weeper" is, ultimately, the *concetto* of most of Crashaw's major religious verse—"the wit of love," the "Truewit" of Crashaw's poetry, Christ and his "conspiracy" of love with human persons. This idea is not explicitly stated in "The Weeper" but infused in the abundant paradoxes and antitheses that are a compression of the ancient Christian tradition of the "wound of love" that informs the poem—a tradition that began with Origen in the second and third centuries A.D. and remained well known in the century during which Crashaw was writing, although certainly less so in our own. The concept of *conspiring*, which provides the structural wit that underlies the varieties of paradoxical and antithetical images, appears in the opening line of the distich:

> Loe where a WOUNDED HEART with Bleeding EYES conspire.
> Is she a FLAMING Fountain, or a Weeping fire?

The emblem that accompanies the poem of Magdalen's weeping eyes and pierced and bleeding heart likewise serves to figure forth the concept of conspiracy between Christ's love that wounds and the sinner's contrition that heals. This concept of conspiracy is present in other poems of Crashaw's, such

11. Laurence Lerner, "Poetry as the Play of Signifiers," *Essays in Criticism* 35 (1985): 240–42.

as the Epiphany Hymn, although the terms are not the same. Toward the end of the hymn, the chorus, addressing the eyes of Christ, seeks a union, a "commerce" between heaven and earth:

> Maintaining t'wixt thy world and ours
> A commerce of contrary powres,
> A mutuall trade
> 'Twixt sun and SHADE,
> By confederat BLACK and WHITE
> Borrowing day and lending night.
>   (ll. 213–18)

The image in the distich of conspiring flame and flood is not lost through the course of "The Weeper": Crashaw is obviously relying on etymological definitions of *conspire* ("to breathe together, to agree in thought, to unite") to provide the key to reconciling the states of contrition and redemption. The heart wounded by God's love produces tears of repentance that lead ultimately to joy and union with Christ. That is what we see in the figure of the crowned Queen of Sorrow of stanza 7, whose contrition and love—which have been inspired by Christ—have led to her enthronement in heaven.

The motto and drawing that were added to the 1648 version of the poem are more than surface decorations. Structurally, they invite consideration of the poem as emblem, that is, the epigrammatic wit of the motto and the elements of the drawing need the longer poem to reveal their full meaning. Further, the iconic presentation of Mary Magdalen suggests it is not her biography that the poem elucidates but what she represents, the nature of the relationship between sinner and redeemer. The motto and emblem establish the context of Mary Magdalen's tears—her heart has been wounded by God's love, and that wound has led to tears, first of contrition, but ultimately of reciprocal love for the sacrifice shown by Christ for sinners. This point bears repeating. The tears of Magdalen are not the same tears as those of sixteenth-century Magdalen poems. Crashaw was given to an emphasis not on the state of contrition but on its aftermath—the joy that arises from a recognition of God's love for humanity in general and for individuals like Magdalen in particular.

This wound of love motif is a tradition as old as the Song of Songs, and its special relationship with Mary Magdalen goes back to Origen and continues on in medieval and sixteenth-century liturgical hymns. Robert Bellarmine, for example, composed the following hymn for the July 22 feast day of Mary Magdalen:

> Source and giver of heavenly light, with a glance
> You lit a fire of love in Magdalen and thawed the
> icy coldness of her heart. Wounded by love of you,
> she ran to anoint Your sacred feet, wash them with
> her tears.[12]

In the seventeenth century, devotional works such as Saint Francis de Sales's *Treatise on the Love of God* continued to use the theme that "Love wounds the heart." Certainly many of the traditional antitheses and paradoxes of this theme are present in Crashaw's poem, along with a richness of additional imagery, such as the classical imagery noted by Stella Revard.[13] But the controlling idea of all the antitheses and paradoxes is that there is a conspiracy between these presumed opposites and what they symbolize—of eyes and heart, of wounds and tears, of fire and fountain, of fountain and garden, of heaven and earth, of contrition and redemption—a conspiracy that unites sinner and redeemer, Church and Christ. The tears of the emblematic Mary Magdalen embody the proper relationship between Christ and human beings: "All places, Times, and objects be / Thy teare's sweet opportunity" (stanza 22, ll. 5–6).

Early in the poem the reader is aware that the tears of Magdalen are supernatural rather than natural, for in stanza 2 her eyes are equated with heaven and her tears with stars that only appear to rain down on earth, because they are really too precious for the dust. Instead, their movement is upward, where they serve to instruct us about the Waters of Heaven (stanza 4). It is not nature that teaches us contrition, but the crowned Queen of Sorrow,

---

12. *Origen, the Song of Songs, Commentary and Homilies*, trans. R. P. Lawson, no. 26, in *Ancient Christian Writers: The Works of the Fathers in Translation*, ed. Johannes Quaster and Joseph C. Plumpe (Westminster, Md.: Newman Press, 1957), 284; Bellarmine, no. 125 in *Hymns of the Roman Liturgy*, ed. Rev. Joseph Connelly (Westminster, Md.: Newman Press, 1957), 214; see also Joseph Szoverffy, "'Peccatrix Quondam Femina': A Survey of the Mary Magdalen Hymns," *Tradition* 19 (1963): 79–146.

13. *Treatise on the Love of God*, trans. Vincent Kerns (Westminster, Md.: Newman Press, 1962), book 6, chap. 13, pp. 253–56; Revard, "Crashaw and the Diva: The Tradition of the Neo-Latin Hymn to the Goddess," in *New Perspectives on the Life and Art of Richard Crashaw*, ed. John R. Roberts (Columbia: University of Missouri Press, 1990), 80–98.

that model of "Sweetnesse so sad, sadnesse so sweet" (stanza 6, l. 6). Nature
has its tears as well:

> Such the maiden gemme
> By the purpling vine put on,
> Peeps from her parent stemme
> And blushes at the bridegroome sun.

But again this natural bride and bridegroom are outdone by

> This watry Blossom of thy eyn, [which]
> Ripe, will make the richer wine.

This stanza (11) puts the poem on a liturgical foundation at the same time that
it uses the terms of the Song of Songs. Continuing the bride/bridegroom
motif, the next stanza alludes to the miracle at Cana, but the setting is
heaven.

The gold and silver, April and May, cheeks and eyes, fountain and garden
of the next three stanzas are contrarieties that find their union in the "wit of
love" of stanza 15. Stanza 18 indicates to us that the lamb had wounded the
heart of Magdalen, and as his chosen one she had followed him—unfortunately
to many readers—as "two faithfull fountaines; / Two walking baths; two
weeping motions; / Portable, and compendious oceans" (stanza 19, ll. 4–6).

Stanza 21 changes our focus from Mary Magdalen to Christ the King—
"Who calls't his Crown to be call'd thine" (l. 2)—and the following five
stanzas refer to the timelessness of the tears. In stanzas 28 and 29, the tears
themselves are questioned about their destination, and their answer is the
concluding two stanzas of the poem, which end, "We goe to meet / A worthy
object, our lord's FEET." The up-and-down movement throughout the poem
establishes a congress between heaven and earth, and that movement is
paradoxically reflected in these last lines. Are these the feet of Christ on
earth, at the moment of Crucifixion? Or are these the feet of the risen Christ,
who has ascended to heaven and is followed by the Queen of Sorrow? Of
course they are both, uniting time and space in a manner dear to the heart of
all baroque artists, and no less so to Crashaw. There is a conspiracy between
heaven and earth in "The Weeper" that is meant to serve as a model for the
proper relationship of sinner on earth and redeemer in heaven. The "wit of

love" is the basis of that relationship, that conspiracy; it is likewise the structural wit or the *concetto* of the poem.

Thus, the wit of Crashaw's poetry consists not just in the ingenious use of image, metaphor, emblem, paradox, epigram, or other rhetorical or poetic devices; one can see that it is all these—but as they are controlled by an ultimate theme in a coherent structure. In all Crashaw's poetry, wit is meant to manifest the "Truewit" of God—Christ and his love of mankind.

The argument on behalf of structural wit is important for an appreciation of what Crashaw intended to do with and through his poetry, for the *concetto* beneath his use of images is sometimes lost on contemporary readers. Crashaw obviously intended at times to shock his readers through some of his conceits, but he did not intend the shock for its own sake; rather, he intended to force the reader into seeking the fundamental truth about the "conspiracy" of the profane and sacred, of the created to the creator. The wit of the poet in rendering this truth can also be seen as a conspiracy between ingenuity and wisdom, fancy and judgment, surface devices and structural concept.

W. A. Sessions

Marvell's Mower

The Wit of Survival

I

Andrew Marvell stands at a point of definition for any theory of wit in the twentieth century.[1] The reason is that Eliot's essay on him (actually a book review) almost seventy-five years ago became itself a major source of wit definition (and controversy) for the rest of the century. Resurrecting Marvell after more than two centuries of obscurity into the forefront of English poets, Eliot proceeded, in a process Frank Kermode has outlined, to give his own theory of wit, sub specie Metaphysical Poets and embodied in the texts of Andrew Marvell: "tough reasonableness beneath the slight lyric grace" dialectically framed within a progression of history in which Marvell, "more a man of the century than a Puritan," spoke "more clearly and unequivocally with the voice of his literary age" than Milton. The historical process of textuality that for Kermode provided the framing of a classic also provided Eliot with his own twentieth-century historicizing. In this essay (and elsewhere) Eliot has certain cultural notions that inscribe Marvell as ideal poet in the midst of social and political breakdown. Within a text of dialectical wit "more Latin, more refined, than anything that succeeded it," the poet can

1. The proof lies in such a comprehensive series of studies as *On the Celebrated and Neglected Poems of Andrew Marvell*, ed. Claude J. Summers and Ted-Larry Pebworth (Columbia: University of Missouri, 1992). Although the focus of that volume is not on wit per se, the complexity of Marvell's dialectical inscriptions is shown in essay after essay. My own study builds on that collection by emphasizing, on a smaller canvas, the relationships of history and text in a way unexamined there.

balance the tensions of his time, notably those of "the great crisis of English civilization" embodied in Marvell's Horatian Ode, the English Revolution prototypic of the modern world. Such wit "involves, probably, a recognition, implicit in the expression of every experience, of other kinds of experience which are possible" so that the maker of such a concentrated dialectical text becomes a kind of cultural hero. Marvell thus inscribes another version of Eliot's Vergilian poet maker, and Eliot's critical focus on "wit's internal equilibrium" can be said to have determined a great deal of later criticism that sees Marvell's poetry operating in terms of crisis.[2]

The essay that follows starts at this same point: Marvell's texts are cultural inscriptions whose dialectical forms present readers with the healing processes necessary for entering history or at least the making of history. I want to argue that, although Eliot's terms may be impossible to recover, the dialectic of wit he suggested can be understood as a theory of cultural action in Marvell. The counterbalances Marvell develops in his texts operate as a formal cathartic means of self-historicizing for reader and audience, a kind of mask put on to prepare the reader for entry (or reentry) into time and history, the clearly marked process, for example, of a poem such as "The Garden." Although this dialectic behind Marvell's ritualizing has been perceived as a purifying process by important psychoanalytic studies, not least that of Jim Swan on the Mower poems or the more comprehensive study by Anna K. Nardo, I shall work from the texts themselves, framing my arguments about this dialectic of wit by a process Gérard Genette calls "transtextualité" or "the textual transcendence of the text," the process by which a specific text arises from transcendent categories like those of discourse or genre.[3] Specifically, I examine the recovery by

---

2. Eliot's essay on Marvell is in his *Selected Essays: New Edition* (New York: Harcourt, Brace and Co., 1950), 251–63, with quotations here from 252, 253, 260, 262, 263. For Frank Kermode's development of Eliot's ideas see *The Classic: Literary Images of Permanence and Change* (Cambridge: Harvard University Press, 1983), esp. 63ff. For the social and political inscriptions Marvell was clearly intending for his Horatian Ode, see Joseph Mazzeo, "Cromwell as Machiavellian Prince in Marvell's 'An Horatian Ode,'" in his *Renaissance and Seventeenth-Century Studies* (New York: Pantheon Books, 1967), 166–82.

3. Swan, "History, Pastoral and Desire: Andrew Marvell's Mower Poems," *International Review of Psychoanalysis* 3 (1976): 193–202; Nardo, *The Ludic Self in Seventeenth-Century English Literature* (Albany: State University of New York, 1991), esp. chap. 6. At the end of this chapter Nardo turns to the inscribing of history through the play motifs of Marvell's text and arrives at many of the same conclusions I have derived from a study of transtex-

Marvell of an original dialectic he found in earlier literary texts, not least those of Vergil (and in his time, Bacon). Although the main focus of my argument will be on the Mower poems themselves, I also deal, but within obvious limits, with the more widely staged (and anthologized) Marvell texts.

What Eliot found, in the first important definition of wit in the twentieth century, was a dialectical poetry for which he could use terms like *wit, reason,* and *urbanity* and utilize Marvell as a signifier for them. For Eliot, not answers but questions were posed in this dialectic of wit whose inscriptions differed from those of Marvell's friend and Eliot's bête noir, the more monologic Milton. Here was language that appeared positively to deflect rigid ideology, counterpointing structures of belief written by a poet who acknowledged in *The Rehearsal Tranpros'd* that he did indeed often write "betwixt jest and earnest."[4] For such an ironic signifier, the very posing of the questions would appear to constitute the poetic act and, with it, the moral stance that Renaissance humanist audiences expected of even the most ironic poetry.

As Eliot knew, Marvell's solutions and closures for his texts could be shocking, even in the twentieth century. Ambiguities could still leave an audience breathless, faced with the absurdity of a Mower, for example, who posed at the same time the most haunting of human dilemmas for which suicide might indeed be preferable. The whole "ideal" of art had to be reinterpreted and with it the necessity of its signs. What did a "serious" poet mean by dramatizing such an anti-heroic figure who was exhibiting heroic dilemmas? Where did the cultural inscription for the posing of such questions come from and how could such a dialectic of wit provide a catharsis? Audiences needed clearer answers for the traditional determinism expected by all social communities of makers of language, especially the therapeutic moral stance all Renaissance audiences desired and demanded of their poets (whether the assurances of "Valediction: Forbidding Mourning," "Inviting a Friend to Supper," or the last book of *Paradise Lost*).

For his post–World War I audience, Eliot took his logic of "wit's internal

---

tuality in Marvell. For the concept of transtextuality, see Genette, *Palimpsestes: la littérature au second degré* (Paris: Seuil, 1982), 7–13; also see "After Genette: Current Directions in Narrative Analysis and Theory," ed. Carl R. Kropf and R. Barton Palmer, *Studies in the Literary Imagination* 25.1 (spring 1992): esp. 29.

4. *The Complete Works in Verse and Prose of Andrew Marvell*, ed. Alexander B. Grosart (London, 1868–1875), 3:295.

equilibrium" a step further: did such wit in the dialectical game of the poem (a literal syllogism in "To His Coy Mistress") enact the process of catharsis intended? Eliot had now implicitly asked the question that critics would continue to ask as they added another: did dialectic then do the work of the more positive assertions of other Renaissance texts and, if so, how? Critics as recent as Nardo, with her perceptive textualizing of play motifs in Marvell, have demonstrated, in fact, that the dialectical questioning does indeed transform the readers of Marvell's texts. It points them toward enactment of social or communal goals after the self-interrogation and reformation (through text) of the ego, personal and social. There were no other "answers," as Eliot's 1920 argument had suggested. Sincerity could only come in the sincerity of the structures asking the questions, a point that Renaissance audiences from Trissino in 1524 on had begun to expect, especially after their encounter with Aristotle's newly edited *Poetics*.[5] Identification with a hero could only come, if it came, from an identification with a dialectically inscribed figure like the Mower, Marvell's only sustained textualizing of a character, a life-text that answered to the Italian and then European reading of Aristotle. If audiences would identify with Marvell's Mower as inscribing a significant act, he had to represent a consciously organized structure, a "readerly" and "writerly" act, in Roland Barthes's terms, whose "equilibrium" of wit, as Eliot defined it, demanded a considerable revision of one's own more limited sense of time and place. With the Mower, at the very least, one's idea of the heroic might have to change; the marginalized and odd and absurd might have to become acceptable voices for the human pain and labor required for all those building a human community like the Rome that Aeneas once built. As so textualized, the clown-Mower could transform and renew with unexpected Aristotelian inscriptions of pity and fear.

In Marvell's texts, this cathartic process stems, as Marvell criticism has never ceased to elaborate, from the poet's considerable simultaneous sensitivity to the power *and* the absurdity of structure, a defusing reductio ad absurdum Marvell brings into the text at almost every crucial enlarging sign of nobility and honor. His therapeutic closures, so ironically balanced between two textualized structures, invert the usual stage choice, the hard social point-

5. Bernard Weinberg, *A History of Literary Criticism in the Italian Renaissance* (Chicago: University of Chicago Press, 1961), i, ii, and chaps. 9–12.

ing of Milton's "one just man," for example, toward an imperative of action. Rather, Marvell's dialectic takes direction inward to the reader's pondering of ambiguities as the heart of history, not certitude. Until ambiguity is recognized, there can be no successful social action of any "one just man." For the reader's inward recognition of historical ambiguity, the represented structure with its voice of dialectic and wit must carry considerable power. That recognition depends on nothing for its healing moral stance except the text itself and the ghosts of other texts that haunt it. Allusion or even ideology will carry little meaning; the dialectic of the text itself must carry the cathartic ritual. In this respect, if the pastoral is supposed to have ended with Marvell, so did the validity of the whole humanist allusion system and its rhetorical supports of which Milton's epic similes are surely the grand finale. From now on, such elaborated allusion can only be absurd and comic, as it is already in Pope and Fielding. Indeed Marvell's lover in "Coy Mistress," Cromwell or Charles, the nymph, all nullify the whole allusive system by pointedly turning cathartic process inward, away from any objective moral stance in his text except the dialectical posing of questions, a "readerly" inscription of both "hell within" and "paradise within" and the terrible choices.

The question then for any reader is twofold: what exactly does the text say? and what can I as reader do with what I am reading and hearing? The two are parts of the same question of the relationship of text to self, both within an ongoing history of interpretation, both of text and of life; and answers to the second part are clearly adumbrated in the first. Indeed, in the kind of trans-textuality Eliot, Kermode, and Genette develop, it will always be this way. The answer to the second part of the question will involve the singular originating text, in this case the Mower poems, but beyond their originality lies another text, one beyond the relationship between Marvell and the reader, in this case, inscriptions by Vergil and Bacon. These operate in a kind of relationship to the reader that only the present originating text (the Mower poems) provides. Only in the originating text can catharsis of the reader be enacted by the "equilibrium" and "recognition" of wit, and the life seeking meaning and action find it. The answer to the second part of the question lies in the answer to the first.

The danger is, of course, that into this singularly originating text the reader may want to bring the maker of the cathartic process, the savior who may provide an answer to the terrible dilemma, Marvell himself, who survives through his wit even in his own texts. If Marvell is read this way, his very witty dialectic inscribes the perfect Stoic of the Renaissance, who had looked at the hells of Revolution and Restoration and whatever else in his personal life only to turn to a life of silence (at least as lyric poet) and parliamentary service, as abnegating an act as Rimbaud's. On the surface such a hero is resigned to a life as simply accepted as that of Wordsworth's noble Michael and underground saints and heroes of the modern world. Whatever the truth of such biography, however, it hardly matters. In fact, interpretation of the texts the poet wrote has hardly been affected, for the simple reason that the dialectic of his texts remains and still inscribes in a way that the life of the poet cannot. The pain and ambiguity, the absurdity and anti-heroic choices, are still there in the lines. Thus the dialectic is part of the text and cannot be integrated into any biographical context without considerable distortion to Marvell's original texts. Like a good mother, Marvell's ritualizing ironizing wit will not abandon his text or its language, for which no biography can answer. The form of the text simply cannot be revised. So the questions of therapy for the audience cannot be separated from the very shapes of their asking. Marvell cannot intervene. The real Andrew Marvell cannot stand up because what composes him composes us, the readers. That is, the terms of the drama express both reader and writer; therapy and healing exist only in those terms, as Aristotle knew. Whatever therapy existed for Marvell himself, whatever levels of psychic "play" charted his own development, the facts are offstage, and glimpsed, at least in his texts, only through a glass darkly, as, in a text Marvell knew well, Saint Paul noted about the whole process of time.

But dramatizations do exist, and in the sustained figuration of the Mower they form, as Richard Wilcher remarks, "a coherent structure in the order in which they were originally printed in 1681."[6] Indeed Marvell sets, within this

---

6. *Andrew Marvell* (Cambridge: Cambridge University Press, 1985), 89. See the arguments for regarding the Mower poems as a coherent figuration in John Carey, "Reversals Transposed: An Aspect of Marvell's Imagination," in *Approaches to Marvell: The York Tercentenary Lectures*, ed. C. A. Patrides (London: Routledge and Kegan Paul, 1978), 142–43; and in the same volume, A. J. Smith, "Marvell's Metaphysical Wit," 69; and Patrides, "'Till Prepared for Longer Flight': The Sublunar Poetry of Andrew Marvell," 42. Also see Donald M. Friedman, *Marvell's Pastoral Art* (Berkeley and Los Angeles: University of California Press, 1970), 120; George de F. Lord, "From Contemplation to Action: Marvell's Poetical Career," *Philological Quarterly* 46:2 (April 1967): 207–24; and Louis L. Martz, *The*

consciously articulated structure, clues for the enactment of healing and for the catharsis required for entering history and transforming it as did Aeneas. An immediate clue is in the name of the new hero; etymologically, as Dean R. Baldwin has indicated, in addition to its meaning of a worker, "mower" also means "One who makes mouths; a jester, a mocker" (*OED*). It may be, in such reductive clues, that Marvell not only ends the pastoral inscription itself by, as Linda Anderson notes, "presenting the pastoral hero not as Pan, but as Peter Pan,"[7] but also presents Peter Pan and the marginalized and the absurd as actors in a new ironic pastoral, whose definitions of action are determined by counterpoint, relationship, tension, a social and communal dialectic. As Milton points out at the end of *Paradise Lost,* it is the "labourer's heel" that becomes the "victor's heel" in a georgics process I have elsewhere suggested. In this sense, E. W. Tayler is right; Marvell does revise his pastoral love complaint in terms of western scriptural history but with a radically new interpretation of the Fall.[8] The absurd and the small may be a source of salvation in a Vergilian georgics inscription Marvell knew well. The Mower thus offers from the beginning a radical revision of the old Abel-shepherd, as Swan indicates, a bloodier retextualizing than the simpler dichotomy of Cain and Abel. Marvell's personal ontogeny may have recapitulated a Christian phylogeny,[9] but not so the Mower's, at least as he is figured forth in Marvell's texts. He enacts a dialectic of choice and time that he cannot seem to escape but somehow endures, and his bloodiness or clumsy actuality comes not through any transcendent gesture or the promise of such transcendence (Aeneas's vision in book 6 of the *Aeneid*) but through absurd and ironic mis(dis)placements of self, often literal but always emblematic.

Wit of Love: Donne, Carew, Crashaw, Marvell (Notre Dame: University of Notre Dame Press, 1969), 177- 79.

7. Baldwin, "Marvell's 'Mower Poems,'" *Explicator* 35.3 (1977): 25–26; Anderson, "The Nature of Marvell's Mower," *Studies in English Literature 1500–1900* 31 (1991): 131–46. Anderson's range of sources and her perceptions make this essay an important analysis of the Mower texts.

8. See my "Spenser's Georgics," *English Literary Renaissance* 10 (1980): 202–38; Tayler, "Marvell's Garden of the Mind," in *Marvell: Modern Judgements,* ed. Michael Wilding (London: Macmillan, 1969), 262.

9. I am using these terms from Swan's interesting interpretation but for different purposes. Cf. Swan, "History, Pastoral and Desire," 200. The earlier Swan reference is on 193–94.

II

Of the four monologues of Marvell's Mower, none recapitulates the Mower experience as precisely as his "Song." It is a good place to begin any look at the Mower figure because its precision of wit balances ingeniously the essential experiences of annihilation and desire not only in the earlier Mower poems but also in the whole pastoral tradition. The Mower can be seen therefore as a complex dramatization rising from a series of texts. The "Song," the last Mower poem in the 1681 Marvell text, distills this Greek experience of *thanatos* and *eros,* first inscribed in the Sicilian pastoral. It carries the same dialectical lightness both Theocritus and Vergil brought to the origins of a tradition Marvell in the Revolution would effectively transform, if not end. In the Greek and Latin originals this lightness springs from a power of emblematic concentration, reducing psycho-historical and cultural experiences (Alexandria and Rome) to the simple tensions of a rural landscape. It is the same reductive process that Horace underscores in his *Ars Poetica,* the epistle to the Piso brothers: "multum in parvo." In Marvell this same originating lightness derives from his particular wit or concentrated balancing of a dialectic of action in the English landscape of eros and thanatos.

This dialectic follows from the three key points I shall be developing in my argument about how the Mower poems focus the cathartic processes of Marvell's texts. First, the meadows, the mower-landscape of eros, have survived as "heraldic" language that recapitulates a richer life before the cultural and natural disaster of Juliana and her total desire; second, as a result of Juliana, the new "courtier" qua mower must enter a world where nature is as dead and malleable as everything else in Juliana's universe; and so, third, for survival of any authenticity of self at all, the old mower/new "courtier" can now only inscribe and act in a society where a georgic like Vergil's, with its dialectic of disaster and rebuilding, Troy and Rome, authorizes "heraldic" language. Without such dialectic inscription of time and work, the sense of self can be lost, entombed, in a Juliana-chaos of history and meaningless eros. This is the dialectical choice posed to the reader.

This definition of wit, the wit of survival as actualized in "The Mower's Song," involves a larger process in Marvell, as I shall argue later. That is, in his highlighting of the Mower experience of desire and annihilation during the English Revolution, Marvell encapsulates this dialectic of wit into a larger dialectic or balancing found elsewhere in his poetry. This wit, or more accurately, this survival of wit, inscribes a new type of hero, a transformation of the Renaissance courtier into a modern georgic figure. On one level in certain Marvell texts, the new mower/courtier/lover is a concentrated variant of Marvell's friend's "one just man" or "wayfaring/warfaring" pilgrim;[10] on another level, Marvell's new hero works in a larger society, on the model of Vergilian and Baconian bees, which bee imagery, one may add, ends the central text of the garden experience. Both are models of hope and survival in a dialectic of action.

None of the other Mower poems has as solipsistic and introverted a text as the "Song." None is as focused on the self or "I." The first two, "The Mower Against Gardens" and "Damon the Mower," have ostensibly objective structures, either argumentative or narrative. They attempt to clarify, through a discourse of distancing, the desire in the garden and the annihilation threatening life and procreation. In the first poem the voice—there is no "I," only an "us"—argues that "Luxurious man" wicked in himself seduces the world but "without a Sex. / 'Tis all enforced." The only hope in this rape/annihilation is that, outside the false garden-society, nature continues its innocent life and "The Gods themselves with us do dwell." This cosmic hope fades with the next poem, the grass under the burning erotic sky "wither'd like his Hopes." Here the more reified Damon, an actual character in a plot, is forced to identify himself as a worker/lover of these fields: "I am the mower Damon, known / Through all the Meadows I have mown." Here the "I" is carefully framed by his song whose lament is proleptic. In fact, the narrator later describes the self-inflicted wound that will allow the Damon figure to see the annihilation at the heart of all desire: "'Tis death alone that this must do: / For Death thou art a Mower too." "The Mower to the Glo-worms" is also a song, in which the animated "Lamps," "Country Comets," "officious" flames, and "courteous Lights," the life and desires of each invoked by apostrophe, disappear in a universal Juliana-darkness, the sheer blankness of mind of the "I" who appears only in the last line and "shall never find my home." The experience of utter desire, distilled as Juliana, has blotted out all other existence.

---

10. Of all the studies of the relationship of Milton and Marvell, Judith Scherer Herz, "Milton and Marvell: The Poet as Fit Reader," *Modern Language Quarterly* 39 (1978): 239–63, delineates the actual working influences of each on the other, even where the two differ in "thematic concerns and artistic problems."

In the fourth Mower poem, a fully identified "Song," the "I" is center stage. The beginning of the poem describes the earlier mind of this "I," a mind not "displac'd" but fully textualized in a topos, a place, even—as the stanzas develop—a chronology and history:

> My Mind was once the true survey
> Of all these Medows fresh and gay;
> And in the greenness of the Grass
> Did see its Hopes as in a Glass.

Then Juliana "came," and all work, all procreation, ceased in the desire that has now turned his mind into a blank. But in the meantime of the plot, its history, "while I with Sorrow pine," the meadows "Grew more luxuriant" and even produced "a Flower on either side." In this ménage à trois of love— worker, meadows, Juliana—the Mower berates the meadows in another apostrophe. He questions them for forgoing his and their "fellowship so true" and having their own "gawdy May-games" in desire and procreation while he is overcome with barren desire. The only answer to his question is the constant refrain of a past narrative: "When Juliana *came*" and, with her, the double death. This is a death not so much to grass and self, but of what she "does to my Thoughts and Me." This strange dichotomizing, doubly solipsistic, sets up a double failure of desire, the Mower as doubly a clown, outside the system of heroes. The fact that the dichotomizing terms appear Cartesian, probably the first such inscription in any significant English literary text, reinforces this alienation. On one hand, in this Cartesian split, if it is that, the self is separated from what Bacon called "things"—what had been reflected so faithfully before in the Mower's mind in the "true survey"; on the other hand, the self is more deeply fragmented, his "Thoughts" now as much the Other to the "Me" as Descartes's "automata" are to his "ego" that performs the act of cognition that alone tells the self it is alive. There is nothing else.

In the penultimate stanza, the violence of this displacement from mind and love leads to the Mower's own plot to revenge himself. His new desire to violate and murder describes the present action of the text, the only direction this unloved self can take: "But what you in Compassion ought," continues the Mower to the meadows, "Shall now by my Revenge be wrought." This is a dialectic of action summed up in Thestylis's reply to Ametas as they are making hay ropes (the same "bloody Thestylis," I presume, who revels in

"Upon Appleton House" at the birds the mowers have accidentally slain). In reply to Ametas's complaint that "Love tyes a Womans Mind / Looser then with Ropes of Hay," Thestylis states her own rhetoric of violence for dealing with time and sexual action: "What you cannot constant hope / Must be taken as you may." So, says the Mower to the meadows that he will now violate, we shall all—himself, flowers, and grass, all sex and signs of desire— "in one common Ruine fall."

In this same stanza, Marvell adds an even greater precision to his dialectic of desire and annihilation: the process is now in the historical present. Juliana and her destruction are ever-present, as time is enacted by a dramatic shift of verb tense in the refrain: "For Juliana *comes*," she *is* in this very moment annihilating his green thought as well as the green shade and the green grass. The disaster is happening now. His desire is now as empty as that in "The Unfortunate Lover," where lines of desire lie *always* parallel. There is no escape from ultimate desire that perpetually destroys. This stanza marks the lowest point in the dialectic of all the Mower poems.

In its last stanza, "The Mower's Song" transforms itself. Here the "Song" concludes Marvell's Mower sequence, which, in its own dialectic, subsumes, as metonymy, both the more empirical Appleton House experience with its very real and not symbolic "tawny Mowers" who "seem like Israelites to be / Walking on foot through a green sea" and the more emblematic "Garden" distillation of that experience. This final stanza of the "Song" inscribes a new type of work and action, and its synecdochal use of a historical motif—heraldry—reveals a new identity for the Mower, one derived from his own aggressive bloody eros. The strategy of the stanza thus unveils a way of surviving the overwhelming force of Juliana-desire by juxtaposing the Mower's own desiring, his own work, the wit of his language or sign making, to her death making. Here also is the Mower's revision of the classical pastoral and its originating dialectic of eros and thanatos that textualized, for both Theocritus and Vergil, all reality.

> And thus, ye Meadows, which have been
> Companions of my thoughts more green,
> Shall now the Heraldry become
> With which I shall adorn my Tomb;
> For Juliana comes, and She
> What I do to the Grass, does to my Thoughts and Me.

The old desires have not been lost, no matter how the Mower-self has sought their "common Ruine" (that pun on the Latin for "fall" Milton also uses for Satan). But the meadows no longer exist as "companions" of green thoughts; they have been transformed into the abstract sign language of nobility, a way of designating his own past, in the universal obliteration Juliana-desire brings. Meadows, once the source of erotic freedom and self-desire, now serve the same purpose as heraldic forms on a medieval or Renaissance tomb: they recapitulate a richer life before the grand disaster came. The older world of chivalry, the old English eros and desire that Surrey and Sidney and Essex flamboyantly displayed, has been transformed into a world where the Mower, who attacks gardens and uses language directly from Bacon, laments how the proud scientist "in the Cherry . . . does vex, / To procreate without a sex." Male display and *gloire* have become Luther Burbank, a Baconian geneticist, the anonymous engineer. In Marvell's own terms as crystallized in the garden experience, the new courtier must enter a world where nature is as dead and malleable as everything else in Juliana's universe. A revolution, greater than the English Revolution, has taken place in the microcosm of the Mower's garden under the disjunctive aegis of Juliana-desire.

Marvell's inscription of this revolution thus carries the wit of surviving in such a time of social collapse and revolution and of finding a role out of it. Marvell's process of catharsis, the process of his texts, is part of the process of finding a social role. In fact, the Mower's dialectic of heraldry enacts one such role. This role describes a task as old as the Greeks: inscribing signs as a way of remembering desire that has been lost or unfulfilled, the perpetual *différence*. The sign maker becomes as much a worker as any other builder of a new civilization. Now the Mower-worker must build a new Rome for which Aeneas had to have the right desires, as Jupiter reminds Mercury, who then warns Aeneas to leave Dido; Aeneas must, in Surrey's translation, "seek honour by some pain," "laude" by "laborem." Vergil gives in these lines familiar to Marvell an essentially georgic inscription, and so, for Andrew Marvell, what resolves the tensions and dialectic of the Mower poems also works for the making of a future world, the invention of signs on tombs of past experience or lost desires, that is, new and appropriate language. This resolution, closure of the entire Mower sequence, develops simply and with terms of wit that have become symbolic, in Marvell's version of the pastoral, of prophetic history: lost "Meadows" of desire become present "heraldry" or language of desire that survives ironically as the erotic ornament of annihilation.

III

Such a resolution and cathartic moment of balance occur elsewhere in Marvell. Often, in a clear moment of prophetic history, the resolution reveals itself as the wit of survival in which an old eros dies and emerges as new desire, all within a dialectic of self and work, the Vergilian dialectic both in the *Georgics* and in the *Aeneid,* as I have shown elsewhere. The inscription of failed desire becomes language for an act of metanoia or conversion in the "I" speaking the text but always in the shadow of annihilation, as in the "The Mower's Song": "Shall now the Heraldry become / With which I shall adorn my Tomb." This language signifies the awareness that comes from Marvell's process of catharsis, the dramatized choices. Thus, for survival of any authenticity of self at all, the old courtier of the meadows must enter another world like Aeneas on his pilgrimage. He must become an actual city builder, an actual parliamentarian restoring and inventing other signs and languages for the survival of the community to which the self is bound, like the bee, for any expression or language of self at all. Such a process and strategy of work and language dominate, at least in my reading, the closure of certain other Marvell texts, as I shall now show.

In these closures, a dialectic emerges that enacts a movement from contemplation to action, from ironic and parodic self-recognition to engagement with the very processes of time. It is a dialectic that recapitulates, in its wit of survival, that odd transformation in Marvell's biography: a professional Latinist of the 1650s (who probably wrote his greatest lyrics in an isolated garden experience) to the Restoration man of parliament, whose only poetic language was bitter satire, in which the terrifying reductions and self-encounters of the Mower poems would have been unthinkable and quite subversive. In the cathartic closures to these poems, as in the text of his life, therefore, a definition of time has been arrived at.

It is precisely time and the uses of time that enact the balancing wit of "To His Coy Mistress" and "An Horatian Ode Upon Cromwell's Return From Ireland." As the making of heraldic signs for his tomb finally engages the Mower as a means of surviving his past and inscribing his future, so in "Coy

Mistress" the language of wooing and the action of seduction not only engage the present but also inscribe an ethic of the future, an ethic of time and work. Thus the lover, the desiring worker, talks not so much about his sexual need—Marvell is making a parody here of Catullus, who was making his own kind of layered Hellenistic joke about the uses of time amid overwhelming cultural eros and thanatos—as about syllogistically dramatizing strategies by which desire survives death. The closure of "Horatian Ode" also enacts a georgic of time and work. The onlooker who has watched the rise of an actualized Cromwell inscribes his origination and its uses of time ("So much one Man can do / That does both act and know") at the same time that the ambiguities of loss, focused in the beheaded "Royal Actor," encapsulate any georgic of action. Thus, in the closure, however Cromwell must keep his phallic "Sword erect," with its "force . . . to fright / The Spirits of the shady Night," nevertheless "The same Arts that did gain / A Pow'r must it maintain." True power always results from a dialectic of wit, balancing desires and annihilation. Power results from a recognition of ambiguity.

In the climactic stanzas of "Upon Appleton House," Marvell's more personally identified self withdraws for its own contemplation and mystic encounter in the midst of a civil war that actualizes the universal Juliana-disaster:

> Oh Thou, that dear and happy Isle,
> The Garden of the World ere while,
> Thou *Paradise* of four Seas,
> Which *Heaven* planted us to please,
> But, to exclude the World, did guard
> With watry if not flaming Sword;
> What luckless Apple did we tast,
> To make us Mortal, and The Wast?

The contemplative's withdrawal, a social death, is necessary if the self is to survive utter historical derangement. In that slow emergence from the woods, in the topos that concludes the poem, the beauty of the human self (actualized as Maria Fairfax) and of natural phenomena with their meadow-desires gives him the surviving unity not just to live but to write the poem, as the flat final simile suggests.

In "The Garden" the strategy of withdrawal and emergence is more elaborately dramatized and, as in Donne's "Canonization," involves three stages: outside the garden; inside; outside again. The last stage in "The Garden," the last two stanzas after the inward "greening" experience of the four central stanzas, inscribes more completely than any other Marvell lyric this conversion experience of the georgic.[11] In the penultimate stanza, the power of the "Such" is equal to the effect of Juliana in the Mower poems. It is simply "beyond a Mortal's share" to exist in a dialectic outside history. For that new dialectic of action, then, a wit is needed, and this can be found in the final stanza's real historical garden: a seventeenth-century sundial of flowers through which an actual sun, the instrument of time, moves. The meadow-desires need be violated only for the fertile work of time, the action of bees. In this transtextualization of the bee image, Marvell enacts not only the Vergilian topos from the powerful fourth book of the *Georgics* and from the description of Dido's rising city in book 1 of the *Aeneid*, originals quite accessible to the Latinist Marvell, but also the Baconian reinscriptions from his *Novum Organon* and the *Advancement of Learning*, the latter dominant texts of the Revolutionary culture. Thus, in this witty closure, as the sundial works, "th'industrious Bee / Computes its time as well as we." Desire has continued, but retextualized, in a disjunctive like "Such" that inscribes an Adam and Eve world of perpetual annihilation. The Fall itself has been retextualized in a world of computing bees. In fact, says the speaker, in a deliberately flat ending after the exalted "greening" stanzas, an ending that reminds all readers of the georgic task ahead: "How could such sweet and wholsome Hours / Be reckon'd but with herbs and flow'rs!"

In the conclusion to this poem, which became one more anthologized classic after Eliot's essay, Marvell completes his dialectic. The reader has been taken through a historical narrative that has dramatized, as in the Mower poems, the price of georgics and the price of Vergilian honor. The witty counterpointing of the two levels of experience can hardly do more than provide a catharsis, however. It can point only to a textual focus where the reader is cleansed, through fear of, and pity for, the formally enacted dilemma of absurdity. In it she or he is prepared for the choices of the next stage of

---

11. For a sense of what this conversion entailed and a basis for this analysis, see Joseph H. Summers, *The Heirs of Donne and Jonson* (New York: Oxford University Press, 1970), chap. 5.

work and action. That is enough. The Mower may provide a negative figuration of the Western hero, but his figuration has cleansed the reader of false illusions of power or eros. Absurdity and thanatos and marginalization are also the hero's unheroic necessary choices. They are also part of the Vergilian dialectic, and it is that dialectic that informs the moral stance at the end of his texts. If anything does, the dialectic points the way to the Aeneas-progression/pilgrimage. But Marvell's terms are formal, witty, as T. S. Eliot first indicated, and it is in their counterpointing of reality that they engage the reader and cleanse. In their dialectic, if anywhere, they give hope. A new text out of the small and absurd might arise.

Katherine M. Quinsey

Religio Laici?

Dryden's Men of Wit and the Printed Word

Truth narrative, and past, is the Idoll of Historians, (who worship a dead thing) and truth operative, and by effects continually alive, is the Mistresse of Poets, who hath not her existence in matter but in reason.[1]

Of all Dryden's poems, *Religio Laici* is the one that seems destined, like *Mac Flecknoe*, to wage immortal war with wit. From the very motto on the title page to the closing lines, Dryden rejects wit in favor of plain speech, negates the power of poetry by equating it with prose, and even makes his own verse into an arbitrary instrument exchangeable with that of Tom Shadwell or Tom Sternhold. Ultimately, the poem presents both human and poetic wit as weak and fallacious, deluded and deluding, in the face of "Sacred Truth."

Although *Religio Laici* thus appears to ally itself with the forces that trivialize poetic wit, it is not in itself far removed from the underpinnings of the debate as articulated in the quotation from Davenant above. Indeed, it might be possible to suggest that *Religio Laici* is more deeply concerned with wit than other poems of Dryden's that are both more witty and more exclusively "literary" (such as *Mac Flecknoe*). The heart of the poem's subject—the nature of religious authority—harbors the same questions of language and truth that lie at the heart of the seventeenth-century debate on wit. *Religio*

---

1. "The Author's Preface," *Sir William Davenant's Gondibert*, ed. David F. Gladish (Oxford: Clarendon Press, 1971), 10–11.

Laici's primary concerns are the criteria for judging and discovering truth and the means of transmission and expression. More specifically, the poem is overwhelmingly concerned with questions of the relation of language to truth, the relation of language and meaning, and the nature of interpretation— that is, the extent to which truth is alive and operative in the minds of readers.

These questions may account for some of the oddities, inconsistencies, and failure of resolution that are generally found in this poem. *Religio* was written and published in a period of intense polemical activity (six months after the excoriating anti-Whig satire *The Medall*, in the midst of the controversy surrounding the production of *The Duke of Guise*, and prior to Dryden's com-missioned and highly politicized translation of Maimbourg's *History of the League*). I have argued elsewhere that in this period of crisis and intensive political writing Dryden was in the process of reexamining himself, his poetic vocation, and his relation to the center of power;[2] this is also the period in which he explored theoretical questions of historiography and of translation,[3] uncovering the same questions of the transmission of truth, the reliability of the linguistic medium, and the nature of interpretation that are central to *Religio*. Recent analyses have dealt in various ways with the extreme minimal-ism of *Religio*'s ending, and with its equivocal treatment of deism, reason, Protestantism, and Catholicism; explanations have focused on the nature of Dryden's skepticism and its role in his eventual conversion to Catholicism, and on the political occasion and purpose of the poem.[4] These political and

2. "Sign-Post Painting: Poetry and Polemic in Dryden's *The Medall*," *Restoration* 16.2 (fall 1992): 97–107.

3. These ideas are most developed in the preface to *Ovid's Epistles* (1680), the dedica-tory epistle and life prefixed to *Plutarch's Lives* (1683), and the preface to *Sylvae* (1685).

4. On religious skepticism see Phillip Harth, *Contexts of Dryden's Thought* (Chicago: University of Chicago Press, 1968), chap. 1; William Empson, "Dryden's Apparent Scepti-cism," *Essays in Criticism* 20 (1970): 172–81; Phillip Harth, "Empson's Interpretation of *Religio Laici*," *Essays in Criticism* 20 (1970): 446–50; Robert D. Hume, "Dryden's Apparent Scepticism," *Essays in Criticism* 20 (1970): 492–95; and Earl Miner, "Dryden's Apparent Scepticism," *Essays in Criticism* 21 (1971): 410–11. For a political rationale, see Stephen Zwicker, *Politics and Language in Dryden's Later Poetry: The Arts of Disguise* (Princeton: Princeton University Press, 1984), 103–22, and Oscar Kenshur, "Scriptural Deism and the Politics of Dryden's *Religio Laici*," *Journal of English Literary History* 54.4 (winter 1987): 869–92.

religious questions are, however, inseparable from the issues of language and interpretation that underlie all Dryden's theoretical and polemical writing in this period, and it is these that produce much of the poem's uncertainty. The poem's unresolved, even negative, ending, its inconsistencies, and its collapsing contrarieties all result from its failure to determine a satisfactory medium for religious authority, from its recognition of and resistance to the implications of subjectivism and multiplicity within its own Protestant reliance on the printed word of Scripture and individual belief, and ultimately from a deep questioning of its own poetic medium, which—like the faith passed on to the layman—relies on the printed word and the critical interpretation of the reader for the transmission of its truth.

Much of this uneasiness is rooted in the fundamental opposition underlying the debate on wit, which informs Davenant's argument quoted above—an opposition between what may be called representational and rhetorical modes of verbal expression. The first is a language that attempts to pin down and fix meaning, to represent a fixed truth; the second is a language that functions as an interactive discourse, working through an interplay of meanings and depending on the reader to complete its meaning. This is, of course, the language of wit.

Davenant locates this opposition in the difference between "truth operative" and "truth narrative": poetic language conveys truth not through straight representation of fixed and discrete fact, but through awakening a principle in the mind: poetic truth is "operative [within the mind of the reader], and by its effects [on the reader] continually alive," existing not in "matter" (its subject) but in "reason" (the principle of order in the mind). By contrast, the historian's truth is separable from his medium of expression; it is a finished fact, observable, discrete. Davenant calls this truth an idol, a dead object that has been falsely invested with meaning, or that pretends to contain meaning in itself; the language of poetry and wit, on the other hand, points in the direction of meaning, depending on the response of the reader to complete *poesis*. Throughout Dryden's critical writings (and, with a peculiar intensity, in his polemical poetry) both views of language are at work, and they are generally resolved in definitions of wit that are comprehensive and flexible, combining representation and conception: wit is "a propriety of thoughts and words," a unifying force linking thought and expression rather than separating them; wit is the means by which poetic form shapes thought rather than merely transmitting it through a neutral medium; wit is both the faculty of imagination and the product of that faculty; wit is both generative and shaping, the power of conception and the power of precise expression.[5]

In *Religio Laici*, however, the representational and rhetorical views generate an unresolved opposition that contributes to the poem's profound uncertainty concerning the nature of religious authority and the function of language as a means to truth. Following a path later trod by Locke, the poem's commitment to an empirical method leads to an awareness that facts are inevitably mediated through perception and expression, and that these are fundamentally subjective and multiple—the historian's objective truth, the poem tacitly admits, may indeed be an idol. Correspondingly, the poem contains the admission that truth may be operative, alive in the response of the readers and approached through a method that is communal and probabilistic rather than one that claims a monological authority. *Religio Laici* resists and ultimately negates this admission, however, by its repeated claims to minimal belief and self-evident truth, and by a conclusion that practically argues itself out of existence.

These questions are sharpened by the poem's peculiar focus on the *written* word in all its aspects, epitomized in its core problem—its claim that the sole authority for Christian belief is Scripture, the Word of God as written in a book. The poem insists on the paradoxes inherent in the nature of any book, deliberately conflating its physical and nonphysical aspects and exploring the duality between the text as a passive exploitable object and the text as an active principle in the mind of the reader. In doing so it raises deep questions about its own description of the authoritative nature of Scripture. Scripture is the self-exemplifying word of God, containing divine power and meaning in

---

5. Dryden's most comprehensive analysis of wit is in the prefatory epistle to *Annus Mirabilis* (1667), in which he defines it as "the faculty of imagination in the writer" and then goes on to unite the faculty with the process ("wit writing") and the product ("wit written"); see *Dryden: Of Dramatic Poesy and Other Critical Essays,* ed. George Watson, 2 vols. (London: Dent, 1962), 1:98–99. (All quotations from Dryden's *Essays* are taken from this edition unless otherwise indicated.) Ideas of the unity of form and meaning occur as early as the dedicatory epistle to the *Rival Ladies* (1664; 1:2, 8–9); the concept of the "propriety of thoughts and words" develops through these assumptions and first appears in "The Author's Apology for Heroic Poetry and Poetic Licence," prefixed to *The State of Innocence: An Opera* (1677; 1:207). This concept combines a representational view of literary decorum ("thoughts and words elegantly adapted to the subject") with much deeper and more comprehensive assumptions about the dynamic unity of form and concept.

itself, while at the same time it is the result of various fallible modes of pro-
duction: authorship, translation, commentary, and print technology. Further-
more, like any book, it depends ultimately on readers' responses in order to
have meaning and power.

Although the poem stretches this dichotomy to its limits (transforming the
Word of God from the fiat of all Creation to a decayed object consumed by a
cluster of maggots), it suggests a possible resolution when truth is removed
from the realm of the fixed fact to the realm of truth operative. This happens
when the poem ascribes a limited authority to the process of critical analysis
and cumulative reading; that is, to the repeated interaction with the text of
"men of wit." Behind this idea is one articulated elsewhere by Dryden (and
discussed in more detail below) that the written word allows for the activity
of mind in a way that performance and visual representation do not: "in a
playhouse, everything contributes to impose upon the judgment: the lights,
the scenes, the habits, and, above all, the grace of action, which is commonly
best when there is the most need of it, surprise the audience, and cast a mist
upon their understandings."[6] The terms of Dryden's argument here are remi-
niscent of Jonson's attack on spectacle when divorced from text (it is notable
that Dryden concludes this passage by declaring that he has "indignation
enough to burn a D'Ambois [the worst example of dramatic imposition] annu-
ally to the memory of Jonson"). The example of *Religio*'s men of wit, however,
echoes more precisely Bacon's claims for the printed word at the end of the
first book of *The Advancement of Learning:*

> But the images of men's wits and knowledges remain in books, exempted
> from the wrong of time and capable of perpetual renovation. Neither are
> they fitly to be called images, because they generate still, and cast their
> seeds in the minds of others, provoking and causing infinite actions and
> opinions in succeeding ages.[7]

The very arbitrariness of print—its dependence on the reader to complete its
meaning, its multiplicity of possible reference—thus links it with rhetoric

---

6. Prefatory epistle to *The Spanish Friar* (1681), 1:275.

7. *Francis Bacon: The Advancement of Learning and New Atlantis,* ed. Arthur Johnston
(Oxford: Clarendon Press, 1974), 58–59 (1.8.6). Dryden is drawing on a tradition also
articulated by Jonson and Milton: the neoclassical idea of books as containing the living
mind of the writer, and of reading as an affirmation of community.

and wit.[8] In *Religio*, as in his other polemical poems of the period, Dryden's most savage satire is reserved for those who arrogate truth to themselves, making it and the text something to which they lay claim. Opposed to this is the activity of men of wit, who approach truth as a mistress, not as an idol, acknowledging that knowledge is fluid and partial, continually engaging truth in engaging the text and each other, in an ongoing communal activity of mind. By admitting this process as a reliable method of interpretation Dryden thus places the language of Scripture in the realm of the discourse of wit rather than that of direct representation, and he does so through its nature as a printed text. It is not a strong affirmation, however. Committed as he is to the idea of "Sacred Truth" as mediated through a representational view of language, Dryden does not sustain this particular argument through the poem, and he backs away from it ultimately into a negation both of witty interpretation and of his own witty expression.

This commitment to directly representational language is emphatically declared in the poem's motto, taken from the third book of Manilius's *Astronomicon:* "impendas animum; nec dulcia carmina quaeras: ornari res ipsa negat contenta doceri" (apply your mind, and do not seek the pleasures of poetry; my subject refuses to be ornamented, content itself to be taught).[9] It is declared as well in Dryden's own claims for "legislative" poetic language at the end of the preface, which anticipate Locke's virulent attack on metaphor as "perfect cheat":[10] "Instruction is to be given by shewing them [readers] what they [objects of passions] naturally are. A Man is to be cheated into Passion, but to be reason'd into Truth." From here, however, the poem itself is structured primarily through alternating claims for a divinely authorized language

---

8. Richard W. F. Kroll, *The Material Word: Literate Culture in the Restoration and Early Eighteenth Century* (Baltimore and London: Johns Hopkins University Press, 1991), locates print as a medium of "negotiation and scrutiny," part of the process whereby "all forms of knowledge . . . [become] known and confessed to be rhetorical" (21–22)—that is, existing in language, so that knowledge becomes a form of active interpretation.

9. *Manilius: Astronomica*, ed. G. P. Goold (Cambridge: Harvard University Press; London: William Heinemann, 1978), 166 (my translation). Manilius is referring to his versified version of the mathematical calculations of astrological operations.

10. *John Locke: An Essay Concerning Human Understanding*, ed. John W. Yolton (London: Dent, 1961), 2:105 (3.10.34). All quotations from the *Religio Laici* and its preface are taken from *The Works of John Dryden*, ed. H. T. Swedenberg Jr., 20 vols. (Berkeley: University of California Press, 1956–), 2:97–122.

that obviates any critical response and suggestions that language is multi-valent and dependent on a community of readers to help complete its meaning. The first section of the poem builds to an assertion that the authority of Scripture encompasses and transcends all human wit, being identifiable with the creating word of God; then it turns almost immediately to questioning such authority being invested in a written book.

> Then for the *Style; Majestick* and *Divine,*
> It speaks no less than God in every Line:
> *Commanding words;* whose *Force* is still the same
> As the first *Fiat* that produc'd our Frame.
> All Faiths *beside,* or did by *Arms* ascend;
> Or *Sense* indulg'd has made *Mankind* their *Friend:*
> This *onely* Doctrine does our *Lusts* oppose:
> Unfed by Natures Soil, in which it grows;
> Cross to our *Interests,* curbing Sense, and Sin,
> Oppress'd without, and undermin'd within,
> It thrives through pain; its own Tormentours tires;
> And with a stubborn patience still aspires.
>
> (ll. 152–63)

Scripture here embodies the ultimate propriety of thoughts and words, as its meaning and its word are one—the ambiguous syntax seems to conflate page and doctrine, style and sense. Its style is invested with the character of its speaker, in the tradition of Cicero and Jonson. The printed word here is imbued with the power of speech, a speech that contains performative power in itself—"Commanding words" with the power to shape and create reality—an ideal of language that Dryden invokes in his other polemical work in an attempt to reinvest mytho-scriptural discourse with monolithic power (for example, to obliterate debate in the ending of *Absalom and Achitophel*). Pointedly, this passage echoes that in *The Medall* on the suffering page of Scripture, in which the text is physicalized and fragmented by Dissenting misappropriations (ll. 158–61); but in the rewriting of that passage here the suffering of the book itself becomes a form of heroic action analogous to that of the Christian martyrs—it is powerful and active, operative and alive in its effects.

What is not stated at this point is that this action is that of a printed book distributed through time and space, and that it can be realized only through the interaction of readers with the text.[11] Uneasiness about such authority being invested in a printed book begins to pervade the poem almost immediately. The complimentary passage to the translator of Pere Simon's *Critical History,* Henry Dickinson, focuses on the nature of the book—on the stages of literary production (text, commentary, translation, response) that made Scripture as Dryden has it—and in doing so rewrites the earlier declaration of the inherent authority evident in Scripture's divine ("spoken") style. Here Dryden acknowledges the role of physical literary production in shaping the text and thus its interpretation. Scripture is no longer seen as growing in Nature's soil but as precariously preserved in nature's soil by fallible human means. The book is reduced to its smaller physical elements—a text corrupted by "gross Errours," with paragraphs missing; the single living word has become multiple copies, maimed and disagreeing. Indeed, what happens to Scripture itself in this passage? It becomes translated into the responses of various readers, mediated through translation, commentary, and the physical exigencies of copying. Simon's book has become a glass through which to view Scripture, wherein "we may see what *Errours* have been made / Both in the *Copiers* and *Translaters Trade*" (ll. 248–49). Scripture is not even referred to directly here but is contained (literally and figuratively) in the "crabbed Toil" of Simon's "weighty Book" (ll. 234–35), which represents the pedantic antithesis of the informing liveliness of wit—"as much as Man cou'd compass, uninspir'd" (l. 247).

Dryden counters the disturbing implications of a text constituted by reading by considering oral forms of authoritative human language: a formulated creed and Church tradition. Ultimately, he rejects both as restrictive and falsifying. The carefully foregrounded critique of Athanasius portrays him as an ideologue associated with a creed—a formulated verbal construct that claims a single authoritative truth and gains its power through being repeated orally. Dryden's linking of Athanasius with the Test Act here—in addition to his immediate political point opposing the act and promoting royal "moderation"—underlines the fact that such oral authority is monological and oppressive, negating witty response of any kind. Similarly, an infallible oral tradition obviates any critical

---

11. Cf. William Frost, "Literacy, Science, and Censorship from the Greeks to Shakespeare and Dryden," *Soundings: Collections of the University Library, University of California at Santa Barbara* 17.23 (1986): 43.

response. It would supersede the authority of the written book ("'Twere worth *Both Testaments*, and cast in the *Creed*" [l. 283]), and communal authority (through time) would replace the activity of individual readers. In this situation truth would be fixed and contained, all doubts resolved, all truth secure (l. 285), lost canon and explication equally fixed and pure (ll. 288–89). In empirically tested reality, however, oral tradition is not only human and fallible but also operates through a physical medium even more subject to decay than that of the printed word:

> If *written words* from time are not secur'd,
> How can we think have *oral Sounds* endur'd?
> Which *thus* transmitted, if *one* Mouth has fail'd,
> *Immortal Lyes* on *Ages* are intail'd.
>
> (ll. 270–73)

Oral tradition negates the ever-renewed critical activity that a written text makes available and thus can perpetuate falsehood in a manner comparable to the transmission of original sin.

Having eliminated any infallible church authority, Dryden falls back onto sweeping (and contradictory) Protestant party statements, both of which equally negate the activity of wit and interpretation: first, the minimalist Anglican orthodoxy of the self-evident truth of the necessary bits of Scripture; and second, Protestant belief in salvation through individual faith. The Anglican position anticipates Lockean dismissals of wit in stating that the necessary parts of Scripture are clear enough to all reasonable people, and that whatever is obscure or ambiguous is unnecessary (and potentially subversive).[12]

> the *Scriptures*, though not *every where*
> Free from Corruption, or intire, or clear,

12. The reliance on the self-evidence of Scripture for the minimal truths of salvation has a long Anglican history; see for example *Richard Hooker: Of the Laws of Ecclesiastical Polity*, ed. Christopher Morris, 2 vols. [London: Dent, 1964], 2:97: "And of things necessary to all men's salvation we have been hitherto accustomed to hold . . . they are in Scripture plain and easy to be understood" (5.22.14). (See also Kenshur, "Scriptural Deism," 879.) The Latitudinarian divines of Dryden's time developed this concept of the reasonableness and self-evidence of Christianity to a complete system of apology; chief exemplar was John Tillotson, who is the "judicious and learned Friend" cited by Dryden in his preface to *Religio*.

> Are uncorrupt, sufficient, clear, intire,
> In *all* things which our needfull *Faith* require.
> (ll. 297–300)

Obviously, the self-evident precludes any critical engagement. Dryden here clearly presents truth as absolute, objective, directly represented by words; in a manner anticipating Locke and looking back to Spratian linguistics, truth is evident to all men of sense, and language should thus be minimal and as neutral as possible. In the lines immediately following, however, Dryden moves away into an almost complete contradiction of this claim for the self-evident and obvious, by presenting all interpretation as necessarily subjective and differing; Scripture is no longer an obvious light representing objective truth, but now a "Glass" where readers see themselves or their own perceptions—"If *others* in the *same Glass better* see / 'Tis for *Themselves* they look, but not for *me*" (ll. 301–2). It is in this context of essential subjectivity that Dryden makes his climactic assertion that "MY Salvation must its Doom receive / Not from what OTHERS, but what *I* believe" (ll. 303–4). This assertion is of course perfectly orthodox in one sense; yet in another it places the activity of the word inside the mind of the reader, claiming the authority of individual belief in the face of the failure of a single and external truth. Like Locke's ideas, authority is doomed to be based in perceptions, not in objective "facts."[13]

The poem is thus left with contradictory positions; one that effectively excludes all multivalent language as irrelevant and potentially subversive, and one that annihilates witty interpretation in the subjective response. In reply to this dilemma, the poem suggests that reliable interpretation is the province of a community of minds over time, combining literary analysis and empirical investigation. Furthermore, this authority depends on the written word and its activity in the minds of readers, not on an oral tradition, in a recognition that "Sacred Truth" requires wit (in all its senses) to complete its meaning:

> Th'*unletter'd* Christian, who believes in *gross*,
> Plods on to *Heaven*; and ne'er is at a loss:

---

13. See John Sitter on Locke's criticism of wit and on responses to Locke by Addison and Prior in "About Wit," in *Rhetorics of Order/Ordering Rhetorics in English Neoclassical Literature*, ed. J. Douglas Canfield and J. Paul Hunter (Newark: University of Delaware Press, 1989), 137–57. Locke's criticism was "sharpened by the suspicion that knowledge and language are inseparable" and that all "facts" are in effect perceptions mediated through language.

For the *Streight-gate* wou'd be made *streighter* yet,
Were *none* admitted there but men of *Wit*.
The few, by Nature form'd, with Learning fraught,
Born to instruct, as others to be taught,
Must Study well the Sacred Page; and see
Which Doctrine, this, or that, does best agree
With the whole Tenour of the Work Divine:
And plainlyest points to Heaven's reveal'd Design:
Which Exposition flows from *genuine Sense;*
And which is *forc'd* by *Wit* and *Eloquence*.

. . . .

Such difference is there in an oft-told Tale:
But Truth by its own Sinews will prevail.
Tradition written therefore more commends
Authority, than what from *Voice* descends:
And this, as perfect as its kind can be,
Rouls down to us the Sacred History:
Which, from the *Universal Church receiv'd,*
Is *try'd,* and *after,* for its *self* believ'd.
                    (ll. 322–33, 348–55)

The entire statement is framed as a reply to a fictionalized objection by Father Simon that without authoritative human interpretation, Scripture remains a mute object of arbitrary manipulation (ll. 305–15). Dryden ultimately locates such interpretation in the activity of men of wit. Initially, he seems even to eliminate the written word, in "th'unletter'd Christian," and he plays off traditional negatives in the meaning of "wit" (deceptive eloquence, artificial cleverness). With the turn whereby wit is transmuted into learning—"Men of Wit" become "The few, by Nature form'd, with Learning fraught"—the passage shifts away from affirming the simple faith of the illiterate and toward an extended development of the role of literary analysis in interpreting Scripture. The methodology of interpretation reasserts precisely those Renaissance artistic values that lay behind Dryden's earlier description of Scripture's divine style: the parts must fit the whole; the order of the work must reflect "Heaven's reveal'd Design"; both text and commentary must be informed by "genuine Sense," the life or soul of the work. These are also the values that inform discussions of wit in Dryden's criticism: unity of thought and expression; the creative spirit passed from one poet to another. As in Dryden's theory of translation and poetic succession, so here the text is re-created in the act of interpretation; as the syntax blurs distinctions and identifies Scripture with commentary, "Tradition written" becomes ambiguous, yet is still the guide to truth.

Above all, the passage emphasizes that Truth is found in the activity of reading the written word and engaging it critically, as opposed to viewing or listening to visual or oral performance. (It is notable that the passage emphasizes the physical nature of the book and of reading; the use of the synecdoche "Page" is habitual.) In Dryden's critical writings, the superiority of reading to performance is most clearly articulated in the preface to the printed version of *The Spanish Friar* (1681): here, performance is fundamentally deceptive and coercive ("In a playhouse, everything contributes to impose upon the judgment"); critical activity—on which wit depends—can take place only in reading ("the propriety of thoughts and words . . . are but confusedly judged in the vehemence of action"). Truth is available through the printed word in a way it is not in performance, being revealed by critical reading over a period of time: "Nothing but truth can long continue; and time is the surest judge of truth" (1:278). In both *Religio Laici* and this earlier preface to his most Protestant play, then, Dryden sees oral delivery or performance as coercive and monological, even falsifying, and as vitiated by time. The written word, on the other hand, contains the living principle of Truth that "by its own Sinews will prevail"—an organic metaphor that appears to describe truth as self-perpetuating through its absorption from the written word by the minds of multiple readers. As in Bacon, the word made printed object becomes the seed of operative truth. This metaphor shows Truth to be Davenant's poetic truth, alive and operative, not an object to be appropriated. In its affirmation of written tradition the passage thus treats Scripture as part of the discourse of wit—not as a self-evident truth to be passively acknowledged, but as a living word to be intellectually and spiritually encountered.

The development of these ideas is cut off almost immediately (ll. 366–69), as Dryden abruptly retreats to his former argument that Scripture is self-exemplifying, containing its good news "in the *Letter*" not in the tradition by which it is transmitted; it is fundamentally oral and monological ("It *speaks* it *Self*"); it is also self-explanatory ("what it does contain, / In all things *needfull* to be *known*, is plain"), thus minimizing the need for language and obliterating the activity of wit. This commitment to a "Sacred Truth" unmediated by human interpretation frames a savage critique of false interpretation, which generates most of the energy of the latter part of the poem. The poem's attitude to "men of wit" and interpretation is thus deeply ambivalent. It documents the failure of all attempts to pin down an objective truth outside interpretation, admitting that the printed word exists in the response of readers. As a corollary, it suggests that true authority may be found in the very fact that the printed word *is* thus constituted by the response of its readers; it is in this realm that truth is operative and alive in its effects. Resistance to the implications of this view, or a strenuous effort to distinguish one view from the other, may explain both the virulence of Dryden's subsequent portrayals of false interpretation by Papists and Dissenters and the evasiveness of his ending, in which the issue is avoided altogether by a minimalist faith that silences not only witty interpretation but also poetic activity.

This extended critique carries the subjectivism implicit in interpretation to its extremes, where it ironically becomes transformed into the very obverse of wit. Dryden presents both Roman Catholics and Dissenters as objectifying both text and meaning, taking the nonphysical and making it physical (whereas the act of interpretation—existing not in matter but in reason—should take the physical and extract the mind existent in it). Both parties lay claim to truth, attempting to make it fixed and discrete, an exploitable or commodified object. For example, the critique of the Roman Catholic church echoes that of the Dissenters in *The Medall*, who inspire the text (literally) rather than being inspired by it (ll. 162–66): "At last, a knowing Age began t'enquire / If *they* the *Book*, or *That* did *them* inspire" (ll. 388–89). In a parodic incarnation, the word is made into a hollow object into which the Roman Catholics blow—it becomes a vessel to contain their subjective meaning, an arbitrary signifier. Dryden supplies an answer to this false claim to prophetic authority in the interpretative act of a "knowing" person reading written documents—"the *Will produc'd*, (the written Word)," l. 392—thus reasserting the primacy of the written text and its operation in the mind.

More savage and more extensive is Dryden's attack on the Dissenters' handling of Scripture, which occupies the climactic rhetorical position in the poem, immediately before the *peroratio*. Here he pushes to the extreme the flaws of print as a physical medium and the implications for Scripture as a printed book, arguing that distorting interpretation fragments the text as surely as violent handling fragments pages, reducing it to an exploitable object empty of meaning except what the holder thereof wishes arbitrarily to assign. Although the written word frees the mind to engage the text in the activity of wit, it is also a passive object separated from its author and subject to multiplicity of meanings. "The *Common Rule*," the latter a word having power to shape reality, and "common" in the sense of "universal," now, in a witty turn, becomes the "*common Prey*" (l. 402), vulgar, undistinguished, a victim to be devoured in a brutish Hobbesian scenario. The closeness of opposites here, the dualities inherent in the nature of the book and of interpretation—the ease with which the book can turn from being an active principle to a passive object—the parodic resemblance between the redemptive activity of critical reading and the subjective and multiple interpretations of the sects: these may explain the intensity of Dryden's rhetoric, as a strenuous effort to distinguish true from false. Interpretation has become a mindless "itching to *expound*" (l. 410)—it has gone wild, not attached to sense or to the whole, being entirely self-referential. Zeal, which claims access to an absolute authority, creates a gap between word and meaning; it invests words with false particularity and specific application, or blurs precise relationships.

The final and most vivid metaphor in the poem picks up the Jonsonian idea of the written word as organically absorbed like food, so that its truth becomes a principle at work in the mind. Here the metaphor is turned to an excoriation of the distorting nature of false and monolithic interpretation, which attempts to grasp language and wrest it to a fixed meaning; in a parody of the critical activity of men of wit, the Dissenters' manipulation of the word creates a subjectivism that eventually devours the living sinews of a text and replaces with a mindless and multiple nonentity that which was once a group of readers:

> While Crouds unlearn'd, with rude Devotion warm,
> About the Sacred Viands buz and swarm,
> The *Fly-blown Text* creates a *crawling Brood;*
> And turns to *Maggots* what was meant for *Food.*
>
> (ll. 417–20)

In the Exodus story, the manna decayed if people tried to save it—analogical exegesis relates this story to the Gospel paradox that he who tries to save his life will lose it. Here, the principle applies to language and to the Word of God: attempting to grasp and contain the word kills it (the letter kills), turning to a decaying and lifeless object what was meant for food. The corollary is that to obtain true nourishment from the word one must accept an ever-renewed meeting with it, that truth may operate in the mind and be alive in its effects. The maggot is a common image of the period for deluded subjectivism and obsession; here, subjectivity replicates itself in the form of mindless hordes—multiplicity and subjectivity end in nonentity, a kind of unison. Ultimately, the text itself is lost, devoured by maggots; in one of literature's more horrific images, the text actually becomes replaced by the maggots, as the crowds replace it with themselves.

This extremely negative view of interpretation helps explain the evasive nature of the poem's conclusion. Where we might expect in the conclusion a climactic reaffirmation of the values of critical analysis and empiricism, we have instead a reassertion of the minimalist position, and even that is practically qualified away. "The things we *must* believe, are *few*, and *plain*" (l. 432), allowing for no critical interpretation; anything else arises from the radical flaws in human nature—"But since men *will* believe more than they *need*; / And every man will make *himself* a Creed" (ll. 433–34)—and thus all doctrinal questions are dismissed as human constructs. Thereafter (ll. 435–50) each question is swept aside (all questions of doctrine should be referred to the Fathers; all problems arising from patristic interpretation should be quietly ignored) until all are drowned in a completely pragmatic social and political consideration—religious questions are dismissed as irrelevant "points obscure," and the ultimate authority is the social body of "Mankind." All interpretative activity is silenced in "Common quiet." *Religio Laici* has written the layman's faith out of existence. And in its signature, the coda of six lines, it writes its own poetic activity out of existence as well:

> Thus have I made my own Opinions clear:
> Yet neither Praise expect, nor Censure fear:
> And this unpolish'd, rugged Verse, I chose;
> As fittest for Discourse, and nearest Prose:
> For, while from *Sacred Truth* I do not swerve,
> *Tom Sternhold's*, or *Tom Sha*——*ll's Rhimes* will serve.
>   (ll. 451–56)

This asserts a strictly representational view, valuing poetry only as it is "nearest Prose" and thus is a transparent medium for "Discourse." In the last two lines Dryden dismisses his poem, utterly separating matter from word and "Sacred Truth" from poetic language, treating verse as an exploitable or exchangeable object, rather in the manner in which Scripture is handled by false interpreters. Dryden's final separation of poetry and its "matter" negates most of his own writing on wit—the propriety of thoughts and words; the union of thought and expression in a generative and shaping process—much as his reduction of the layman's faith to passive assent and social utility negates his own ideas on critical response to the written word.

In his *peroratio*, then, Dryden dismisses both his poem and his subject: the advice of the layman to his readership is to be quiet and ask no questions; his claim for his own poem is that it need not be a poem at all. The philosophy that negates the activity of poetic language seems also to be that which renders the layman's faith inactive. Thus, two different views of language as a means to truth are at work in the poem: one view sees truth as fixed and discrete, existing separately from the medium of expression, to be passively transmitted through a neutral medium, and passively acknowledged by a neutral mind. The other view—resisted and ultimately suppressed—sees truth as realized through the word, depending on an active response and indeed upon an interplay of responses and significations; in this process truth becomes itself an active principle in the mind. Centering on the Word of God as printed artifact and the layman's faith as a critical response to the printed word sharpens this dichotomy, and digs through to deeper perceptions by which wit and poetry are judged.

Notes on the Contributors

Matthew C. Allen, a doctoral fellow of the Social Sciences and Humanities Research Council of Canada, recently completed his dissertation on the relationship between Herbert's poetry and prose. Currently a seasonal lecturer at the University of British Columbia, he has published an article in *Milton Quarterly* on the pedagogy of *Paradise Lost*.

Jim Ellis teaches at York University, Canada. His doctoral dissertation, entitled "Negotiating Male Subjectivity in Elizabethan Narrative Poetry," is a psychoanalytic reading of narratives in the work of Spenser, Marlowe, Sidney, and others.

Robert C. Evans, Professor of English at Auburn University at Montgomery, is the author of four books on Jonson (*Ben Jonson and the Politics of Patronage; Jonson, Lipsius, and the Politics of Renaissance Stoicism; Jonson and the Contexts of His Time;* and *Habits of Mind: Evidence and Effects of Ben Jonson's Reading*). He is also the coeditor, with Barbara Wiedemann, of *"My Name Was Martha": A Renaissance Woman's Autobiographical Poem,* the first printing of the 1632 "Memorandum" of Martha Moulsworth.

Lee M. Jonson is Professor of English at the University of British Columbia. He has published books on Wordsworth, including *Wordsworth's Metaphysical Verse: Geometry, Nature, and Form,* and has written on Milton and Vergil. He is currently writing a book on *Paradise Lost*.

Erna Kelly, an Associate Professor at the University of Wisconsin–Eau Claire, has published essays on Walt Whitman, Alice Walker, and technical writing. Her current research focuses on seventeenth-century women writers and self-definition.

Catharine Gimelli Martin is Associate Professor of English at Memphis State University. Specializing in Milton, the seventeenth-century lyric, and literary theory, she also writes on the theater of Jonson and Shakespeare. A book-length study of the role of allegory in *Paradise Lost* is forthcoming.

Ted-Larry Pebworth is William E. Stirton Professor in the Humanities and Professor of English at the University of Michigan–Dearborn. He is author of *Owen Felltham;* coauthor of *Ben Jonson;* and coeditor of *The Poems of Owen Felltham* and of collections of essays on Herbert, on Jonson and the Sons of Ben, on Donne, on the seventeenth-century religious lyric, on poetry and politics in the seventeenth-century, on Marvell, and on Renaissance discourses of desire. A textual editor and member of the Advisory Board of *The Variorum Edition of the Poetry of John Donne,* he has served as president of the John Donne Society of America.

Katherine M. Quinsey, Associate Professor of English at the University of Windsor, has published a number of articles on Pope and Dryden, as well as on seventeenth-century poet and translator Sir Edward Sherburne, on biblical tradition in the canon of English literature, and on Canadian poet Margaret Avison. Currently, she is working on a book on Pope's religious thought. Shorter projects deal with feminism, narrative, and rhetoric in George Lillo and Samuel Johnson, and with Dryden's historiographic theory.

Lorraine Roberts is Associate Professor of English at Saint Mary's College of Minnesota. She received her Ph.D. from the University of Missouri–Columbia. She is author of essays on Crashaw and Southwell and has in progress studies of Crashaw, Southwell, Milton, and Marino.

Roger B. Rollin is William James Lemon Professor of Literature at Clemson University. His revision of his 1966 critical study, *Robert Herrick,* has recently been published by Twayne. He is coeditor (with J. Max Patrick) of *"Trust to*

Good Verses": *Herrick Tercentenary Essays*. He has also published essays on Donne, Jonson, Herbert, Marvell, and Milton, as well as on popular culture. He has served as president of the Popular Culture Association in the South and of the American Culture Association.

Sharon Cadman Seelig is Associate Professor of English at Smith College. She is the author of critical essays on Donne, Browne, Milton, and Shakespeare and of *The Shadow of Eternity: Belief and Structure in Herbert, Vaughan, and Traherne*. She is currently completing a book on questions of rhetoric and genre in seventeenth-century and later English prose.

W. A. Sessions is Regents' Professor of English at Georgia State University. A founder and editor of *Studies in the Literary Imagination*, he edited the special issues on Bacon, seventeenth-century prose, and Sidney. He is author of *Henry Howard, the Poet Earl of Surrey* and has recently edited *Francis Bacon's Legacy of Texts*. He has published essays on Surrey, Bacon, Herbert, Milton, Spenser, and the seventeenth-century religious lyric, as well as a monograph, *Spenser's Georgics*, in a special issue of *English Literary Renaissance*.

P. G. Stanwood, Professor of English at the University of British Columbia, is the author of many essays and reviews on Renaissance poetry and prose, a selection of which appears in *The Sempiternal Season: Studies in Seventeenth-Century Devotional Literature*. He has edited a number of texts, including John Cosin's *A Collection of Private Devotions*, Richard Hooker's *Laws, Books VI-VIII*, Jeremy Taylor's *Holy Living* and *Holy Dying*, and *Of Poetry and Politics: New Essays on Milton and His World*.

Claude J. Summers, William E. Stirton Professor in the Humanities and Professor of English at the University of Michigan–Dearborn, has published widely on both seventeenth- and twentieth-century literature. Coeditor of collections of essays on a wide variety of seventeenth-century topics and author of book-length studies of Marlowe, Jonson, Isherwood, and Forster, his most recent books are *Gay Fictions: Wilde to Stonewall, E.M. Forster: A Guide to Research,* and *Homosexuality in Renaissance and Enlightenment England: Literary Representations in Historical Context*. His essays include studies of Marlowe, Shakespeare, Donne, Herbert, Herrick, Vaughan, Forster, Cather, Auden, Isherwood, and others.

Helen Wilcox is Professor of English Literature at the University of Groningen, The Netherlands. Her research interests are in seventeenth-century literature, particularly devotional writing, and Shakespeare studies. She is editor of the Longmans Annotated Herbert and coeditor of *Her Own Life: Autobiographical Writings by Seventeenth-Century Englishwomen*. She is currently writing a study of the seventeenth-century religious lyric and editing *All's Well That Ends Well*.

Index

This index includes only primary works. Lengthy titles are abbreviated, and anonymous works are alphabetized by title.